In the Spirit of Ubuntu

# TRANSGRESSIONS: CULTURAL STUDIES AND EDUCATION

Series Editors
  Shirley Steinberg, *McGill University, Canada*
  Joe Kincheloe, *McGill University, Canada*

Editorial Board
  Heinz-Hermann Kruger, *Halle University, Germany*
  Norman Denzin, *University of Illinois, Champaign-Urbana, USA*
  Rhonda Hammer, *University of California Los Angeles, USA*
  Christine Quail, *SUNY, Oneonta*
  Ki Wan Sung, *Kyung Hee University, Seoul, Korea*

Scope
Cultural studies provides an analytical toolbox for both making sense of educational practice and extending the insights of educational professionals into their labors. In this context *Transgressions: Cultural Studies and Education* provides a collection of books in the domain that specify this assertion. Crafted for an audience of teachers, teacher educators, scholars and students of cultural studies and others interested in cultural studies and pedagogy, the series documents both the possibilities of and the controversies surrounding the intersection of cultural studies and education. The editors and the authors of this series do not assume that the interaction of cultural studies and education devalues other types of knowledge and analytical forms. Rather the intersection of these knowledge disciplines offers a rejuvenating, optimistic, and positive perspective on education and educational institutions. Some might describe its contribution as democratic, emancipatory, and transformative. The editors and authors maintain that cultural studies helps free educators from sterile, monolithic analyses that have for too long undermined efforts to think of educational practices by providing other words, new languages, and fresh metaphors. Operating in an interdisciplinary cosmos, Transgressions: Cultural Studies and Education is dedicated to exploring the ways cultural studies enhances the study and practice of education. With this in mind the series focuses in a non-exclusive way on popular culture as well as other dimensions of cultural studies including social theory, social justice and positionality, cultural dimensions of technological innovation, new media and media literacy, new forms of oppression emerging in an electronic hyperreality, and postcolonial global concerns. With these concerns in mind cultural studies scholars often argue that the realm of popular culture is the most powerful educational force in contemporary culture. Indeed, in the twenty-first century this pedagogical dynamic is sweeping through the entire world. Educators, they believe, must understand these emerging realities in order to gain an important voice in the pedagogical conversation.

Without an understanding of cultural pedagogy's (education that takes place outside of formal schooling) role in the shaping of individual identity–youth identity in particular–the role educators play in the lives of their students will continue to fade. Why do so many of our students feel that life is incomprehensible and devoid of meaning? What does it mean, teachers wonder, when young people are unable to describe their moods, their affective affiliation to the society around them. Meanings provided young people by mainstream institutions often do little to help them deal with their affective complexity, their difficulty negotiating the rift between meaning and affect. School knowledge and educational expectations seem as anachronistic as a ditto machine, not that learning ways of rational thought and making sense of the world are unimportant.

But school knowledge and educational expectations often have little to offer students about making sense of the way they feel, the way their affective lives are shaped. In no way do we argue that analysis of the production of youth in an electronic mediated world demands some "touchy-feely" educational superficiality. What is needed in this context is a rigorous analysis of the interrelationship between pedagogy, popular culture, meaning making, and youth subjectivity. In an era marked by youth depression, violence, and suicide such insights become extremely important, even life saving. Pessimism about the future is the common sense of many contemporary youth with its concomitant feeling that no one can make a difference.

If affective production can be shaped to reflect these perspectives, then it can be reshaped to lay the groundwork for optimism, passionate commitment, and transformative educational and political activity. In these ways cultural studies adds a dimension to the work of education unfilled by any other sub-discipline. This is what transgressions: cultural studies and education seeks to produce—literature on these issues that makes a difference. It seeks to publish studies that help those who work with young people, those individuals involved in the disciplines that study children and youth, and young people themselves improve their lives in these bizarre times.

In the Spirit of Ubuntu
Stories of Teaching and Research

Diane Caracciolo
Adelphi University

Anne M. Mungai
Adelphi University

SENSE PUBLISHERS
ROTTERDAM/BOSTON/TAIPEI

A C.I.P. record for this book is available from the Library of Congress.

ISBN 978-90-8790-841-6 (paperback)
ISBN 978-90-8790-842-3 (hardback)
ISBN 978-90-8790-843-0 (e-book)

Published by: Sense Publishers,
P.O. Box 21858, 3001 AW
Rotterdam, The Netherlands
http://www.sensepublishers.com

Printed on acid-free paper

All Rights Reserved © 2009 Sense Publishers

No part of this work may be reproduced, stored in a retrieval system, or transmitted in any form or by any means, electronic, mechanical, photocopying, microfilming, recording or otherwise, without written permission from the publisher, with the exception of any material supplied specifically for the purpose of being entered and executed on a computer system, for exclusive use by the purchaser of the work.

TABLE OF CONTENTS

Acknowledgements vii

Foreword ix
Ngũgĩ wa Thiong'o

Introduction: *Becoming Human* xi
Diane Caracciolo

                                Ubuntu   1

Chapter 1   *Where have all the Fishes Gone? Living Ubuntu as an Ethics of Research and Pedagogical Engagement* 3
Dalene M. Swanson

Chapter 2   *Towards an African Peace Epistemology: Teacher Autobiography and uMunthu in Malawian Education* 23
Steve Sharra

Chapter 3   *Ubuntu: From Poverty to Destiny with Love* 39
Anne M. Mungai

                                Healing   51

Chapter 4   *Being Otherwise, Teaching Otherwise* 53
Michael O'Loughlin

Chapter 5   *Even When Erased, We Exist: Native Women Standing Strong for Justice* 69
Frances V. Rains, Ph.D.

Chapter 6   *Growing Up Gay Deep in the Heart of Texas* 89
Rob Linné

                                Respect   101

Chapter 7   *Closing the Distance: Partnering with the Indigenous Peoples on Whose Lands We Earn Our Living* 103
Diane Caracciolo

Chapter 8   *Paths In: Transformations of a Painter* 117
Kryssi Staikidis

TABLE OF CONTENTS

Chapter 9	*Bicultural Journeying in Aotearoa* 135	
	Jenny Ritchie	

Community   147

Chapter 10	*Confessions of a Reluctant Professor: In Gratitude to Service Learning* 149	
	Diana Muxworthy Feige	
Chapter 11	*Place-Conscious Learning: Bringing Local Culture and Community into the Curriculum* 165	
	Donna Grace and Rhonda Nowak	
Chapter 12	*Today I am Proud of Myself: Telling Stories and Revaluing Lives* 183	
	Elite Ben-Yosef	

About the Authors 195

Index 199

ACKNOWLEDGEMENTS

We would like to acknowledge our community of authors. Without their humanism and vision, as well as their patient support and graciousness during the writing and editing process, this work would not have been possible. Additionally to those individuals and community members whose lives inform these projects, we send our heartfelt gratitude. Special thanks go to Esther Kogan, for providing the original photograph for the front cover, George Mungai for his poem "We are" and to Shirley Steinberg for her belief in this book. Last but not least, we thank our families for their unconditional love and enthusiastic support of our lives and work.

NGŨGĨ WA THIONG'O

FOREWORD

In his book, *Discourse on Colonialism,* Aime Cesaire has made the apt observation that culture contact is the oxygen of civilization, that cultures that don't make contact shrivel. I think one could say the same thing about stories; that sharing stories is the oxygen of the human spirit. But the stories told here are not fictional but rather stories of personal encounter in the quest of the truly human embodied in the term Ubuntu. Every individual no matter the culture and community they come from has experienced reality in a unique way and therefore each person has something unique to contribute to the common spirit of our being. Such stories then become like the streams that make up rivers that flow into the common Sea.

The stories here are united in a common quest for Ubuntu but in the process they become an important contribution to that common quest. Ubuntu has to be seen, not as an abstract term that has no base in material existence, but rather as an expression of the highest being of that existence. This is important in a global society that has become divided into a majority of nations in Africa and Asia and Latin America that live in poverty even as they see ninety percent of their natural and human resources consumed by a minority of rich nations. They are the most needy yet they are the most giving. But within each and every nation there is also the division between the wealth of a social stratum at the top, and the poverty of a vast social majority at the bottom. The ever increasing demographic of the homeless, the beggar, and the prisoner in nearly all nations of the earth is really a metaphor of a world divorced from its being.

These divisions between and within nations have left wounds in the human heart. An economically, politically, culturally and psychologically liberated Ubuntu is the only way of healing the wounds and the scars. These stories, *In the Spirit of Ubuntu*, tell of personal journeys in the quest of such healing practices. They should be read as an expression of the common quest for a more humane world.

DIANE CARACCIOLO

INTRODUCTION

Becoming Human

> When we stay with a story, refusing the impulse to abstract, reacting from the source of our own experience and feelings, we respect the story and the human life it represents.... (Bochner, 2001, p. 132)

From the perspective of the early 21st century, becoming *human* seems more than ever a work in progress rather than a given. With this in mind, we offer a book of stories because we believe that sharing stories can help us grow into our humanity. Taking the narrative turn in research and teaching frees us to let go of the master narrative of academic power and privilege in order to learn, humbly, from the diverse peoples with whom we share our lives and the world. If we take care not to lose ourselves in isolation, but unite our search for self-knowledge with an equally strong commitment to community well-being and transformation, stories can offer powerful tools for the renewal of educational scholarship and practice. They provide much needed warmth within the too often chilly byways of academe.

In the Spirit of Ubuntu: Stories of Teaching and Research is a collection of experiential narratives representing a range of voices and styles, grounded in different communities, landscapes and personal histories, yet united in a desire to join self-reflection and engaged storytelling with the social justice agenda that informs each author's particular work. With our stories we search for ways to reintegrate the individual with the communal and the secular with the sacred. Out of a feeling of deep respect and gratitude, we associate these ideas with the spirit of *Ubuntu*—a Southern African worldview that Desmond Tuto (1999) describes as "the very essence of being human":[1]

> It is not, "I think therefore I am." It says rather: "I am human because I belong. I participate, I share." A person with ubuntu is open and available to others, affirming of others, does not feel threatened that others are able and good, for he or she belongs in a greater whole and is diminished when others are humiliated or diminished, when others are tortured or oppressed, or treated as if they were less than who they are. (p. 31)

Our opening chapters draw directly from three lived experiences of Ubuntu. The remaining nine chapters offer a selection of autobiographical narratives, research reflections and educational projects from around the globe. We have organized these narratives by three themes—*healing, respect,* and *community*—interlocking dimensions of our shared humanity, embodied here by the single word *Ubuntu*.

Ubuntu

The spirit of Ubuntu was in the air at the Second International Congress of Qualitative Inquiry held at the University of Illinois, Urbana-Champaign in 2006. It was here that I was fortunate to be scheduled for a panel with South African author Dalene M. Swanson, whose presentation, "Humble Togetherness and Ubuntu," stayed with me long after the conference ended and was one inspiration for the concept behind this book. In her chapter, "Where have all the Fishes Gone: Living Ubuntu as an Ethics of Research and Pedagogical Engagement," Dalene weaves the concept of Ubuntu into a many-layered story of her lived and educational research experiences in South Africa. For Dalene, Ubuntu offers a generative pathway toward understanding and transcending the paradoxes of positivist research and neoliberal politics to arrive at a place where the deeply human is discovered and cherished, forming a basis for a transformed ethics of research and pedagogy.

Discovering a way of knowing with the potential to revitalize educational philosophy and practice is at the heart of "Towards an African Peace Epistemology: Teacher Autobiography and uMunthu in Malawian Education." In this chapter Steve Sharra offers the story of how his educational research evolved from a study of teacher autobiography to a profound search for a unifying philosophy and pedagogy of peace arising from uMunthu, the Chichewa word for Ubuntu. Along the way, he traces the historical, political and theological roots of a Sub-Saharan worldview that challenges us to draw the well-being of the human community to the center of our educational thinking.

In "Ubuntu: From Poverty to Destiny with Love," Anne Mungai describes how the shattering loss of her daughter inspired her family to return to Kenya and initiate a grassroots community project to serve countless children orphaned as a result of disease, violence and poverty. During this journey, she rediscovers the spirit of Ubuntu as fundamental to traditional Kenyan society, yet undermined by the social ills engendered by colonialism. She describes how the Caroline Wambui Mungai Foundation revives the spirit of Ubuntu in her Kenyan community and provides a replicable model for addressing the needs of orphaned children throughout the world.

Implicit in these stories of Ubuntu is an urgent need for healing—healing within self, community, and the wider socio-political and educational contexts in which we live. Finding ways to uncover and speak the buried histories of those that have been "othered"—denied their essential humanity through oppression, becomes an essential tool to begin the broader healing of both the oppressed and the oppressor. Authors in the next section explore the experience of being othered from three unique perspectives.

Healing

In "Being Otherwise, Teaching Otherwise," Michael O'Loughlin recounts his experiences growing up as a member of the working poor in a rigidly class-stratified Ireland. Marked early by "sanctioned inferiorization" Michael's examination of his personal history generates a multileveled narrative that explores issues of social class, race, and migrant status and how broader historical and biographical legacies contribute to the development of our subjectivities. Building on his experiences as an educator and therapist, he explores the importance of inner work, and the value of forms of pedagogy that allow children to engage with spectral memories and historically transmitted trauma. His approach has particular relevance for marginal groups in our world, most particularly Indigenous groups and groups who come from long historical lineages of oppression.

As a Native American scholar and woman, Frances Rains (Choctaw/Cherokee & Japanese) carries the responsibility and promise of generations of Native women whose courage, leadership, and steadfast devotion to their lands and peoples have been erased from history. In "Even When Erased, We Exist: Native Women Standing Strong for Justice," Frances traces the outstanding contributions of Native women to their Nations, both before and after the onslaught of cultural genocide and land theft by Western colonizers. In the very act of writing these lives back into history, her scholarship uncovers the devilish work of racism, sexism, and greed that has rendered their important voices silent until now. Recovering these stories is a profound act of historical healing that offers lessons, not only about the past, but also about the present, as Native women continue to speak out forcefully against the injustices that rob all of us of our humanity.

In "Growing Up Gay Deep in the Heart of Texas," Rob Linné describes his early confusion at learning his sexuality marked him as other within his own family, school and church. Through a series of autobiographical vignettes he traces how this othering launched him on a journey to understand the dynamics of love and hate we are taught as young people. This journey informs his life as a teacher educator where he searches for ways to discover the healing and forgiveness that are at the heart of being truly human.

The act of othering is central to the critique of Western research practices explored by the authors in the next section. Decolonizing the research act involves a radical rethinking of many of its basic premises and power imbalances, and a search for new methodologies. Such rethinking is both a challenge and a source of important new learnings for nonindigenous scholars seeking respectful partnerships with Indigenous peoples. At its heart, decolonization strives for Ubuntu's open spirit of respect and the honouring of all members of the human community as part of the research act.

Respect

"Closing the Distance: Partnering with the Indigenous Peoples on Whose Lands We Earn our Living, tells the story of my research journey from ignorance to an evolving understanding of the Indigenous peoples of my birthplace—Long Island, New York. Along the way I retrace my early stumbles and discoveries and show how my original project changed from a traditional graduate school "problem statement," to one more resonant with the ideas encountered in multiple conversations with the Shinnecock people who became my teachers and ongoing research partners rather than the "subjects" of a study.

In her self-reflexive narrative, "Paths In: Transformations of a Painter," Kryssi Staikidis recounts her experiences being mentored by two Maya artists in their Guatemalan studios. She examines her positionality as student, artist, cultural outsider and ethnographer. Her artistic apprenticeship in an Indigenous context becomes a unique method of decolonizing art education inquiry. Along the way the three artists transform their research relationship into one of shared artistry and mutual discovery, learning together that the language of art can foster deep understandings, reciprocities and friendships across cultures as well as life-long transformations within the self.

Jenny Ritchie describes herself as "a Pākehā, a citizen of Aoteaora/New Zealand of European ancestry, committed to social justice and cultural equity within education." As a scholar, educator, and mother of six bicultural children and grandmother of one, she is deeply committed to exploring collaborative educational research methods that centralize Māori worldviews and values within a Western monocultural educational context that has excluded such understandings. In "Bicultural Journeying in Aotearoa," Jenny traces an academic journey that led her to enact decolonizing practices in early childhood educational research. Along the way, she and her Pākehā and Māori co-researchers articulate pedagogical approaches that are profoundly grounded in Māori ways of being, knowing and doing. Her story demonstrates ethical research methodologies that flow from generous hearts and open minds.

The authors in the final section are teacher educators reflecting on their own practices. All three model the importance of honouring community in the teaching and learning process, where both teacher and learner are united in a search for meaning and a commitment to human flourishing.

Community

In service learning, Diana M. Feige has found liberation from a troubling, disquieting sense of the inauthentic in the role of university professor. "Confessions of a Reluctant Professor: In Gratitude to Service Learning" is a deeply personal account of her struggle to integrate her spiritual and professional lives. Through stories of how service learning—a pedagogical option that marries academics with action, curriculum with compassion and community—Diana weaves a deeply reflective celebration of how we can expand the boundaries of our classrooms to include the wider world of the human community.

As language arts teacher educators at the University of Hawai'i, Donna Grace and Rhonda Nowak work to enliven curriculum that is increasingly divorced from children's lived experiences due to the culture of standardized testing generated by the United States No Child Left Behind legislation. In "Place-Conscious Learning: Bringing Local Culture and Community into the Curriculum," they share two projects that demonstrate how critical and creative inquiry into local issues awakens teachers to the role community can play in engaging high level learning within language arts classrooms that dare to expand beyond their four walls.

INTRODUCTION

In "Today I am Proud of Myself: Telling Stories and Revaluing Lives," Elite Ben-Yosef describes the work of a weekly literacy class she taught in a recovery home for women who live together while working to reclaim their lives after prison stays, substance abuse and other traumas. Through sharing stories, tentatively at first, and then with increasing power and expressiveness, the women embark on a communal journey toward finding their voices, coming to new understandings about their self-worth, and forging new spaces for themselves and the world.

It is our hope that the readers of this book will find encouragement for engaging in new ways of writing and thinking about research and education. Most importantly, we present this work as one way to move from isolation to interconnectedness and to move the human spirit—the spirit of Ubuntu—to the heart of our discussions, lives, and work.

NOTES

[1] Out of respect for the term *Ubuntu* and the human ideals toward which it points, the editors have chosen to use the initial upper case when employing this word.

REFERENCES

Bochner, A.P. (2001). Narratives virtues. Qualitative inquiry, 7 (2), pp. 131-157.
Tutu, D. (1999). No future without forgiveness. NY: Doubleday.

Diane Caracciolo
Ruth S. Ammon School of Education
Adelphi University

UBUNTU

DALENE M. SWANSON

WHERE HAVE ALL THE FISHES GONE?

Living Ubuntu as an Ethics of Research and Pedagogical Engagement

In the Spirit of Joseph

Deeply disappointed, I stood looking at the gate, chained and bolted closed. There was a fine stillness that threaded itself diaphanously through the soft zephyr of early afternoon, like the breath of dissipated anticipation. The red brick school building stood there empty and alone as if mocking my memory of the happenings within it some years prior. I could discern the dappled shadows of the past behind the veil of an existent manifestation of reality. I could feel the sunlit-afternoon ghosts of that present intruding on the past,[1] trying to trick my consciousness, attempting to reconstitute history and replace it with current phantasms of a vacant school and post-apartheid South Africa, like simulacra, as if they were the new 'real'. The background white noise of nearby traffic and the faint lull of waves against the barnacled pier in the nearby harbour seemed, for a moment, to pause, and the audience of my consciousness hushed as if some premier performance was about to begin....

I had been very excited to revisit this school, one of the schools in which I had engaged in my doctoral research[2] all those years ago and in which I had dreamed, wished, aimed to go back and give back for so long now. Even a quick visit would suffice, at least for now. And here I was, finally standing in front of the main entrance of the school, and it was empty! The whole school was steeped in the silence of absence. My word-thoughts of what I had wanted to say when I greeted him again, the principal of this school that I had admired so much, and to the teachers and the people and the humanity within the community herein, were now lying as splintered shards of discarded possibility on the ground, and the fragments disintegrated and seeped into the red dust like playful demons of failed intent.

There was a nation-wide public sector strike on. I knew that many schools had closed their doors in sympathy and in safety to their community. Teachers were striking too. There had been strike action when I had engaged in my research in this region of South Africa years ago, but it had not really impacted these schools in this bay. Nor had the historic fishing village with her mixed-race community been directly affected at that time. Now, I was in the country for such a short ten days before I had to move on and return to Canada. I'd hoped beyond hope that there would at least be some staff present that I'd known before in the school, characters that I'd written into my narratives. Even if the school were closed for classes, perhaps they would still be there bustling about. I played with the mental images of the faces from my narratives, from my past lived experiences, hoping for them to come alive and become re-embodied in the flesh outside of the words.

As I drove my hired car up the same unchanged winding roads towards the school, I wondered what their reaction would be to seeing me again after so many years. While the possibility of disappointment dampened the sense of excitement, hope, and anticipation of seeing the people of this schooling community again, my thoughts were primarily focused on an existential question of consciousness: What would it be like?

But…there were just ghosts for me.[3] Just the remains of objects of past activities marking in similitude where happenings might have occurred, of phantom events within school buildings, along pathways, behind closed doors, closed meshed windows, closed metal gates, bolted and chained: just the remains of memories; the remains of the day before me; and with it, the shattering disappointment of lost opportunity to fill the substance of that space.

Only the haunting caw of a seagull as it flies (fore) shadowingly overhead breaks the silence that has pervaded this static moment, as it also signals a change of scene. It is as if the seagull is heralding some new emergence, reminding me to be ready and open to receive new messages, to expect a visitation, to recognize a harbinger of sorts, and to stand as internuncial witness.[4] As I stay standing, longer than I needed to, trying to capture a sense of past presence and place, grasping at an illusory real, I am aware that I am in fact waiting for something, something to happen. I stand still in front of this school as if in expectant anticipation of the unexpected…and as I do so, he enters from the left.

"Goeie middag, mevrou! Kan ek mevrou miskien help met iets?"[5] I turn to look at him perplexed. I had not seen him appearing from the wings into the vision of this scene of absent presence. He is wearing the blue overalls that designate workmen and workwomen in South Africa, but in contradiction to this class referent, he is carrying a black leather report folder under his one arm. His face is wrinkled with years of sunburn and his hair shows hints of grey. He smiles, turning his head to one side deferentially, and I see his mixed-race heritage with the signs of Khoi-San descent in his facial structure. I extend my hand to shake his, and I reply to his greeting: "Goeie middag, meneer! Ek wou kom kuier. Ek was lank gelede hier."[6]

He nods his head as I explain that a few years back I had come home from Canada to engage in my doctoral research in this school and two others in the vicinity (Swanson, 2004). He sees the resignation in my face and responds sympathetically, with an "ag, shame, mevrou,"[7] as I explain my reason for being here at this moment. I tell him that I had come back for a conference and a quick visit to South Africa, and had hoped to visit the school, the principal and teachers that I had befriended here before. I knew that the students would be new and that the other students I'd known would have passed on to other things and left the school by now, but I had hoped to visit with some of the school community members that might still be 'holding the fort', so to speak. He laughs with me over my last comment. He nods with understanding and compassion in his eyes, recognizing my disappointment as if it were his own. He sighs and drops his eyes to the ground as if to think about this situation a little longer and afford it the quiet gravity of this moment. We both look at the ground where my thought words had disappeared, and there is a moment of silence again. The breeze stirs little dust balls on the ground and about his dusty workman shoes, sturdy with large laces, that have been worn well with several years of walking in this community. We stand and are both thoughtful.

Choosing the appropriate moment to speak again, he lifts his eyes with the intentness of issuing important words. Converting to English, probably because he had heard that I was now living in Canada and my Afrikaans was less than fluent, or because he recognized that I spoke it with the accent of an English speaker, he tells me that he remembers the principal and teachers speaking about me, "the South African teacher from Canada," and how they had spoken so highly of me. "Ja, for a long time," [8] he says, with an accent on 'time' to give it importance and with another nod of the head.

This compliment comes across most sincerely, but I also understand it in the cultural parlance of graciousness that I remembered as being so prevalent within this fishing community, their heart-felt politeness, their sensitivity to the feelings of others, their careful deference and bestowing of honour on people they deeply respected. Speaking slowly, which, from my perspective, is a cultural code borne from humility and intended to give each word the weight of meaning and respect it was intended to bear, he says: "I wasn't here at the school at the time, but I came to be more involved with the school soon after you left, and they used to speak of you, and you left a good impression. They would be very disappointed to know that they missed you today. Ag, siestog! What a shame! I am sorry!" [9]

I reply with a gracious 'thank you' and tell him what an honour it had been to be welcomed into this community, that I often thought of the people I had come to know in the community and wished them all well, and that I had been very grateful for the opportunity to engage in research and with such a wonderful community. I explained my gratitude for the gift of their wisdom and hospitality, and that I looked forward to meeting them all again. And then as if we both simultaneously realize that we had not formally introduced ourselves, we exchange names with a "nice to meet you" at the end of the greeting.

It is then that he begins to share his story. At the time, I was not prepared for what was to come. I was still caught up with my own disappointment, but as he spoke in deliberate and carefully formed words, I soon realized that I was again being given something very precious. My senses initiated a shift of consciousness that opened me to humbly receiving what was to be one of the most sacred gifts of humanity I could ever have been given, the sharing of an important narrative, the telling of a precious life story, full of reverberating meanings and wisdoms that that telling entails.

"I am Joseph Hendriks,[10] that same Joseph Hendriks that was in all the newspapers. I am the one," he says with a hint of pride, and realizing that I probably have no idea of what he is talking about as I would not have had access to local provincial papers in Canada, he continues:

> I am the caretaker at this school, but on Sunday's I am the community pastor. Over the last few years I have become increasingly involved with the school, because I am concerned about our youth here. I pray for them on Sundays and I try to take care of them during the week. I support our teachers and principal because I know what hard jobs they have here in this community and the difficulty with our youth. It is because of our youth that it happened. They tried to get rid of me because I was speaking up for our youth.

I look perplexed at his last statement and he continues his narration carefully and slowly, undeterred:

> You see, the skollies[11] and the drug dealers, they are damaging our youth, corrupting them and ruining their lives before they have a chance for anything in life, and I was trying to stop them. Because I was close to the kids in the school, I could see what was going on, and I was telling the police, and they didn't like me as an informant, the drug lords that come into our community. They come here because our community is poor and our kids are so vulnerable. There are no prospects for them because there is no fish in the harbour. No fish! Where have all the fishes gone? They have been plundered, the big boats come from elsewhere, and the fishermen have ransacked the seas, so there are no fish. They did not stop until the fish were all gone. And as you know, this is a fishing village that has grown around this harbour. It has been our way of life for many, many decades.

He stops to clear his throat then continues, meticulous in his explanation:

> So the fathers of the kids, they have no work. There is terribly high unemployment and the fathers just lie about and drink, and so the alcoholism is very bad. So the kids get neglected. And then we have other social problems here, the violence with the gangs, and domestic violence and rape.

Resonating with the despairing discourse the principal had deployed all those years back during my doctoral research in relating the conditions of the community, he continues to explain with a sigh:

> There is lots of it. It is very bad. The kids have no prospects and there is not much hope of getting a job or doing better than their parents, so they get involved with drugs. And for the drug dealers, this is easy money because there are so many kids they can get their hands on. So our community suffers and we can't get out of this vicious cycle. We are dependent on the fish. The fish is our hope and there is no fish.

He turns for a moment towards the harbour and looks wistfully at the sea beyond the school as if imagining a harbour brimming with fish and a community 'saved' and 'healed' by the emergence of prospect, hope and possibility. But reality intrudes; it is a messianic wish, and he turns back and continues:

> That is why they plotted to get me, those skollie drug dealers, because I tried to stop them and I kept on telling the police. So they tricked me. One day, I

> was driving in my old car and at the stop street, a car pulls up next to me and a youngster turns down the window and asks me if I am the pastor, and I say "yes," and he says he has good, cheap parts for my car and I must follow him and he will take me to the place where I can get the parts cheap-cheap. I followed him because I thought they were being kind to me because I was the pastor and next thing I am on a lonely road towards one of the beaches here and the youngster stops the car. As he does so, three men jump into my car and hold a gun at my head and tell me to drive. They tell me where to go and the next thing we are driving towards The Strand.[12] They hold the gun below the level of the window and tell me not to try any tricks. I try to flick my lights and drive onto the wrong side of the road to get the attention of passing cars, but they threaten me that they will kill me if I try that again.

He stops for a moment to fidget with his report folder then tucks it back under his arm. The sun is hot and I can feel the sweat running down my back. He must feel it too and he takes out a handkerchief to mop his face:

> Then at a place that is very remote they make me stop along the road and they force me out of the car and shove me in the boot,[13] and then they drive again, and I know they are driving towards The Strand.

He pauses again and I imagine that the flood of memories of the situation he was in, of his own fear, must be difficult to relive and retell. But he continues, intent on his story:

> I prayed. I cannot tell you how much I prayed in the boot of my car, because I knew what they were going to do with me. I lay there in the dark and I prayed, and I knew I must try to do something before it was too late. And you know, The Lord was with me because I decided to flip the boot open, but I just happened to do it at exactly the time when the car came to a stop at an intersection, and because of that, I managed to jump out and I ran and I ran as fast as I could. They tried to come after me and they were shouting and shooting but they did not get me, and I managed to get away. I ran through the dunes and just kept on running. I've never run so fast in my life. I was covered in white sand like a ghost but I kept on running until I eventually got to a roadside store. I went in there and the people helped me phone the police and they came right away. They sent out a squad to look for the skollies but they could not find them, and they took me home and made sure I was safe with my family. It was a terrible thing and the whole community was badly shocked. Everyone was in fear, but they were very supportive and ready to protect me. Everyone was very kind and they were very concerned about the skollies coming back to murder me. And one day I get a phone call and I am asked to meet a man down by the docks, so I go down there and he tells me that he was told to tell me that they did that because I was telling on them to the police and they wanted me dead as a result.

> So I kept very low for about a month or so, and I said nothing and I did not go many places, and I just kept a low profile. You know, I was scared for my

> life. It did not feel good having to look behind your back every moment, worrying about the safety of your family, imagining every moment when you hear a sound, that they are coming to get you.... It was not good.

I was trying to take in the full horror of his story, and for a moment I tried to imagine his situation. The breeze stirred again and it was like warm breath on my clammy face, but my sweat turned cold down my neck. I made a comment about how sorry I was and how awful it must have been. The story was shocking! The afternoon turned, and shifting his feet and tucking his report folder under the other arm, he again continues:

> You know, I could not live like that. For a while I kept low, but I realized that this was not the way. I could not keep on living like that in fear and that I wasn't helping anyone. So I changed my approach. I started to get out into the community again. I spoke up for our youth in church again. And I realized that working against the drug dealers like that wasn't the right way. It wasn't going to work. So I actually approached them. I arranged to meet with them and I invited them to talk with me. I showed them I wasn't afraid and that I had changed my approach. And many of them agreed to speak with me, and slowly I befriended them and asked them, "Please, look what you are doing to our youth! You are destroying these young people's lives. This is not right!" And I appealed to them to please change their ways, and some of them came over to the right side, and they stopped their drug dealings with the youth here. Some of them even came to our church. So now I am back in the community and I continue to help our youth. Recently we started a job training centre for the unemployed youth here to try to find them other work because there is no fish. I am praying it will help a lot. I pray for our youth everyday.

It is often difficult to grasp the full impact of a narration and to understand what has been given, the preciousness of the gift. From disappointment, I was given an unexpected offering of learning. He gave me so many gifts of wisdom, the meanings from this tale and from their telling unfold in layers and across time. The telling offers moments of insight and sagacity in each pondering and remembering, in each epiphany it evokes, and in each recasting of the narration in my mind and spiritual communion with it. Like a textured coat of many colours, the story holds multiple understandings of ways of knowing and being that we can only be humbled by its generative living power.

This Joseph, like his biblical counterpart, forgives his brothers that sell him off. He, like his counterpart, wears a coat of many colours, but he has given this as a gift of himself to his community and through the telling of his story. The interrelated lessons of this tale are many and each holds importance and position in how we engage with our lives, of its purpose, of education, of approaches to community engagement and research, of society, ideology, justice, and our earth. It gives us more than any of this. It gives us hope.

One of the foremost lessons I gained from Joseph's story and which, for me, is manifest in daily other revelations, is the understanding of how social justice cannot be slathered off from the larger ecological concerns that impact issues of poverty, opportunity and cultural epistemic access and affirmation. They work together as a whole, and like other binaries of Western thought, their separation is ideologically problematic. The particular and the universal, the local and the global require being understood as multi-articulate, reciprocal, concomitant and intermeshed. The subjugation of people, their way of life, their knowledge systems and wisdoms, their socio-economic, political and cultural aspirations, are part of a broader global historical discourse of subjugation that marks the land and people in localized ways through geographies of difference, and it enacts its violence across time and space. "Where are all the fishes gone?"[14] Joseph asks, delineating the relationship between the devastation of the seas, the denial of a community's livelihood and historical way of life, and the drug addiction and despair suffered by the youth of this community.

Just as holism and a larger vision of humanity and ecology as being ever-interrelated[15] is nurtured back into life through Joseph's story, so the appreciation of that which Joseph was expressing in his actions of care, compassion, forgiveness, and an expansive inclusivity, was, in fact, Ubuntu. His encompassing sense of humanity and his great generosity of spirit bore these out. His capacity to transcend personal fear and self-interest, to overcome the limitations of an oppressive context and step aside of the mocking shadows of despair, was the life and spirit of Ubuntu. It was with Ubuntu in his heart that he had the courage to approach the drug dealers, those who would have him murdered, and win them over. It was a show of Ubuntu that he succeeded. It was (with) Ubuntu that he gave back to his community and to the care for its youth. He *modelled* Ubuntu for these youth. It was with Ubuntu that he shared his story with me, and he gave Ubuntu in its telling and in the lessons I received from the giving. Joseph's story was the spiritual *gift* of Ubuntu.

Ubuntu: An African Philosophy of Being

I come to an understanding of Ubuntu through lived experiences, having grown up in apartheid South Africa. I attended university there during the height of the liberation struggle, witnessed the release of Nelson Rolihlahla Mandela, and with fellow South Africans and others around the world, I celebrated the transition of my country of birth to democracy. I became aware of the concept of Ubuntu from an early age. My mother, who spoke conversational Zulu and who had experienced close relationships with Zulu people since birth, was careful to expose me to the responsibilities, contributions and consciousnesses of citizenship and community in an African context. I experienced Ubuntu, first hand, through love and friendship with Xhosa, Zulu and Sotho South Africans, and other Southern Africans I knew, and was often welcomed into indigenous communities. Nevertheless, I was *also* acutely aware of the difficulty and near impossibility of achieving Ubuntu in many contexts of segregated South Africa, as well as *my* role and responsibility as being collectively implicated in this as a white South African (Swanson, 2006; 2007a; 2007b).

While an ongoing project of 'nation building' draws on the political aspirations of a strong, united South Africa, renewed and healed from a divided and ruptured past, it highlights the challenge of incorporating Ubuntu as a pan-political philosophy of engagement, not only operating in the interstices of human relationships but at the institutional, structural and national levels, a somewhat utopian endeavour (Swanson, 2007a; Marx, 2002). Nevertheless, Ubuntu as a guiding principle for nation-building in South Africa serves as a signifier of commitment to a collectivist program of healing, redress and forgiveness, as has been exemplified in the *Truth and Reconciliation Commission's (TRC)* mandate (see Tutu, 1999; Battle, 1997), even if this has been critiqued as being via a glorified and imagined past (Marx, 2002).

Nobel Prize laureate, Archbishop Desmond Mpilo Tutu, who, in 1995, became the chairman of post-apartheid South Africa's *TRC*, was a strong advocate of Ubuntu. For Tutu, the spiritual power of Ubuntu humanism served as an important platform for providing rules of engagement in TRC hearings. The ethos and tone of proceedings were critically important to the hearings in order to enable, in an ethical manner, the recovery of "truth" through narratives of atrocities from the apartheid era. These terms of engagement were also necessary in the subsequent processes of *forgiveness*, reconciliation, transcendence, and healing that arise, cathartically, through the humbling process of truth-telling.

As I have grown to understand the concept, Ubuntu is borne out of the philosophy that *community strength* comes of *community support*, and that dignity and identity are achieved through mutualism, empathy, generosity and community commitment. The adage that 'it takes a village to raise a child' is an African wisdom borne from an understanding and way of being aligned with the spirit and intent of Ubuntu. The obsessive Western focus on individualism and the continued colonization of African indigenous peoples through the new forms of global capitalism have served to diminish the importance of African collectivist humanism and Ubuntu as a philosophical and communal way of life. The increasing verticularity of Western dominant norms over indigenous wisdoms and perspectives has, through the modernistic project and the dominance of Western-interested techno-centricism, subjugated such knowledge forms and undermined their resurgence (see Swanson, 2007b).

In the South African context, just as apartheid threatened to erode this traditional African way of life – although in some instances it ironically strengthened it through galvanizing collectivist support and creating solidarity amongst the oppressed—so increasing industrialization, urbanization and neo-colonial globalization, threatens to do the same.

South Africa's ready embrace of global capitalism and globalizing neo-liberalism, post-democracy, has set back the project of Africanisation. The global project of progressivism set the course for South Africa in its desire to be competitive on the global stage and significantly participate in global affairs. This came at a cost. At the time when South Africa came out of isolation and was welcomed back into the international arena, a new wave of imperializing capitalism disallowed the possibility of community healing and restoration by preventing the "insurrection of subjugated knowledges" (Foucault, 1980, p. 80) of the Southern African peoples and an abandonment of "a historical knowledge of struggles" (ibid., p. 83) and its earlier politico-ideological purposes. This has been despite Thabo Mbeki's initiative, as previous President of South Africa, to engender an African Renaissance, whose said purpose is to assist in 'ending poverty and oppression' and to 'regain dignity' for all South Africans. In this sense, incompatible ideologies have resulted in contradiction and fragmentation rather than the unification ideals of nation-building. Ubuntu is a victim of this incommensurateness and rupture. It struggles for recognition, realization and legitimacy within (indigenous) communities, and against misappropriation and complete subjugation on a national, political and institutional level. But, to appreciate the complexity of this, we need to understand Ubuntu more fully as an important historical thread of Africanist knowledge systems. It is to be appreciated as the salt of much of African philosophy, an African way of life, and as a norm and value within African community contexts.

Ubuntu is short for an isiXhosa proverb in Southern Africa, *Umuntu ngumuntu ngabantu*; a person is a person through their relationship to others. Ubuntu is recognized as the African philosophy of humanism, linking the individual to a collective of 'brotherhood' or 'sisterhood'. It makes a foundational contribution to indigenous 'ways of knowing and being'. With differing historical emphasis and (re)contextualization over time and place, it is considered a spiritual way of being in the broader socio-political context of Southern Africa. This approach is not only an expression of a spiritual philosophy in its theological and theoretical sense, but as an expression of daily living. In my own work (Swanson, 2004, 2005, 2006, 2007a, 2007b), I have spoken of it in terms of a 'humble togetherness.' For Tutu, Ubuntu is a way of knowing that fosters a journey towards 'becoming human' (Vanier, 1998) or 'which renders us human' (Tutu, 1999), or, in its collectivist sense, a greater humanity that transcends alterity of any form (ibid.).

This 'transcendence of alterity', as I understand it, is not the collapsing of difference in the sense of ignoring the social and political effects of power that 'difference' and discourses on difference constitute in daily lived realities within communities across the world, where the arbitrary nature of constructed 'difference' enacted on diverse geographies of the body are made to appear 'normal' and 'real.' Instead, it is a conscious attempt to reverse these effects in bringing together an understanding of the common investment of humanity as being inextricably bound up together, in 'a bundle of life' (Tutu, 1999), whose pleasure and pain, survival and demise, recognition and subjugation, are all part of a common responsibility, a trans-phenomenon of collectivist concern for earth and other. In recognition of an interconnectivity with the land and all of Earth's citizens, a disposition in consonance with Ubuntu would mean becoming receptive to others and other ways, while offering a generosity of heart and spirit. It is centered on an accepted communal obligation to justice rather than 'individual rights.' It would mean a way of seeking inner sanctum that gives rise to compassion, self-effacement, mutual understanding, and humble spirituality. It attests to a belief that the individual is implicated in the whole and that the self bears witness to a transcendent, trans-phenomenal capacity for human good, no matter how complicated and ethically complex that 'good' might be(come).

Ubuntu's Contribution to the Global Politic, Pedagogic Engagement with 'The Other,' and the Ethical Commitments of Research

Most saliently, and in great consciousness of the complexity of global politics and contemporary social problems we face in the world as ever interconnected humanity, Archbishop Tutu remarks that: "You can never win a war against terror as long as there are conditions in the world that make people desperate – poverty, disease, ignorance ..." (in Lloyd, 2007, p.1).

A notion of 'humble togetherness' or Ubuntu in facing the shared responsibility of world poverty, may go a long way to addressing these problems and provide alternatives to the way governments act in response to 'threat' and 'fear' as well as to the perceived need to 'protect their own interests'. Ubuntu undoubtedly emphasizes responsibilities and obligations toward a collective well-being. On a global scale, greater co-operation and mutual understanding is very necessary to a sustainable future for all with respect to the ecological, moral and social well-being of its global citizens, human and otherwise. Ubuntu provides legitimizing spaces for transcendence of injustice and a more democratic, egalitarian and ethical engagement of human beings in relationship with each other. In this sense, Ubuntu offers hope and possibility in its contribution to human rights, not only in the South African and African contexts, but across the globe. In support of this final assertion on human rights, Tim Murithi, Programme Officer at the United Nations Institute for Training and Research, writes on a culturally inclusive notion of human rights and its implications for a new international charter. Murithi (2004) asserts that the global campaign for human rights needs to be given new life. He believes that this needs to be achieved through reformulating the Universal Declaration of Human Rights. In reference to the universal ideals of social, economic and ecological justice, Murithi avers that we need to re-articulate our aspirations to human rights far more in the 'language of obligations', which would commit more unambiguously to action. He notes: "In essence, a re-articulation of human rights from an ubuntu perspective adds value to the human rights movement by placing more of an emphasis on the obligations that we have towards the 'other'" (p. 15).

Ubuntu is not to be taken as another meta-narrative for global engagement, however. It should not take on the dominant position of yet another scatological Truth. It should not become the new 'said' in Levinas's terms, 'the said' being that which strives for universality, solidarity and closure, but should maintain the openness of ambiguity and uncertainty that resides uncomfortably with the tensions, challenges and possibilities of the 'Saying' in relation to encounters with global 'others' (See Edgoose, 2001). Its misappropriation and recontextualization (Bernstein, 2000) might also become dangerous in its new configurations through prevailing power relations in the contexts of its adoption. These are always the dangers of philosophy at the level of 'implementation' or as universalized ideology. Much like Hegel's (1820) owl of Minerva, who spreads his wings only with the falling of the dusk, philosophy can only speak of events in their hindsight, rather than command a power to project prescriptively on a generalized future. In the same sense, Ubuntu should always find its source and rootedness at the level of one human being to another, of a human being to the earth, of a human being within community, as difficult as that is to understand or define or as complex as its various constitutions may become. While Ubuntu values obligation and responsibility, it is also defined by acceptance of difference and sacrificial care for another. Ubuntu's power is with its ethical spiritual commitment, its propensity to value humility and human dignity, not with its capacity to impose a set of values on an-Other.

Nevertheless, as principles for pedagogic engagement, and as a guide to living within an ethic that places responsibility for social and ecological justice within a web of interrelated collectives, Ubuntu has much to offer, not only within the Southern African context, indigenous peoples and historical location from which it arises and has lived and breathed, but in what it offers for all humanity across the globe as to be interpreted and embraced variously within their situated contexts. On a personal level, it has also offered a way for me to understand the importance of an ethics of engagement in educational research. It is to this that I turn my attention now.

A Research Journey as Pedagogic Journey of the Self

I completed my Ph.D. at The University of British Columbia. As previously introduced, my dissertation is a critical exploration of the construction of disadvantage in school mathematics in social context. It provides a reflexive, narrative account of a pedagogic journey towards understanding the 'pedagogizing of difference' (Swanson, 1998, 2004, 2005) in mathematics classrooms and its realizations as *lived disadvantage* in and across diverse socio-political, economic, cultural, and pedagogic contexts. As mentioned, I returned to South Africa some years back and stayed for several months to engage in fieldwork in schooling communities there.

Two of the communities in which I engaged in research were situated in contexts of relative and extreme socio-economic poverty. Consequently, ethical issues associated with respectful ways of being in research with such communities, the moral dilemmas faced through research engagement, the positionality of research relationships, the power relations invested in such relationships and through institutional engagement, as well as the researcher's 'ways of seeing', all became critical issues of concern in the research process. It was necessary for me to find less objectifying ways of being in research; ways which would disrupt and decolonize dominant meanings, not contribute to 'deficit discourse' (Bernstein, 2000) and 'disadvantage'—meanings produced from privileged perspectives.

It was here that Ubuntu provided a vision and framework for me for respectful engagement in research of this nature; one that permitted reflexivity, reciprocity, community connectedness through a sense of 'humble togetherness', and cross-cultural understanding. It also provided opportunities for life-enriching and transformative experiences, and, importantly, spiritual growth. A focus on Ubuntu in its socio-cultural and political context, helped to *highlight* the multitude of interrelated moral, ethical and ideological dilemmas faced in fieldwork experiences in a context of 'poverty', while paradoxically also serving to provide a way *through* the quagmires and contradictions, and achieve transformation through a transcendent spirituality. It is through my narrative exploration of research issues, ambiguities and contradictions in their full, often irresolvable and ungraspable complexity – narrative that often bordered on autoethnography – that Ubuntu was drawn into my research, shaping my research experiences, in ways that offered lived pedagogies of hope and possibility.

The Narrative in Context

To exemplify only a small aspect of this research engagement with Ubuntu and how, through a reflexive narratizing, it might deconstruct hegemonic meanings and allow for other possibilities of being in the world, I will offer an extract from a narrative in my dissertation. I have elaborated on this in Swanson (2005, 2006, 2007a, 2007b, 2009a, 2009b).[16]

To set the scene, I am sitting in the office of a principal at a missionary elementary school situated in a shanty or informal settlement. The conditions of poverty are evident everywhere.

The Narrative Excerpt...

"You mathematics education researchers," he says, half jokingly. "I don't know." He laughs and shakes his head a little self-consciously or to be polite perhaps. He knows he is positioning me now as one of 'Those.' He is congenial and friendly about it and I can see that he hopes I don't mind! I *don't* mind...I understand and appreciate this in context of this cultural aspect of South African humour. "All these new methods and this progressive education thing," he continues after a long pause, "and these kids *still* don't know their times tables! So what is the good of all of it?" At first, he assumes the posture of someone in debate, but then he jumps up and starts to stride across his office, gesticulating as he talks. I sit on the other side of his desk as he performs for me, explicating his argument against progressivism in an extemporaneous and agitated dance. "When I grew up, we did it by rote, and *at least* I can work out my budget and do multiplication without having to reach for a calculator...But these kids today, if you ask them what is two times seven, they don't know." He goes on: "But we have to embrace this progressive education thing."

I realize that this statement has more to do with his positioning of me as "a white South African mathematics teacher," or *even more* so, "a white Canadian researcher," and his own relational positioning in this context, than it is about the pedagogics or politics of educational progressivism itself. And despite this...for a moment...I want to ask what I think are crucial questions, which, for me, highlight the contradictions of the statements I have just heard from the principal of this elementary school. I want to ask him why it is, that from my perspective, I have not *really* evidenced any real attempt to engage in any progressive education practices within these classrooms...why I have seen *so much* rote learning...when any pedagogic learning took place at all...or why I have seen, from my perspective, so much apparent indifference...why it is that corporal punishment is still used here when it has been made *illegal* to engage in physically punitive practices in South African schools...why so many of the teachers are so seldom *in* the classroom when the National Minister of Education at the time, Kader Asmal, has made urgent and repeated appeals to teachers across the country to take their jobs seriously for the country's sake, for the sake of our youth and the future generation of South Africa now in creation? Where does the proverbial 'buck stop,' who is responsible, who cares, why not, and how can we make a difference?

I want to ask him why he closes the school early so frequently, causing very small children to have to walk home alone, often unescorted back to their homes in the informal settlement where they are not attended to or protected because their parents or caretakers are at work? Where does his responsibility to the community end ... or where does it start? Why does he use class time to have meetings with his staff, and why so frequently is learning interrupted for apparently, *from my perspective*, inconsequential issues? Why does he legitimize teachers' missing classes by engaging in these practices himself? Why can't meetings take place after school?

A part of me wants to speak out. I want to tell him what I think. I want to tell him that I think it is not right. That this is 'just not good enough'! Is this what we were all liberated for...? Wasn't it to try and make a difference, to turn it around, to 'fight the good fight'! Not to give in to oppression; not to submit to the authority of poverty and consequently the authority of privilege that establishes the poverty; not to succumb to the worst form of oppression, in Freirian terms, when the oppressed begin to oppress themselves.

I want to ask him why? Why he is not seeing it, why he is so bound by this model of oppression, this discourse of poverty and situated experience that he cannot step outside of it, even for a moment, to see what it is like.... Is it that poverty is so rooted in 'situatedness', that it is so delimiting, so strangulating, that we cannot create even a momentary spark of insight? Does it require a stepping aside, a looking awry, a new platform, another place, a firm patch of new ground, to find it, to visualize it, to imagine? Does envisioning require the separation or abstraction from local context and its firm rootedness to be able to provide perspective, generate new interpretations and conceptualizations, provide them with the flesh of real hope, of tangible possibility?

And I know at this moment that there is no Ubuntu here...there is only me – the researcher, and him – the principal...And then the blinding moment of anger passes and I am back within this situated reality. I look out of the window. I see two girls scuffing their shoes in the red dirt. The dry dust rises in a small wisp of smoke. Then one girl suddenly grabs the other girl from the back by her hair and pulls her down into a kneeling position. There is anguish on the victim's face, but she doesn't resist. And it appears to me that this has happened to her many times before and she is no longer indignant, resistant, affronted. Was she ever otherwise given the space to be such, I wonder? Her hopeless resignation angers me.

I jump up and move to the window looking down onto the scene in the courtyard, the crisscrossing Euclidean grid of the window frame between us. The bully turns her eyes towards me and looks through the pane...looks through her own pain...even with a blank undaunted stare...staring into my face contorted with a horrible mixture of anger, disappointment and pity. The Principal sees my reaction and he too jumps up to have a look at what I am looking at. He swears under his breath in Afrikaans, "Darrie blêrrie boggers van graad sewe kinders... uit die blêrrie klasskamer alweer."[17] His composure is broken, the posturing has disappeared...we are back to the immediacy and brutal 'reality' of the moment, and partially recovering his previous tone, he relays to me in English: "Their teacher isn't here again today," as if I might not have known this self-evident piece of information. "Excuse me a minute," he says brusquely, and walks hastily out of the office, across the courtyard, up the steep steps and stops in the open doorway of the offending classroom.

From my visual perspective, the classroom behind the principal's dominant form is dark, unseeable and formless, like an auditorium when the lights have gone down – ready for the performance...a performance on a 'stage-in-the-round'. The two girls have already disappeared back into the same room, caught out, scampering like a pair of frightened rabbits back into their dark burrow. I can see the principal shouting and gesticulating threateningly. He is silhouetted against the dark doorway, delineated by the door, and through the windowpane I can hear nothing of what he says...there is only silence...and it is loud in my ears...it is as if I am watching an old-fashioned silent movie, being played out before me...a performance in silence on the theme of silence...visible, audible silence...

I am trying to comprehend the scene. I think back on what precipitated the current chain of events, to make sense of it. I think of the two rabbit girls scurrying away when the Voice of Authority entered the scene...I am a schoolgirl again... waiting in the principal's office. I am remembering the fear of bullies, bullies that took all forms, classmates and teachers. I am remembering the smell and taste of fear...the fractured, brutal, images of authority and its violent sting. I feel the same sick feelings coming back...deafening fragments of memories. I feel like a bewildered animal caught in the headlights of this strange blinding reenactment of repeated repressive realities...

At that moment...and it was not an epiphany...but a slow blurred form taking root... re-rooting in my mind. It was a slow re-realization of what I had done by wanting to 'speak out' and to tell this principal that I thought it was 'just not good enough.' It was a re-cognition of my *own* voice of violence, of what brutality I had done in feeding into the discourse on "disadvantage." I re-realized that my thoughts, framed within the discursive roots of my socialization, my education and knowledge, my own perceived empowerment as an adult, and my experience of teaching mostly within the context of privilege – which, through the temporal and spatial, defines the moment and place of poverty – had established that "disadvantage" as "plain to see" (McLaren, Leonardo, & Allen, 2000, p. 113).

I began to re-realize that in my initial thought-words of anger, I had been taking on the colonizing voice which produces the deficit, and that creates, validates and establishes 'the problem' from outside...from a place out there that can speak unmonitored by its own surveillance...I had been doing the same thing as that which I had surveyed in the courtyard. I was producing and reproducing the very conditions that produced the bully/bullying in the first place, ensuring its reproduction through my own voyeuristic perspective and reproductive deficit language, albeit a silent language of thoughts.

I too had become a bully. I was complicit with a system or discourse and a well-entrenched paradigm of thinking that constructs 'the problem', establishes the 'truth' on 'deficit', and *lays blame...*

I realize that my vantage point was at fault. These are the power principles that inform not only the political gaze from the perspective of the self, but also control the distributions of the spatial/temporal dichotomy and that define the political economy of context by assisting in the production of the poverty/privilege hierarchy, and which define the roles of subjects in context...

I hear the deficit voices again...bullying voices...some voices of educationalists, specialists, and well-known people in authority in South African Education...people in the 'new arena' of post-liberation education...people I interviewed. "The problem lies with our teachers...they are underqualified, demotivated, lacking experience and expertise, and there is not enough of them. Our failures in mathematics can be directly attributed to the teachers...*they* are our problem..."

I realize that in my own way, I was feeding into this, re-creating this monster, re-establishing this deficit discourse. I realize that in creating the teachers, principal and their pedagogic practices in this "disadvantaged community" as *lacking*, as the "real problem," it was an *escape*, a way of not facing up to not understanding, not seeing the source of power and how it threads its way into the repressive web.

Yes, I had become the bully. And the bully in the courtyard was as much, if not more, my *victim* of constructed "disadvantage" and the pedagogy of pain and poverty that it produces as she was a bully in herself. The principal was a victim of it too, and I had not even *begun* to imagine the strangulating and delimiting conditions that this discourse served to produce and in which he was constrained to operate. This was the 'pedagogizing of difference' (Swanson, 1998; 2005) indeed, and a discourse in which I had participated.

The principal came back into the room, looking a little harassed. A 'sideshow' had interrupted and seemed to detract from 'the conversation.' But, in fact, it was a critical fragment of the whole, a necessary contribution to understanding the resolution of the narrative, and in which our initial 'polite' conversation preceding 'the sideshow' had been the essential exposition. I, myself, had moved through several modes of *looking*, premised by various experiential podiums of perspective. Consequently, when I had been angry and critical, my vantage point had been the context of privilege in which I had gained much of my own teaching experience. When I had overcome my anger and realized my role in the co-constructed authorship of power, I had returned to my early youth and to remembering, remembering what it was like to be bullied and to feel the hand of violence and the voice of humiliation...and it was only *then* that I could begin to understand-feel with a *deeper listening* – the kind of deeper listening that renders one human.

It had required a range of senses as it had required a shift in perspective. I had moved from a 'looking on' and the voyeuristic power instantiated in perspectives of 'seeing', to a 'listening to', where the eyes are quieted and humbled by the sights and sounds within darkened silence, and the sense of hearing is peaked...tuning *into* silence...

This had been my route. Instead of trying to find the "root *of* the problem" and trying to "root *out* the problem," like a cancer from living tissue, I was moving towards searching for "*the source.*" The source of the problem lay silently *behind* the construction of "the problem" itself and threaded its way, like a tributary, to my very doorstep...I too was complicit, a collaborator of deficit discourse, a root of "the problem's" routedness. Now I became responsible as well, through acknowledging that responsibility.

The I-you dichotomy [which Buber's (1996) *I-Thou* relationship would oppose] had been broken by the emergence of a new bond of responsibility, a *humbling togetherness, a sense of Ubuntu*. I needed to *listen* collaboratively to that "source" in collectively finding a way together of "re-sourcing" towards non-impoverishment, other possibilities and mutual healing. With the sense of responsibility and humility came the opportunity for transformation and transcendence, both political and spiritual. It was the kind of calling in which one could recognize oneself in the image of the other as an organic relationship of 'humble togetherness'.

In Closing

Ubuntu offers a contribution to an ethic of engagement with the other. It provides a lens, through the embrace of critical reflexive narrative methodology, that helps foreground existing positions of dominance and deficit in discourses in ways that open up opportunities for resisting them. It offers the possibility of dialogue about the nature of transformation and transcendence beyond personal, political paradoxes informed by neoliberalism and neocolonialism. It creates a rootedness with the daily, local and lived. A disposition of Ubuntu facilitates the exploration of less objectifying ways of being in research through the inclusion of the self and the self's role in achieving humble togetherness with the research community. It offers hope of engendering pedagogies of possibility away from dichotomous discourse and positivist approaches to qualitative research. By confronting our colonizing ways of seeing, a transcendent spirituality may be found through 'humble togetherness.' Ubuntu, therefore, contributes to decolonizing hegemonic meanings, heralding the opportunity for renewal and personal transformation. It offers guidance in terms of our responsibilities and obligations to egalitarianism and human dignity. It affords a way of knowing that helps us learn to become human.

NOTES

[1] This has resonance with Hannah Arendt's (1968) assertion that the past always intrudes on the present. There is no objective present divorced from a historical context. It brings in to play the understanding that what precedes us influences how we engage with the world, the choices we make, our values and beliefs in and understandings of that world, and how we proceed with what we claim to know about it. We are always within (con)text, as Derrida implies in his comment: "'Il n'y a pas de hors-texte' (There is no outside-text). Extrapolating this to a question of ethics and

responsibility, we can never be independent of or 'free' from obligation in our relationship with others. This would be consistent with Emmanuel Levinas's philosophy that he calls a 'first philosophy', (where philosophy is defined for him as a 'wisdom of love'). In this philosophy, an ethical responsibility towards the Other precedes subjectivity. There is strong resonance with this other-centered ontology and many indigenous philosophies that espouse that the individual only exists in consummate interrelatedness with many others that constitute a whole with nature and the Earth. Ubuntu rests on this deep humanistic philosophy of obligatory interrelatedness.

2   *Voices in the Silence* is a critical exploration of the construction of disadvantage in school mathematics in social context. It provides a reflexive, narrative account of a pedagogic journey towards understanding the pedagogizing of difference in mathematics classrooms and its realizations as pedagogized disadvantage in and across diverse socio-political, economic, cultural, and pedagogic contexts. Fieldwork occurred within the Cape Province of South Africa, in schooling communities with socio-economic, cultural and historical differences. Research took the form of interviews, discussions, narrative-sharing, and participant observation, in a recent post-apartheid context. In resistance to perpetuating hierarchized, linear or scientistic approaches to research within traditional social sciences and mathematics education, I embrace an arts-based methodology. Through narrative and poetry, I engage with the socio-political, cultural and pedagogic implications of the social construction of disadvantage in school mathematics practice. The dissertation, therefore, offers interdisciplinary approaches to critical concerns of inequity and access, calling on the emotive, spiritual, embodied, and personal domains of experience in problematizing the (re)production of disadvantage. Consequently, I broaden the scope of interpretive possibilities to encompass interrogation of dominant discourses and universalizing ideologies within the social domain, which colonize meanings. These include globalization, neo-liberalism, neo-colonialism, and aspects of progressivism and pedagogic constructivism, in the way in which they compete for hegemony within mathematics classroom contexts as sites of struggle for meaning, informing discursive positions of disadvantage, delimiting practice and disempowering students constructed in terms of social difference discourses such as ethnicity, gender, class, race, poverty, and ability, amongst other positions. The incommensurability of certain social domain discourses produce disjunctions, paradoxes, contradictions and dilemmas, experienced as a lived curriculum of pedagogic disadvantage in the lives of students and teachers within contexts of constructed disadvantage.

3   The metaphor of ghosts is purposeful in that it has resonance with Derrida's ghosts that are ever present and absent as they haunt us in our engagement with 'the other.' In this narration, I make conscious in my own writing the interlocution with ghosts as a way of exposing how, in Derrida's (1994) terms, the author or narrator is never fully present to themselves, that we dance with absences we can neither capture nor see, only as shadows of what might be, and that these absences are ever present in what we do affirm as real, always-already erasing that presence. In this sense, absence is ghostliness. I have given more depth to this discussion in reference to the complexities of research and research ethics in Swanson (2007a).

4   I am reminded of Derrida's (1994) words in his concluding paragraph in Specters of Marx: "We, in a sense, become mediums, allowing the ghosts of the past to tell their stories, our stories, through us" (p. 176).

5   Afrikaans for: "Good Afternoon, (Mrs.) Ma'am. Can I perhaps help you (madam) with something?" [This is the polite way of addressing a stranger. The use of 'you' would be considered impolite.] Many of the mixed-race communities in the Cape Province of South Africa speak a dialect of Afrikaans as their mother tongue.

6   Afrikaans for: "Good Afternoon, (Mr.) Sir. I wanted to come and visit. I was here a long time ago."

7   "Oh, what a shame, Ma'am": The Anglicization of Afrikaans is commonplace in these communities, so that a mix of English and Afrikaans in the same sentence is often heard.

8   "Yes, for a long time." "Ja' is slang for 'yes' in South African English and is borrowed from the Afrikaans.

9 "Ag, siestog! What a shame! I am sorry!": 'Ag, siestog', is an Afrikaans expression of sympathy. To say "I am sorry' in this context in South African culture does not mean that you claim responsibility for harm done to another as in 'I apologise'. It simply means that you are feeling for that other person and you understand how they must be feeling. In other words, you are sorry to see that they are suffering.

10 This is a pseudonym.

11 Skollie: from the Afrikaans, a common street criminal; someone up to no good; a deviant person.

12 The Strand: A remote stretch of beach with white ancient-marine sand, where a number of murders of this nature have taken place over the years. 'Strand' means 'beach' in Afrikaans.

13 Boot: South African and British English for 'trunk' of a car.

14 "Where have all the fishes gone?" acts as a double entendre in particular reference to the famous song, "Where have all the flowers gone?" Like the original antiwar folk song written by Pete Seeger and Joe Hickerson, it reminds us of the lyrics in the chorus, specifically the line that asks: "Oh, when will they ever learn?" In respect of the global responsibility of environmental devastation suffered within local communities, reinforcing oppressive social and political relationships within and between them, perhaps we also need to ask, "When will they ever learn?" or more inclusively of the global community, "When will we ever learn?"

15 It is a web of 'glocal' interrelations; an ever-interdependent global mesh of influence and effect that impacts local communities.

16 Please note that a version of the original narrative appears as Roots/Routes I & II in Swanson, D. M. (2009a & b).

17 Those bloody buggers of grade seven children ... out of the bloody classroom again!

REFERENCES

Arendt, H. (1968). Men in dark times. New York: Harcourt Brace and World.

Battle, M. (1997). Reconciliation: The Ubuntu theology of Desmond Tutu. Cleveland, OH: Pilgrim Press.

Bernstein. (2000). Pedagogy, symbolic control and identity: Theory, research, critique. New York: Rowman & Littlefield.

Buber, M. (1996). I and thou. (W. Kaufmann, Trans.). New York: Touchstone.

Derrida, J. (1994). Specters of Marx. London: Routledge.

Edgoose, J. (2001). Just decide! Derrida and the ethical aporias of education. In G. J. J. Biesta & D. Egéa-Kuehne (Eds.), Derrida and education. New York: Routledge.

Foucault, M. (1980). Power/Knowledge: Selected interviews and other writing 1972–1977. New York: Pantheon Books.

Hegel, G.W.F (1820). Elements of the philosophy of right [S. W. Dyde, Trans. (1896)]. Hegel's Philosophy of Right, Preface: found at http://www.marxists.org/reference/archive/hegel/works/ pr/preface.htm {partially hyperlinked, needs removing}

Marx, C. (2002). Ubu and Ubuntu: On the dialectics of apartheid ands nation building. Politkon: South African Journal of Political Studies, 29(1), 49–69.

McLaren, P., Leonardo, Z., and Allen, R.L. (2000). Epistemologies of Whiteness: Transgressing and transforming pedagogical knowledge. In R. Mahalingam & C. McCarthy (Eds.), Multicultural Curriculum: New directions for social theory, practice, and policy (pp. 108–123). New York: Routledge.

Murithi, T. (2004). Towards a culturally inclusive notion of human rights: The African world view known as Ubuntu. Human Rights Tribune, 10(1), 14–15.

Swanson, D.M. (2009b). Roots / Routes II. Qualitative Inquiry, 15(1), 58–78.

Swanson, D. M. (2009a). Roots / Routes I. Qualitative Inquiry, 15(1), 49–57.

Swanson, D.M. (2008). States of Nature: Creating "The Normal" Through the Tale of a Farm School in South Africa. Journal of Curriculum and Pedagogy, 5(2), 95–133.

Swanson, D. M. (2007b). Ubuntu: An African contribution to (re)search for/with a "humble togetherness." The Journal of Contemporary Issues in Education, 2(2). University of Alberta, Special Edition on African Worldviews. [Online] Retrieved from http://ejournals.library. ualberta.ca/index.php/JCIE/issue/view/56

Swanson, D.M. (2007a). Shadows between us: An A/R/Tographic gaze at issues of ethics and activism. In S. Springgay, R. Irwin, C. Leggo, P. Gouzouasis, & K. Grauer (Eds.), Being with a/r/tography. Rotterdam, Netherlands: Sense Publishers.

Swanson, D.M. (2006). "Humble togetherness and Ubuntu": An African contribution to a reflexive, critical, narrative journey. Paper presented at the Second International Congress of Qualitative Inquiry, University of Illinois at Urbana-Champaign, U.S.A.

Swanson, D. (2005). Ubuntu: An African contribution to a narrative journey of seeking a 'humble togetherness.' Paper presented at the annual conference of the Comparative and International Education Society (West), The University of British Columbia, Vancouver, Canada.

Swanson, D. (2004). Voices in the Silence: Narratives of disadvantage, social context and school mathematics in post-apartheid South Africa. Unpublished Doctoral Dissertation, University of British Columbia, Vancouver, Canada. [To be published by Cambria Press].

Swanson, D. (1998). Bridging the boundaries?: A study of mainstream mathematics, academic support and "Disadvantaged Learners" in an independent, secondary school in the Western Cape, (South Africa). Unpublished Master's Dissertation, University of Cape Town, South Africa.

Tutu, D. (1999). No future without forgiveness. New York: Doubleday.

Lloyd, M. (2007). Tutu: Poverty fueling terror. Retrieved June 17, 2008, from http://www.cnn.com/2007/WORLD/asiapcf/09/16/talkasia.tutu/

Vanier, J. (1998). Becoming human. Toronto: Anansi (CBC).

Dalene M. Swanson
Department of Secondary Education,
University of Alberta

STEVE SHARRA[1]

TOWARDS AN AFRICAN PEACE EPISTEMOLOGY

Teacher Autobiography and uMunthu in Malawian Education

INTRODUCTION

When I was growing up, my father liked to tune in the British Broadcasting Service (BBC) soon after the seven o'clock evening news on the Malawi Broadcasting Corporation. He would do this either before or after dinner, depending on what came first, the news or the dinner. One evening we were listening to the BBC after dinner, and my father motioned everyone in the house to shush up. This was always an indication that something about Malawi was being mentioned in the BBC's world news, or something with relevance to Malawi, or to the world. My siblings would scamper off to play moonlight games, but I would stay to listen. On this particular evening, the BBC were interviewing Kanyama Chiume. I was about 10 years old or so at the time, and I do not remember what Kanyama Chiume said in the interview. But after the interview ended, my father admonished me not to mention to anyone that we had listened to Kanyama Chiume being interviewed on the BBC. When I asked why, my father said Kanyama Chiume was enemy number one of the Life[2] President Ngwazi Dr. Hastings Kamuzu Banda. As a result, he was a wanted man, and the government wanted to keep track of his every movement.

I asked my father if he was going to report the interview to the authorities. He said they had probably listened to it too. "Does that matter?" I wondered to myself. Wouldn't the government in fact be happy that here was one good police officer doing his part to report the country's enemies to the authorities? Such was my innocence that were I to spot Kanyama Chiume on the street, I would surely report him to the authorities myself. He was one of the people said to be plotting to assassinate the Life President and overthrow the one-party Malawi government. These were people who wanted to bring war to the country, and they deserved to be arrested, or worse, as the government told us. When the news broke on Christmas Eve 1981 that the government had arrested Orton and Vera Chirwa, another dissident couple "wanted" by the government, and put them on trial for treason, most of us felt they deserved it. Who wanted war in our country? Why would anybody want to kill the Life President, a generous, wonderful leader who brought us independence from the British?

AUTOBIOGRAPHY AND MALAWI'S STRUGGLE FOR INDEPENDENCE

This chapter recounts stories from my dissertation research, which arose from a personal passion as a writer whose main subject, broadly speaking, had been the Malawi I grew up in, and its place in the world. Initially I was unaware of how the research would intertwine questions of writing, identity, peace and violence, with those of what in Chichewa, Malawi's primary language, is known as uMunthu, or ubuntu in other Southern African societies. This story also entails my personal search for identity through literary effort, leaving Malawi and Africa for a diasporic sojourn in the United States, adopting an Africa-centered intellectual framework, and returning with that framework to discover uMunthu peace epistemology, which had been lying in plain sight all along.

The specific goal of my dissertation study was to better understand the role of teachers in interpreting Malawi's political and social history, and Malawi's contemporary problems of structural violence. More centrally, I was interested in exploring how those definitions and interpretations of political and social history, and contemporary problems of structural violence might contribute to curriculum and pedagogy in ways that promote peace at the local and national levels, and beyond.

Part of the field work for the study involved conducting writing workshops with Malawian primary school teachers. I worked with 21 selected teachers who came from five schools from different parts of Malawi. We experimented with personal life writing, and then observed how these exercises affected the content of what they taught in the classroom, and how they taught it. I was interested in finding out how the personal narratives the teachers wrote rendered definitions of peace, conflict, and various typologies of violence and dehumanization.

The teachers also used the writing workshops to read excerpts from some of the Malawian autobiographies I had selected, and also to write their own autobiographies. During my preparations for the field work I had read several Malawian autobiographies, and continued to read a few more upon returning from the field.

I found the Malawian autobiographies that I read as part of the process of developing my research proposal exceptionally exciting and inspiring. It became clear to me how as Malawians, the dictatorial imposition of official histories during Malawi's 30 years of one party rule had deprived us of a much richer and fuller heritage of how the Malawi nation, and Malawi's Pan-African identity, came into being. Seeing how personal narratives combined individual insights with national aspirations for independence from British colonialism led me to see the power of autobiographical narrative as a methodological tool, as research data, and as a contribution toward educational policy in peace building (Barash & Webel, 2002).

Realizing how this tool had not been well investigated in Malawian education, I began to think of the challenges and opportunities posed by autobiography in educational practice. I started looking around for studies that explored the intersection between autobiography and teaching, and my search started off with a researcher who was in fact one of my own professors at Michigan State University, Susan Florio-Ruane. I drew inspiration and motivation from Florio-Ruane's (2001) study of pre-service teachers who formed a book club and read autobiographies.

Called the Future Teacher Autobiography Club, the prospective teachers read, met and discussed autobiographies for a six month period, during which time they dug into several conversations about many issues surrounding culture and their identities as students, teachers, members of a race, gender, various ethnic groups, and citizens. More inspiration for my approach to the study also came from my experiences in the Michigan State University's chapter of the National Writing Project, the Red Cedar Writing Project, to which I was kindly invited by the director, Dr. Janet Swenson. My participation in the 2002 summer invitational came at a crucial time when I was putting together ideas and resources for my proposal. Both ideas, a teachers' autobiography club, and the summer invitational writing institute, became important parts of the methodology for the eventual study I did with Malawian teachers.

I read Henry Masauko Chipembere's 2001 autobiography, *Hero of the Nation: The Autobiography of Henry Masauko Chipembere*, published posthumously, and Kanyama Chiume's *The Autobiography of Kanyama Chiume*, published in 1982. Reading the two autobiographies took my thinking in new directions regarding the role that education played in preparing Chipembere and Chiume to contribute towards the emancipation of their country and the continent of Africa from colonialism. Both Chipembere and Chiume were in their twenties when the struggle for Malawi's independence gathered momentum in the mid-1950s. They had just returned from universities—Chipembere from Fort Hare University in South Africa, and Chiume from Makerere College in Uganda. They became actively involved in the movement for independence. Both of them became very close to Dr. Banda, first corresponding with him through letters while he was in Ghana and in Britain. They convinced Dr. Banda that he was the person best placed and best suited to lead the people of Nyasaland, as Malawi was then known, into independence.

Dr. Banda returned to Malawi in 1958, spearheaded the independence movement, and Malawi became independent on July 6, 1964. Within three months, Dr. Banda's first cabinet underwent a crisis, and many of those who had helped establish the new nation of Malawi, including Chipembere and Chiume, resigned and were forced into exile. What followed thereafter was a thirty-year period about which much has been studied and written. Chipembere's and Chiume's autobiographies are two of the most important narratives written about how Malawi's dictatorship started. Reading the two books, I developed a new sense of connectedness to and affection for my country, leading to a feeling of self-empowerment in understanding not only how one major period of my own life was shaped, but also how that period remained unanalyzed, and its tensions unexpiated. I included chapter excerpts of these two autobiographies on the reading list of the writing workshop I used as part of the methodology for the project. Out of the twenty-one teachers who accepted the invitation to participate in my study, the eight who wrote their own autobiographies took their cue from Chipembere and Chiume, and wrote some of the most illuminating stories that I encountered in the course of the study.

In addition to the autobiographies of Chipembere and Chiume, I also included the second chapter of Paulo Freire's (1970) *Pedagogy of the Oppressed* on the reading list. Freire's contributions to the study were twofold. First, his admonitions against a *banking* education had pedagogical implications for how to teach in a way that freed the creativity and imagination of students. Second, his discussion on how a critical pedagogy can educate an oppressed people about their oppression, and mobilize them for community projects of liberation offered a pertinent definition of what the teachers agreed was a peace education approach to curriculum and pedagogy. Subsequently, Freire's notion of *praxis* as action and reflection informed the thematic framework of my study, as a culmination of the process of constituting uMunthu as a peace epistemology, through peace-themed curricula and pedagogy.

'I AM, BECAUSE WE ARE'

That this work would end up with uMunthu as its intellectual framework was not apparent during my early months of field work. I thought of my research question as dealing with how to use creative writing as a way of approaching the primary school curriculum and its pedagogy. A peace education perspective arose from the infusion of historical and contemporary problems of violence and conflict in Malawi in the curriculum.

On Saturday, April 17, 2004, two months into my field work, the Catholic Diocese of Zomba ordained a new bishop, Rt. Rev. Fr. Thomas Msusa, to take the place of Rt. Rev. Bishop Allan Chamgwera who had retired. I went to witness the auspicious event at the grounds of the historic Zomba Catholic Secondary School. In his speech, Bishop Msusa, who had left Nankhunda Seminary just months before I set foot there in 1988, spoke of the problems Malawi was facing, and how we needed to "become as one," his guiding biblical verse from his seminary days. "The African worldview is about living as one family, belonging to God," he said. "We say 'I am because we are', or in Chichewa *kali kokha nkanyama, tili awiri ntiwanthu*." The raw, literal translation is that an animal of the bush is on its own, but human beings have community. Community is the essence of being human. In his reflections on how he experienced the Truth and Reconciliation Commission (TRC), *No Future Without Forgiveness*, Archbishop Tutu (1999) explains *Ubuntu* as the philosophical essence that propelled the TRC. In the book the former Anglican archbishop offers a list of examples where Ubuntu was the driving philosophy for many southern African countries that chose forgiveness over retaliation against white minority regimes upon attaining independence. Included on the list are Zimbabwe, Kenya and Namibia.

Bishop Msusa's reference to *uMunthu* in his speech that Saturday afternoon would become a turning point in my search for an intellectual framework for the study. That search would later lead me to the scholarship on uMunthu, written by Malawians, Zimbabweans, South Africans, and other scholars elsewhere. In my search, I took a closer look at John Mbiti, the late Kenyan philosopher of African religion, who turned French philosopher Descartes' dictum "I think, therefore I am" on its head to demonstrate the African philosophy of being, "You are, therefore I am." My introduction to the Cartesian dictum had come from Joe Kincheloe's 1993 discussion of individualism and the postmodern deconstruction of scientific rationality and its Enlightenment ideals. Alongside Malawian philosophers and theologians Harvey Sindima and Augustine Musopole, I found it eye opening to read critical pedagogues such as Kincheloe pointing out how the Cartesian dictum forms the basis of neoliberal individualism and the Western worldview.

But Bishop Msusa's reference also brought back to my mind Jason Carter, grandson of the former US president Jimmy Carter, who spent two years in South Africa as a peace corps volunteer in the late 90s. On his return, Carter (2002) wrote a book in which he narrated his experiences in South Africa. I was struck by an interview with National Public Radio in 2002 in which Carter offered that the African worldview of 'Ubuntu' was an important philosophy that Americans could do well to learn from Africans.

I was walking to church on the morning of April 18, 2004, when it occurred to me that I had stumbled upon a concept that had the potential to tie together the many pieces of inquiry I was engaged in through the study. Here I saw two projects merging into one: the dissertation research study, and my own ongoing epistemological study. We had ended our first week in the writing workshop with the participating teachers, during which time we had grappled with the question of what peace education looked like in a Malawian classroom. Could what we were doing in the workshop, and in the larger context of the entire study, be usefully termed 'uMunthu education'? Could it be broad enough to incorporate peace education? If so, how would a teacher go about it in a Malawian primary school classroom? How would this unraveling of uMunthu in the journey so far affect the autobiographical writing I had used as part of the methodology for the study?

'INTELLIGENCE IS ONE THING, UMUNTHU ANOTHER'

As I read the teachers' autobiographical narratives resulting from the writing workshops, I began to see aspects of Malawi's history reflected in the lives the teachers had lived while growing up. I also saw the contemporary aspects of Malawian society in their teaching lives at that moment in time. I began to wonder to what extent the particular aspects of Malawi's recent history of dictatorship and contemporary life could provide insights into how a peace curriculum and pedagogy might look like in a Malawian classroom. Not all of the narratives discussed uMunthu, but those that did saw it as a part of the analysis in understanding what lay at the root of Malawi's contemporary problems of structural violence and injustice. Even for those that did not, my later analysis of the narratives grappled with the question of how the absence of uMunthu could be seen as part of the context in which physical and structural violence was a part of daily life for the teachers, both as young people growing up, and as practicing teachers.

According to two of the teachers in the study, Nduluzi and Pinde,[3] the problems of exploitation and injustice that teachers were working against in

27

Malawi were problems brought about as a result of the breakdown of uMunthu in Malawian society. Thus one way of addressing the problems was through the promotion of the concept of uMunthu. As Pinde observed, uMunthu was something that both the home and the school needed to emphasize in order to prepare young people for a future in which problems of structural violence and social injustice would be minimized. As I read the scholarship on uMunthu, I was struck by how much Pinde's and Nduluzi's explications resonated with that of the theologians and religious philosophers, especially Harvey Sindima. According to Sindima (1995), uMunthu stands for "basic values of human life, or that which gives human life meaning" (p. 175).

The dynamism of uMunthu is grounded in the moral agency characteristic of being a full human, giving people the recognition that "they can be agents of change when given a chance or when recognized as persons. To be recognized as a person is to have self-respect, or to realize self-determination" (p. 175).

In his narratives, Nduluzi recounted a particular incident that occurred during a curriculum development workshop session. As he recounted the event, I could visualize the incident and the setting in which it took place. It was a place I was familiar with, with tall windows that opened to let in the cool dry wind of April. When you were in that room the sound of the Domasi River could clearly be heard coursing down its way to Lake Chirwa. If you stood up and looked outside through the tall windows, you could see the tall blue gum trees standing erect along the grassy banks of the fresh water river.

In Nduluzi's narrative, a group made up of curriculum specialists, teacher educators, education administrators and one primary classroom teacher was meeting in the Humanities Laboratory of the National Curriculum Center. They sat around tables that had been rearranged to form a large, square-shaped working area.

The group was working on the scope and sequence for a unit on literacy around the home. They decided to use fictional stories that conveyed messages about health and nutrition, as a way of integrating various disciplines into language and literacy. On one particular story, the consensus was that Malawian students needed to learn about the three dietary groups of food needed for a balanced nutrition. Nduluzi raised his hand and said he had an observation to make. He had recently read in a science journal that nutritionists were now suggesting that rather than the conventional understanding that there were three dietary groups of food, there were in fact six. He went on to list them. There was a silence in the room before one of the members in the group raised an objection to Nduluzi's suggestion. Nduluzi was asked to provide a credible source for his information, and according to his narrative, he did. Before very long everyone else in the group refused to accommodate Nduluzi's suggestion. They said they were not aware of these changes in the scientific community, and therefore, they did not trust the suggestion. Someone pointed out that Nduluzi was a "mere" primary school teacher, how could he know such details? Another one wondered, slyly, when Nduluzi was going to go to university and study for a first degree. "He is uneducated, yet he wants to dominate," was another remark.

Nduluzi's autobiographical narrative recounts the ways in which he had to endure put-downs and demeaning attitudes by his superiors in the education system. In most cases he was the only primary school teacher in groups of experts mostly boasting university degrees and high government offices. The attitude of many of the experts was that they deserved to be considered experts by virtue of their higher education. People like Nduluzi, mere primary school teachers without any university degrees, did not know much, and therefore did not deserve to be included in such important activities. Nduluzi wrote about having had to persevere against an onslaught of ridicule and disdain. But his narratives also celebrated the encouragement and positive attitudes of some of his superiors, who recognized his hard work, and promoted his endeavors.

Nduluzi's comments on uMunthu addressed specific abuses directed at him by his superiors, especially during his participation in the curriculum development workshops he was a part of. He wrote about his views being subjected to scrutiny and ridicule with specific reference to his not possessing a university degree. Nduluzi pointed out that it was the absence of uMunthu ethics from which sprang the abuse he was subjected to by fellow educators who held senior ranks and higher educational qualifications, and looked down upon primary school teachers.

> uMunthu is an act of doing something for anybody as you would want anybody to DO the same for you. Usually the uMunthu act has self-giving and a total equalization of somebody's being, by way of valuing and looking at somebody as a human being. It does not emphasize who this person is, who is this, kodi akuchita ngati ndani....Akufuna akhale ngati ndani ameneyi....Kodi kamwana kameneka [who does he think he is. . . this little child]. uMunthu is self-realized in very few people. Many do not have uMunthu qualities. Usually those practicing this mentality do not themselves realize that when somebody's being is realized and valued, that particular person reaches his or her full potential.

Pinde was another teacher who also provided a direct perspective on uMunthu and its place in the peace education curriculum and in the school system. Pinde was unable to undertake the autobiographical writing exercise, so instead of producing a piece of writing, we conducted an autobiographical interview in her classroom. Pinde pointed out that the injustice visited upon Malawian teachers stemmed from the lack of appreciation for the humanity of other human beings. When one is able to appreciate and respect others, one is said to have uMunthu, she told me. Pinde spent a considerable amount of time giving examples of what uMunthu was, and pointed out that it needed a combination of cultural upbringing and educational opportunity for one to develop uMunthu. Many of the education officials at the district, division and ministry of education headquarters levels were better educated than most teachers. Yet there were those in their midst that had not developed uMunthu, she pointed out. These officials did not regard teachers as people worthy of dignity and deserving of opportunities. Pinde's own words are worth reproducing at length:

> Ethical responsibility is not the responsibility of the school alone. 'uMunthu' starts at home. uMunthu is when you can do things that make other people say you are a human being; you have certain characteristics that make you a human being—to listen to what other people say, to associate with other people—elements like those are what make a human being. And there are times when uMunthu disappears. And one becomes a thug. And these forces can have nothing to do with education. A person can be highly educated, but have no uMunthu . . . So this uMunthu, as a teacher you can do your best, but the environment at home can cause uMunthu to disappear. . . Education is one thing, uMunthu is another. Intelligence is one thing, uMunthu another.

While the other participants did not directly address uMunthu in their autobiographical narratives, they wrote about their lives growing up and becoming teachers. They wrote about a societal context that begged explanations for the causes of the violence, conflict, inequality and injustice that were a part of their day to day lives. Their narratives revisited images of what schooling looked like under the dictatorship. They wrote about the types of physical violence they experienced, and participated in, with peers, during play, and in boarding school. They described the socio-economic conditions in which they grew up. In some cases they nearly dropped out of school because their parents could not afford the tuition fees, and wealthy relatives refused to help out of envy. They wrote about gender relations and the victimization some of them experienced as girls. To bring their narratives to their lives today, they described the conditions they worked in as teachers, analyzing the hierarchies of exploitation, inequality, class and social injustice.

Schooling Under a Dictatorship

These teachers were young and in school when Dr. Hastings Kamuzu Banda was life president of Malawi. Dr. Banda ruled Malawi from 1964 to 1994. There is a considerable amount of disagreement about Dr. Banda's rule, with many Malawians holding him as the visionary father and founder of the Malawi nation who built a strong foundation for the country. There are as many Malawians who argue that Dr. Banda's dictatorial rule suppressed freedoms that were necessary for the development of the country. These argue that Dr. Banda's rule did not prepare Malawi for the benefit of the majority of the population. For these teachers, going to school during the dictatorship meant having to deal with a specific set of challenges, some of them peculiar to the dictatorship, others peculiar to Malawi's status as a newly independent, Third World country caught in the geopolitics of the Cold War.

The political nature of schooling under Dr. Banda's dictatorship and its effects on social justice and human security was aptly illustrated in the autobiographical narrative provided by Wembayi, a teacher in his late forties. In the year 1972, eight years after Malawi's independence and one year after Dr. Banda was declared state president for life, Wembayi was expelled from school, and banned from attending any school in the country. He was a standard 8 pupil at the time. What happened was that his seat in the class was directly below the portrait of the president, Dr. Kamuzu Banda. One morning the classroom opened to the discovery that somebody had desecrated the portrait by painting it and adorning it with sunglasses. "All the blame came to me. Because I was young, I was not arrested." However the school's administration was not prepared to close the case without somebody being punished, regardless of the absence of evidence. Wembayi wrote that he was "suspended from school for good." He stayed home for two years, and then an idea came to him. He changed all his names and re-enrolled in a school some fifteen miles away where no one knew him. He did well and was selected to attend a respected national secondary school.

The "Torturing Profession": Life as Teachers

Several of the teachers wrote and talked of being treated with disregard and disrespect by superiors in the schools, the community and in the government. They wrote about being denied deserved promotions, being denied good housing, and not being consulted on important decisions affecting their lives. They also talked of being denied opportunities for further education, and of being passed over for foreign study tours that usually go with attractive allowances paid for by the government. The teachers' descriptions of these issues are vivid and detailed. The tone deployed in interviews, discussions, and in the narratives shows how strongly and passionately the teachers feel about their grievances, and how, in their view, nobody is listening.

According to Sakina, the Teaching Service Commission of Malawi stipulates that if a teacher has gone for eight years without undergoing an interview for promotion, they should be awarded a promotion. Sakina wrote of how it took fourteen years before she could receive her first promotion, and another seven before the second promotion came. "Such things in my life have been very painful," she wrote. She added: "The profession which indeed is teaching became a torture," alluding to a saying common amongst Malawian teachers that the teaching profession should really be renamed the "torturing profession."

In addition to discussing teachers' lives and analyzing their autobiographical narratives, I also participated in their lesson planning preparations, and observed some of them teaching in their classes. Two particular lessons stood out for how they addressed the question of teaching a given primary school lesson from a peace and social justice education perspective. In one lesson, the textbook required the teacher to teach students how to fill out a bank deposit form, while in the other the textbook required students to be taught how to use the mathematical concept of ratio. In preparing to teach both lessons, the teachers struggled with the problem of how to bring peace and social justice education perspectives into the lessons. In the bank deposit form lesson, the teachers invited the students to discuss the larger implications of banking operations in Malawi. The recent privatization and sale of a government owned bank to a foreign company had led to retrenchment of workers. This had repercussions on the extended families that depended on the workers. In the ratio lesson, the teacher led the students in a discussion on the ratio between boys and girls in the school, and the gender contexts that presented particular problems to female pupils. The relevance of these particular lessons to uMunthu lies in the broader ideals of the importance of appreciating the humanity of others, rather than in sacrificing people's wellbeing for the sake of the bottom line.[4]

TOWARD AN AFRICAN CONCEPT OF PEACE: UMUNTHU AND THE HUMAN COMMUNITY

Four years after the field work, I can not claim to have answered the questions I set out to investigate. However it became more obvious that there was something about the concept and definition of who a human being is in Malawian and Southern African ways of being, that required more theoretical reflection and investigation, especially in the school system. The autobiographical narratives written by the teachers reflected that need, as did the discussions with students on how theories and skills propagated in curriculum content needed to relate to people's daily lives in a real and meaningful way.

As the study progressed, I became eager to find more applications of uMunthu to the autobiographical narratives produced by the teachers, and to curriculum and pedagogy in peace education. I felt that I needed to dig deeper into what the introduction of uMunthu perspectives meant for the trajectory of the study. To do that, I undertook further literature review studies of the available, relevant scholarship on uMunthu. I ended up selecting four Malawian studies done on the concept of uMunthu, three of them in theology, and one of them in political science. I selected these four to enable a discussion of what an African peace epistemology might look like, and how it might inform curriculum and pedagogy.

The first study I looked at was Rev. Dr. Harvey Sindima's 1995 work, *Africa's Agenda: The Legacy of Liberalism and Colonialism in the Crisis of African Values*. I had discovered Rev. Dr. Sindima's work before leaving for the field. I was aware of Sindima's rigorous analysis of uMunthu in the philosophy of African culture and religions, but at this early point of the project I was more interested in Sindima's historical dissection of Western liberalism and its role in the disruption of Africa's indigenous systems. In Sindima's words, *Africa's Agenda* "examines the impact of liberalism on African thought and values which resulted in a serious identity crisis" for Africans. Sindima's argument is that an agenda for Africa's recovery lies in the "recapture of traditional values" and the opening of "possibilities for a deeper understanding of self and society" (p. xiv).

Another source was Gerard Chigona, whose master's thesis, titled *uMunthu Theology: Path of Integral Human Liberation Rooted in Jesus of Nazareth*, was published as a book in 2002. Chigona's study aimed to provide a local context for a theological interpretation of Jesus Christ, observing that "any neglect and sidelining of the African cultural heritage in doing theology is a neglect and negation of oneself in history" (p. 14). Chigona's study presents a model of Malawian life based on uMunthu, embedded within it an "inbuilt critical analysis at both [the] individual and social level" in which individuals and communities can measure themselves

(p. 76). For Chigona, uMunthu provides a basis for education that involves the head, the hands, and also the heart.

A third source was the Association of Theological Institutions in Southern and Central Africa (ATISCA) Bulletin, a journal of African theology. The journal's edition was a compilation of papers presented at a 1996 conference, held in Swaziland. Rev. Dr. Musopole had been the keynote speaker, and I soon learned that Rev. Dr. Musopole had written a master's degree thesis on the topic of uMunthu theology. I later learned that he had in fact continued this focus into his doctoral research, which he had published as a book, *Being Human in Africa: Toward an African Christian Anthropology*.

Musopole's (1996) study pursues the question of "How does African Christianity define and understand African peoples in a way that is humanizing, and, how can that view influence the shaping [of] a humane life for the African people in the totality of their existence?" (p. 1). In answering that question, Musopole analyzes the theological and philosophical work of John Mbiti (1969). In Musopole's words, Mbiti adopts a dynamic view of African humanity that "takes into account the changes that have affected and continue to affect African humanity as a result of western Christianity, imperialism, colonialism, modernity and capitalism" (p. 12). While Musopole finds "serious flaws" and inadequacies with Mbiti's concept of time in African thought, he sees Mbiti's dictum "I am because we are, and since we are, therefore, I am" as "an excellent summary of what it means to be human in Africa" (p. 13).

Although most of the available literature on uMunthu in Malawi arose from theological and religious studies perspectives, some of it adopts a political studies perspective. In "Can African feet divorce Western shoes? The case of 'uBuntu' and democratic good governance in Malawi," Richard Tambulasi and Harvey Kayuni (2005) use the concept of uMunthu to evaluate Malawi's first two governments since independence in 1964. They analyze the thirty-year dictatorship under Dr. Hastings Kamuzu Banda, and the multiparty government led by Dr. Bakili Muluzi from 1994 to 2004. Tambulasi and Kayuni conclude that based on the common understanding of what uMunthu entails, the thirty years of dictatorship failed to live up to the ideals of uMunthu. In that regard, the ten years under Bakili Muluzi and the United Democratic Front did start out as governance with uMunthu ideals but soon deviated by doing away with principles of good governance and democracy.

One thing I found significant in the theological studies by Musopole, Sindima and Chigona was that they interrogate liberal Christianity and its dehumanizing effect on Africans, without, as Chigona puts it, attempting to romanticize Malawi's religious heritage. In being able to use the concept of uMunthu in discussing theology, colonialism, history and politics, the authors make a remarkable contribution that marks a turning point in locating intellectual sources for uMunthu as an element of African epistemology in Malawian scholarship.

Although none of the studies use the Malawi education system as their central context, Musopole's study addresses the individualism of modern education, brought to Malawi as missionary education, as being responsible for the suppression of uMunthu as the basis for educating young people. Musopole makes mention of an autobiographical motivation for the origins of his inquiry, starting when he was made principal of one of Malawi's earliest schools, Robert Laws Secondary School. Musopole's experiences as principal caused him to reflect on how the influence of the British school system remained unchanged even after Malawi's independence, with no effort, as Musopole (1996) puts it, to "radically indigenize the educational philosophy" (p. 13). Musopole, therefore, wondered what was being left out of the education system by divorcing Malawian education from Malawian values. Musopole's perspective on uMunthu boldly describes the atrocities committed by the dictatorship as part of the context in which the values of humanness were not considered as part of daily life in Malawi. He further points out that humanness was missing, as evidenced by the politics of oppression, fear and harassment that characterized the dictatorship. He states,

> As I reflected upon the aim of traditional Malawian education, I realized again that traditional education was centered around the concept of humanness. Humanness is that essential character defined by our culture as the sum of what makes a person essentially human. I also realized that the western type of education, as received and practiced in Malawi at least, placed less emphasis on humanness in its curricular content and focussed on intellectual knowledge for its own sake (p. 2)

From the four Malawian studies on uMunthu described above, as well as other studies from other parts of Sub-Saharan Africa, I was able to discern how African conceptions of the human being locate personhood in a community of other persons. I have since found it instructive to use uMunthu as part of the analysis of problems of violence and conflict that have unraveled in parts of Africa, including current and recent examples in South Africa, Kenya, Zimbabwe, the Congo and Sudan, among others. I found it quite intriguing that one could recast the Cartesian dictum "I think therefore I am" into an African perspective, turning the very idea of personhood from an individualist gaze into a communal one. Musopole points out that Mbiti's I am because we are, and since we are, therefore I am "makes an excellent summary of what it means to be human in Africa" (p. 13). What did all this imply? If one was human in relation to other human beings, why was it a significant notion? How could we achieve, as the Zimbabwean philosopher M. B. Ramose (1996) implored, the restoration of the humanness of our existence, constituting a fundamental step in envisioning a world peace that encompassed our relations as individuals in a community, as well as with nature?

That uMunthu could usefully be termed an epistemology became part of the answer provided by the Malawian philosophers of theology, including Musopole, Sindima, and Chigona. In their scholarship I sought confirmation of the hypothesis that part of the problems contemporary Africans were having to deal with today were a result of a lost dignity and identity, a racialized dehumanization brought about by the historical encounter between Africa and Europe. Europe brought to Africa a theology that claimed to be based on equality, yet in practice dehumanized Africans. Musopole's (1996) argument went to the heart of the matter:

> It is false theology to claim that all people are made in the image of God and then live to oppress a whole people just because they were created black or women or because they did not discover and manufacture both guns and gunpowder in time to conquer and dominate. (p. 175)

As I would also learn from another African peace scholar, Hizkias Assefa (1996), the period of colonization and imperialism especially in Africa changed the endogenous dynamics of defining 'progress' and 'modernity,' so that most African societies ended up being in an intractable difficulty. According to Assefa,

> They have given up much of what they were, but are unable to attain what they aspire to. No doubt this frustration will be a constant source of disruption, conflict and disillusionment at both the individual and societal levels. (p. 65)

I read Assefa's essay in 2004, whilst still in the field. I found Assefa's explanation quite perceptive in diagnosing the root causes of the problems of conflict and violence in Africa, and of global injustice in the larger international system. It was a diagnosis that begged a prescription. According to the teachers I worked with, uMunthu provided a part of that prescription. None of this is meant to argue that all of Africa's problems have external causes, nor that African people do not dehumanize one another. Africans are as human as any other people, with all the virtues and vices that come with being human. However being an African in the world also means having to deal with a particular history of the world that has affected Africa in a specific way, thereby calling for specific analyses.

An important part of the answer therefore focused on how an Africa-centered concept of 'peace education' needed to allow for a historically-rooted inquiry into the contexts of contemporary problems Malawians and many other sub-Saharan Africans face today. With problems of poverty, violent conflict, exploitation, and even the spread of HIV/AIDS and other dangerous diseases, the stories the teachers told pointed to the alienation of the majority of Africans in the production of knowledge from the day to day running of their societies. This is a consequence of the perpetuation of governance structures put in place during colonial times, and maintained by a neo-liberal paradigm.

The stories also portrayed a picture in which the lives of teachers could be seen in various contexts, dealing with problems implicated in the erosion of the ideals of uMunthu. The teachers portrayed their lives in contexts that were personal, political, economic and historical. As reflections of the teachers' understanding of their world, the autobiographical narratives produced by the teachers add to the emergent scholarship on uMunthu and contribute to the beginnings of a development of an African peace epistemology framework.

This was one of the most important things I learned from the study, something that in hindsight appeared rather obvious and not that complicated: peace derived from uMunthu, the humanness and dignity of a person. This was where a four-thematic framework of my study emerged: 1) Autobiography, 2) uMunthu, 3) Peace curriculum and pedagogy, and 4) Peace praxis. The autobiographical narratives produced by the teachers captured Malawi's history and contemporary society, and helped contextualize Malawi's problems in the terms of structural violence. In this way, an organic definition of uMunthu, the second theme, emerged from the autobiographical narratives. The erosion of uMunthu in contemporary Malawian life defines the contexts of the problems the teachers reported encountering, a reflection of problems facing the larger Malawian society. This contextualization led to the third theme in the African peace epistemology framework, providing content for a curriculum that exposes problems of structural violence, and emphasizes a peace and social justice education approach. The peace curriculum enables a pedagogical imperative, another arm of the third theme. At the pedagogical level, the framework becomes a guide to action and reflection, *praxis* in Freirean terms, for social transformation by teachers, students, and the community.

TOWARD A NEW UMUNTHU CONSCIOUSNESS

As I finish this chapter in July, 2008, there has been a trail of violent conflict in Kenya, Zimbabwe, and now in South Africa. In Kenya and Zimbabwe the violence has been related to presidential elections in those two countries, while in South Africa the violence has been perpetrated by groups of poor South Africans against poor immigrants, mostly from Zimbabwe, Mozambique and Malawi, and also from other parts of East and West Africa. More violence has already claimed thousands of lives in Sudan, and millions in the Congo. One thing I have learned from this entire process of studying contexts of violence is how not to be content with the surface appearance of the violence, without asking probing questions about underlying causes, and the structures of the power relations in which the root causes lie. Knowing that conflict and violence thrive in situations in which fellow human beings are dehumanized, stripped of their uMunthu and their lives regarded as dispensable, we see how root causes lie in complex structures that straddle global, historical, political, social, cultural and economic relations.

While it would be naïve to promise that an educational paradigm based on uMunthu would solve all problems of conflict and violence, it is also obvious to peace educators that its absence in curriculum and pedagogy makes it harder for education to be relevant to the understanding and solving of those problems.

This is what happened in the Malawi in which I grew up, where heroes and heroines of the independence struggle such as Kanyama Chiume, Masauko Chipembere, Rose Chibambo, Orton and Vera Chirwa, and many others, were declared enemies of the state, and the majority of the country had no way of learning the suppressed truth. The political transformation that Malawi underwent in the early 1990s offered a new opportunity for a new political consciousness based on uMunthu, as argued by Tambulasi and Kayuni (2005). There being no deliberate effort to make uMunthu the center of educational policy, political practice and community ethic, the old problems of conflict and violence were merely replaced by new forms of competition, suffering and intolerance. But there is little use in acknowledging all that has gone horribly wrong, and then stopping there. The question is how to use our knowledge of what has gone wrong, and how it happened, to build new programs.

On May 8, 2008, I was fortunate enough to listen to Mandivamba Rukuni, a long time professor of agricultural economics in Zimbabwe. Professor Rukuni talked about how our future lies in relearning the strengths of our ancestors and the heritage they built based on the ideals of uMunthu. I read Professor Rukuni's (2007) book, *Being African: Rediscovering the Traditional Unhu-Ubuntu-Botho Pathways of Being Human*, and found in it ideas that I had been developing in my own work since 2004.

Like the other books discussed in this chapter, Professor Rukuni's book contributes to the inquiry into uMunthu as an important part of the search for an African identity that restores dignity and hope to people long oppressed and marginalized by an unjust global order. The teachers in the story narrated above offer some of the ways in which the endeavor can be approached. While not promising any panacea to Malawi's, Africa's and the world's contemporary problems, these teachers have at least attempted to show what is possible when autobiographical narratives are at the center of educational efforts to try and make curriculum and pedagogy relevant to the day to day lives of students, teachers and their communities. Since embarking upon this study, the bigger lesson for me has been how to shift from the preoccupation with the gloomy analysis of how bad things are in Africa, to asking how to use Africa's own heritage and diverse knowledges, which include uMunthu epistemology, in creating new social, cultural, economic and educational policies and programs that restore hope and optimism, and build a stronger foundation for the future.

NOTES

[1] This chapter is derived from my dissertation field work of 2004, funded by the Compton Peace Foundation in Palo Alto, California, through the African Studies Center and the Center for Gender in a Global Context, at Michigan State University. I sincerely thank Lynn Fendler, my dissertation director, Jack Schwille, my dissertation committee chair; John Metzler, Susan Florio-Ruane, and Ernest Morrell, members of my dissertation committee, for their guidance.

[2] Life President was a title bestowed Dr. Banda, making him president of Malawi for as long as he lived. He stepped down in 1994 after losing an election, the first one in 30 years.

[3] Where relevant, names of people, places and institutions have been changed to protect the identity of participants in the study.

[4] These and other lessons are discussed in greater detail in my dissertation, S. Sharra, (2007), *Teaching Lives: Autobiography, uMunthu, Peace and Social Justice Education in Malawi.*

REFERENCES

Assefa, H. (1996). Peace and reconciliation as a paradigm: A philosophy of peace and its implications for conflict, governance and economic growth in Africa. In Assefa & Wachira (Eds.), *Peacemaking and democratisation in Africa: Theoretical perspectives and church initiatives* (p. 65). Nairobi: East African Educational Publishers.

ATISCA Bulletin no. 5/6, 1996/1997, Special Volume. K. Fidler, P. Gundani & H. Mijoga (Eds.).

Barash, D., & Webel, C. (2002). *Peace and conflict studies.* Thousand Oaks, CA: SAGE Publications.

Carter, J. (2002). *Two years on South Africa's borders.* Washington, DC: National Geographic Society.

Chigona, G. (2002). *uMunthu theology: Path of integral human liberation rooted in Jesus of Nazareth*. Balaka, Malawi: Montfort Media.

Chipembere, H. M. (2001). *Hero of the nation: Chipembere of Malawi: An autobiography* (R. Rotberg, Ed.). Blantyre, Malawi: Christian Literature Association of Malawi.

Chiume, K. (1982). *Autobiography of Kanyama Chiume*. London: Panaf Books.

Florio-Ruane, S. (2001). *Teacher education and the cultural imagination: Autobiography, conversation and narrative*. Mahwah, NJ: Lawrence Erlbaum Associates.

Freire, P. (1970). *Pedagogy of the oppressed*. New York: Continuum.

Kincheloe, J. (1993). *Toward a critical politics of teacher thinking: Mapping the postmodern*. Westport, CT: Bergin & Garvey.

Mbiti, J. (1969). *African religions and philosophy*. Oxford: Heinemann International.

Musopole, A. (1996). *Being human in Africa: Toward an African Christian anthropology* (p. 1). New York: Peter Lang.

Ramose, M. B. (1996). Specific African thought structures and their possible contribution to world peace. In H. Beck & G. Schmirber (Eds.), *Creative peace through encounter of world cultures*. New Delhi, India: Sri Satguru Publications.

Rukuni, M. (2007). *Being African: Rediscovering the traditional Unhu-Ubuntu-Botho pathways of being human*. Arcadia, South Africa: Mandala Publishers.

Sharra, S. (2007). *Teaching lives: Autobiography, uMunthu, peace studies and social justice education in Malawi*. Unpublished doctoral dissertation, Michigan State University, East Lansing.

Sindima, H. (1995). *Africa's agenda: The legacy of liberalism and colonialism in the crisis of African values* (p. 173). Westport, CT: Greenwood Press.

Tambulasi, R., & Kayuni, H. (2005). Can African feet divorce Western shoes? The case of 'uBuntu' and good governance in Malawi. *Nordic Journal of African Studies, 14*(2), 147–161.

Tutu, D. M. (1999). *No future without forgiveness*. New York: Doubleday.

Steve Sharra
Department of Philosophy
Michigan State University

ANNE M. MUNGAI

UBUNTU

From Poverty to Destiny with Love

We are

Standing at the beach, watching waves upon waves
From shoreline to eye's limit
Waters upon waters
Delicately joining hands

Drop by drop, molecule by molecule

Rushing to the shore as one
While floating on their back—
Gigantic steamers, warrior aircraft carriers
Hiding in their depths, whales, silent submarines

The ocean prides in being one big giant

The ocean is—because
The drops are

The shoreline defines another expanse
From continent to continent
Peoples upon peoples
Invisibly joining together

Male and female, white and black, young and old

Tackling and conquering myriads of issues
In synergetic oneness, tackles and topples
Hidden natural laws on land, sea and air
Propelling bullet trains, floating ocean liners, flying air buses,

I am—because
We are

GsnMungai 2009

My journey into Ubuntu

I was born and raised in Kenya, East Africa. Since I was one of ten siblings, our family had a dozen people. Growing up in such a large family, I learned early the need to share with others, no matter how small the item. My parents were low income and my father was the breadwinner. My mother did a marvelous job bringing us up single handed. I remember how she taught me to take care of my younger siblings, and they in turn were taught to care for the youngest ones.

I remember my grandmother as she gathered us in the evening to tell us stories and give us African riddles to solve. The fun was solving the riddles as a group; it was never to compete as individuals. She would invite other children from the neighborhood who did not have a grandmother nearby, and together we would have dinner. Then, seated around the fire, she would share stories that left us breathless while tales of giants and animals filled the air.

I grew up at a time when a parent was any adult in your village, and everyone raised and disciplined the children. We children witnessed sharing on a daily basis. If you had visitors and there was no sugar or milk in the house to make tea, it was not unusual to ask your neighbor for some. And villagers shared not only property but relationships too. It was not unusual to take in a stranger and feed him until he was back on his feet. This is still an acceptable practice in the rural areas. Being individualistic was frowned upon as one was seen as anti-social and selfish. For me, this belonging and sharing as a community is central to my understanding of Ubuntu.

In the country of humankind

Among our many diverse African cultures, there are some key commonalities. In their discussion of the social and moral significance of Ubuntu, Mnyaka & Motlhabi (2005) single out this concept as perhaps one of the most important aspects of a shared African world view. Central to this world view is the notion of humanness, which is reflected in the word itself. "Buntu" in the Bantu language means "the country of humankind" (Van Binsbergen, 2002). From this comes the notion that all men are assumed to be equal and good natured. Mnyaka and Motlhabi (2005) describe the equality assumed by Ubuntu when they state, "Regardless of their social status, gender or 'race', persons are recognized, accepted, valued and respected for their own sake (p. 219). Through pleasant interaction and cooperation with others in the community, individuals act with Ubuntu and therefore, are of good nature. Even when individuals in the community act in a selfish, individualistic manner (i.e. without ubuntu) they still have self-worth. Despite this fact, acts of individualism are greatly discouraged and people who act this way are "akangomntu", or without an inner being.

Ubuntu not only focuses on humanity, but also on community and morality. In Ubuntu, the individual person is inextricably linked to the community (Mnyaka & Matlhabi, 2005). The communalism found in Ubuntu is essentially the essence of the traditional African way of life (Venter, 2004). Since birth, African children are taught that the welfare of the community takes precedence over individual enterprise. This sense of community that is presented in ubuntu is shown in the Xhosa saying, "umunu ngumntu ngabany' abantu", which translates to, "a person is a person through other persons" (Mnyaka & Matlhab, 2005). This saying is in direct accordance with the idea that African people identify themselves through the community they live in. Further examples of this notion are found in the saying, "I am because we are" (Tutu, 1999, p. 31).

The moral aspect of Ubuntu is shown in the caring and hospitable nature of many African people. There are many moral virtues that are associated with Ubuntu such as: thoughtfulness, consideration, sensitivity, generosity, wisdom, humbleness and understanding (Venter 2004). A person who acts with Ubuntu utilizes moral virtues to act humanely to others, thereby improving the quality of life within the community. This notion shows that the main aspects of Ubuntu are not mutually exclusive of each other, but are linked in a web of social causality and reciprocity.

But how do you reach out and practice Ubuntu in times of pain and sorrow? This is the story of my journey towards extending my ubuntu to others and inviting others to join me in this journey. I hope that this journey will come full circle as the children, whose stories I will share with you, learn to extend their Ubuntu to others. Ultimately, this is a journey of turning pain into joy for someone else and finding inner peace by reaching out to others.

Ubuntu extended beyond pain

My journey started when our second daughter, Caroline W. Mungai, passed away at the age of twenty-five. Caroline was concerned about the plight of disadvantaged children. She was a passionate teacher who believed that every child needs to be encouraged to reach his or her destiny. Through her graduate studies in early childhood education, she hoped to become a teacher and eventually establish a school for children whose futures are at stake. She believed she could steer children without hope to their destiny. Caroline was often heard saying: "Children are the most innocent beings on earth. One can make them or break them by how you treat them."

The Caroline Wambui Mungai Foundation (CWMF) was started as the act of Ubuntu that Caroline lived for and hoped to perpetuate in her profession. In 2005 the CWMF started a children's home on a three acre piece of land in Wangige, Kenya to serve orphans who were desperate and in need of shelter and basic needs. Wangige is twelve miles from Nairobi, the capital city of Kenya. Eighty percent of the orphans are from the capital city Nairobi and other urban areas. The other percentage come from rural areas. These children have no family to take care of them. From the age of three they were either abandoned in the street or left alone in abandoned houses. They have no uncle, no grandmother, and no cousins. A social worker is always involved to check whether there is a family that can take care of the child. Inevitably, these children have no one. When found, they are usually digging in the garbage for food.

Currently 43 children aged between 2½ and 8 years have been accepted at the Home from five of the seven Provinces of Kenya including one from Tanzania. We hope to have 160 children when the first dormitory is completed. The children receive medical care and upkeep and attend Kindergarten through grade 3 in the newly completed classrooms. The vision of CWMF is to have a home for 400 children, and create a model for other countries.

There is a saying in Kenya, "a child belongs to the society." In the traditional society a child was raised by the whole village. Whether or not the parents were able, the villagers came together and helped where needed. As a result, orphanages are a foreign idea to the African community. Traditionally when a parent died, others stepped in and brought the child up as their own. If a relative was not available to take in the child, then a neighbor or someone else in the community would step in. Because of westernization and the movement from rural areas to urban in search of jobs, this tradition has died down. Also with civil wars and the aids epidemic in Africa, there are more orphans in the community. Currently the number of orphans in Sub-Saharan Africa is over 12 million.

Orphans and vulnerable children are deprived of their first line of protection and guidance – their parents. According to a biennial report on global orphaning released by USAID, UNAIDS and UNICEF, by 2010, sub-Saharan Africa will be home for an estimated 50 million orphaned children, and more than a third will have lost one or both parents to AIDS. Children without the guidance of their primary caregivers are often more vulnerable and at risk of becoming victims of violence, exploitation, trafficking, discrimination and other abuses. Unaccompanied girls are at especially high risk of sexual abuse. Meanwhile, unaccompanied boys are at high risk of forced or 'involuntary' participation in violence and armed conflict.

Poverty plays a large role in this seeming neglect of children. With more mouths to feed and little money, families opt not to take on other children who are orphaned. Taking on orphaned children means that you have to worry about their education in addition to their basic needs. This puts a strain on any willing person as education can be very expensive. Though primary education is supposed to be free in Kenya, there are a lot of hidden fees that many parents have a problem meeting. Secondary education is very expensive so parents struggle to pay for their own children and do not want the responsibility of other children.

Despite such hardships, Kenyan society has always expected that when there is a need, people will come and help out without expecting to be paid. Children are the future of our society, and this sentiment has been engraved in the hearts of many Kenyans. When the Caroline Wambui Mungai home started we asked for help and four young women volunteered to stay at the home and take care of the first 15 children. This is indeed Ubuntu at work.

Begin with the children

If we are to reach real peace in this world... we shall have to begin with children.
– Mahatma Gandhi

As a young boy my grandfather was stolen from the Massai people during a tribal war. He was then brought up by a Gikuyu couple who loved him as their own son. There is a great value placed on children in the African culture and the belief that each child is a life worth saving. Children are most vulnerable, however, when the Ubuntu concept is not honored by society. Gandhi places the realization of sustainable peace on a grassroots approach, beginning with children to create a culture of peace. In order to perpetuate a peaceful environment, each generation must pass on the baton of peace to the next. This is, for me, the moral essence of Ubuntu.

When my husband and I first returned to Kenya after opening the CWF Home, we were surprised by the beautiful voices that meet us there. The children sang, "Welcome daddy, welcome mommy. We know everything is gonna be alright" Coming from little boys and girls who had such hope for their future brought tears to my eyes.

Coming to the Home is a life changing experience where healing takes place and the children have a sense of belonging and feeling safe, often for the first time in their young lives. After only two weeks one can see the difference as they start to feel comfortable about being with others and not having to scavenge for food. The fact that they have three meals a day is difficult for them to grasp at first. Having a bed at night is a new concept for most of them. Having people who care for them, hug them and love them, is also a new experience. I will share some of their stories with you. (All of the children's names have been changed.)

"Nate" is seven years old and is HIV positive. His single mother died soon after his birth. Nobody wanted to take care of this sickly child. Nate was picked from the slums almost at death's door, and we were not sure he would survive even for a week. When he came to the Home he was too weak to walk or talk. Two weeks into his stay, however, he regained his energy and was able to stand on his feet. Since arriving, Nate has undergone extensive treatments to improve his weight and energy. Though he is HIV positive, he is going to school and is doing very well. He has been nicknamed the "usher" at the Home. He is the first person to welcome you when you visit. He will usher you in style and show you around. He is now playing with other children and he has achieved the normal weight for his age. He has a sweet smile and a peaceful look that tells you without words that he is happy and content to have a home.

Danet who is eight and a half arrived with raw wounds on her head. Danet's mother died from sickness and left her with a grandmother who did not want her. The grandmother is poor and so having another mouth to feed was impossible for her because she could not even fend for herself. So one day she decided to get rid of this little girl rather than see her suffer. She boiled water and poured it on Danet hoping that it would be a quick death. Fortunately the determination to live was on this little soul, and she did not die from the wounds. She was rescued by a Good Samaritan who took her to hospital, and then she was brought to the Home. When she arrived she used foul language and was cruel and unfriendly. She was a bitter little girl who did nothing but fight and call the other children names. She did not accept love or warmth from anyone and was aloof to any show of kindness or friendship. She was suspicious of anyone who tried to befriend her, and it was clear that she did not trust adults. After about six months, Danet is a changed person because she has learned to give and receive love. It is interesting to see how she takes care of the younger children in the home with kindness. Truly she has experienced the true nature of Ubuntu—that her being happy and making it in this world depends on the other people around her, and she has a part to play in helping others succeed and thrive.

Vinny is seven years old and he came from Tanzania which is a neighboring country of Kenya in East Africa. Vinny was brought by a church group that has connections with churches in Tanzania. He was abandoned and some church members took him in, but they knew that they could not take care of him for a long time, so they were looking for a home. When Vinny came to the Home he was very weak and sickly but aggressive. He was not able to sleep and had a lot of nightmares. Now he loves being in the Home and sleeps very well. He is a playful boy who likes to be included in group games. It is not unusual to hear Vinny asking "Nije tujeze?" which means, "May I join in the game?" His exuberant belly laugh now fills the Home.

For three days 2½ year old Rebecca was outside a store in Nairobi, where she was abandoned. She has no idea of the whereabouts of her parents or relatives. She was brought to the Home with documents from the Kenya police. Rebecca is a joy to the home as she mingles very well with the other children, who see her as one of the "babies," and so they all compete to take care of her. The older children like to pick her up and hold her on their laps. She is a sweet, beautiful child who loves to laugh and enjoys her new life to the full.

Njeri and Njoroge are twins and they were brought to the Home after their mother passed away. They are eight years old now. Their mother died leaving the twins and a baby. These children were traumatized by the death of their mother who had passed away at home. The children thought she was asleep for three days. A neighbor found the children crying for food and the baby was almost dying. The twins were brought to the home where we had to deal with the emotional trauma. The baby was taken to Mama Ngina Children's home that caters for abandoned babies.

When the twins were brought to the home, they would stick together and did not want to socialize with anyone else. They never talked or played with other children. After experiencing love and care from the assigned "mother" they began to adjust to being at the home because of the attention and care they received. Eventually they started to mingle with the other children and within five months they started to make friends and socialize with others. I believe that the behaviour of these children changed as they felt the love and the care they were getting form the "mothers who were taking care of them. Being in a secure home also gave them a sense of security and a feeling of belonging. Safety and security is a real issue for most of these children either because they were abandoned by their mothers or because they were left with relatives who abused them and misused them. Njeri and Njoroge have come a long way they are now in grade 3 and doing well in their school work. They have learned to socialize and have made friends with other children in the Home.

Ben was brought by the local leaders in Wangige. His mother was mentally ill and she could no longer take care of him. This boy was staving to death because the mother did not feed him. There were no relatives who wanted him, so he ended up in the Home. Ben has forgotten his earlier experiences with a mother who never rested but was always in the street walking from one place to another. He has adjusted to the life at the children' home and he loves to play ball and likes to be the teacher's helper. He likes to read books and loves to sing.

The saddest case we have ever had was little girl, Monny, aged one and half years, but she looked like a six months old baby. This little toddler was found in a dumpster in the worst slums in Nairobi. These slums called Kibera slums are the poorest areas of Nairobi slums. She was HIV positive and had tuberculosis. She was malnourished and could not even crawl or even sit down. She was very underweight and we feared that she would not live through the night. Though our policy is to not take very young children the social worker told us that if we do not take her in she would not last through the night. So Monny became ours and though she literally lived in and out of the hospital we saw a great change in her for a good eight months. Monny did not survive the problems her little body carried, but she was cared for and loved for the eight months she lived at the home. The other children called her the "baby" and loved her as their sister. Monny did not live her full life but for the eight months at the home she had a bed and someone to love her for twenty-four hours a day. We shared our Ubuntu with Monny, and she became a worthy, loved human being for the duration of her short life.

Growing into our humanity through community

A sense of Ubuntu permeates the Home and this is shown very well by the way the children interact with each other. The vision of the Caroline Wambui Mungai Foundation is to keep the children at the home until they are eighteen years old. At eighteen years of age the young adults will have developed their own identity and have career and professional aspirations of their own and we will be able to help them achieve their goals. We hope that after they finish high school we will sponsor them to go to colleges or trade schools, to be able to make a livelihood for themselves. Once they are able to take care of themselves then they will be free to live on their own or to stay and help out with the younger children.

Once these children arrive, we expect the community to rally together to help. I have seen the Ubuntu concept at work in the community around the children's home in Wangigi, Kenya. We find it in the women buying cabbages and bringing it to the Home. Other women bring bread. Some women will even volunteer and come for a day and do some cleaning and laundry for the children. We have had young people help clean the compound. That is the Ubuntu concept. In the spirit of Ubuntu the children do not belong to the Caroline Wambui Mungai Foundation; the children belong to the society. Therefore it is expected that where there's a need, the society will come together and help. In the same spirit, it is expected that every member of the community will help in bringing up the children. If the child fails the whole community has failed and if the child succeeds the whole society has succeeded. And if the child belongs to the community it means that the community has a part to play in the future of the child. And as the children grow older, they will learn that they need the community to survive. Without the spirit of Ubuntu that fills the Home, these children would not survive. We believe that these orphans of Kenya will become someone because of the community. We view these children as future leaders of their country.

The Ubuntu concept is also at work through the people who volunteer at the Home. From the beginning we have had many people, coming from all over the world – from Australia, Mexico, the USA, China, Korea, Amsterdam, and Sweden - to give their time and love to the children. The volunteers typically stay for two weeks at a time, though some have stayed for a month or more. Many of the volunteers are career people who use their vacation to help out. We also have had some retired teachers visit and volunteer their time. A few university students have used their summer vacation to help.

The airline ambassadors have had the largest group of volunteers. The organization took a large group of twenty volunteers to work with the children and they were there for one month. Airline Ambassadors International (AAI) is a non-profit organization affiliated with the United Nations and recognized by the US Congress. It began as a network of airline employees using their pass privileges to help others and has expanded into a network of students, medical professionals, families and retirees who volunteer as "Ambassadors of Goodwill" in their home communities and abroad. It provides a way for members to share their unique skills and talents to care for others and bring compassion into action. AAI provides humanitarian aid to children and families in need as well as relief and development to under-privileged communities worldwide.

A young adult from Mexico stayed for two months and helped in the kitchen and in the classrooms. She was a helping hand in whatever chores she was given. This is Ubuntu in reality; the Ubuntu concept that says, "I am because we are." After leaving, the volunteers write to us and say things like, "I went there to change the lives of the children but instead the children changed my life." And others say, "I left a part of me in Wangige, Kenya." The Ubuntu concept works both ways; "I am because you are" and "You are because I am." In helping and reaching out to others you don't just change the other person you are reaching out to, you change yourself. You grow into your own humanity.

We have one child, Sarah, who nobody could get through to. People tried to talk to her, but she never interacted with anyone. She never smiled; she never played with the other children, not even with the workers or the teachers. When you looked at her you could see the sadness in her eyes.

In summer 2007 an Adelphi student named Billy went to Kenya for two weeks. Billy was touched by the sadness in Sarah's eyes. He tried to talk to Sarah but she would not say anything. Finally, after three days, there was a breakthrough. Nobody understands what happened; Billy does not understand what happened. There was simply a connection between Billy and Sarah. For the first time in a year, Sarah was smiling. She was playing and laughing. By the time Billy left Sarah was a happy little girl. And she is still happy. She smiles and plays with the other kids and interacts with everyone. Sarah "is" because of Billy and Billy "is" because of Sarah.

Ubuntu and Education

According to Venter (2004), many Africans struggle through their schooling, because the curriculum is not geared towards their societal beliefs and practices; it does not connect to real life issues. The subject matter that is taught in African schools is very similar to what is taught in Western societies. African students cannot relate to the material that is presented to them. Venter suggests that education in Africa should come to encompass the values that are presented in the philosophy of Ubuntu. Therefore, African curriculums should focus on interpersonal skills, cooperation (community), emotion, welfare of others (humaneness), kindness and compassion (morality). This type of education should not be limited to children. Adult Africans, who have embraced more individualistic values as a result of the globalization of Africa, can get I touch with their roots by means of spreading the good word of Ubuntu.

In *Affirming Unity in Education: Healing with Ubuntu*, Goduka & Swadenar, (1999) position ubuntu as an avenue for critical and reflexive teaching and research focused on community well-being. They encourage teaching and learning that fosters a climate of mutual co-operation, respect, dignity and confidence in what each individual brings into the learning environment. From my own perspective as a teacher educator, the lessons of Ubuntu infuse much needed humanity into our educational spheres.

Coming full circle

At the roots of African culture is a philosophy that promotes community, generosity, and stresses human worth (i.e.: equality). Although some might dismiss the notion of Ubuntu as utopian, no one can argue that the ideals proposed in this philosophy contain what Africa needs and what the world needs. In a time where Western society's individualistic nature has infected the enterprise and goal orientations of the rest of the world, the notion of Ubuntu sheds a light of hope on what seems to be an increasingly bleak future.

My journey toward Ubuntu started with the pain of losing a loved one at a time when her dreams of life were at their fullest. It was at a time when any parent is proud of what her child is about to achieve. Pain has a way of igniting a fire that may either burn you or become a redemptive force. Pain can birth energy in us that we never knew we had. The pain of losing Caroline became a drive for us as a family to reach out and help children who have not experienced the love, comfort and security a home and family bring. These children have become a joy in my life as I look into their eyes and see hope for the future. This is not only their future but my future as well as the future of the whole community. When the younger generation is cared for, they in turn take care of others, both younger and older, and this completes the circle of Ubuntu. So I have become a mother of forty-three children in Kenya and each one of them has brothers and sisters at the Home. Together all of us—children and volunteers—are learning to become human beings; we "are" because of each other.

Figure 1. Children during Physical Education class

Figure 2. The New dormitory under construction. This will hold 160 children

Figure 3. The whole group of 43 children with the author at the Home

REFERENCES

Barben, T. (2006, January). UMNTU NGUMNTU NGABANTU ('A person is a person because of other persons'): the ethos of the pre-colonial Xhosa-speaking people as presented in fact and young adult fiction. Quarterly bulletin of the National library of South Africa, 60(1/2), 4-20. Retrieved November 4, 2007, from Academic Search Premier Database.

Children on the brink, 2004: A joint report of new orphan estimates and a framework for action. UNAIDS, UNICEF USAID, July 2004.

Coertze, R. (2001). Ubuntu and nation building in South Africa. South African Journal of Ethnology, 24(4), 113. Retrieved November 4, 2007, from Academic Search Premier Database

Coughlan, S. (2006). All you need is ubuntu. BBC News Magazine. Sept. http://news.bbc.co.uk/2/hi/uk_news/magazine/5388181.stm

Enslin, P., & Horsthemke, K. (2004, November). Can ubuntu provide a model for citizenship education in African democracies? Comparative Education, 40(4), 545-558. Retrieved November 4, 2007, from Academic Search Premier Database

Goduka, I.N.M. & Swadenar, B. (1999), Affirming unity in education: Healing with ubuntu. Kenwyn, South Africa: Juta and Company, Ltd.

Mnyaka, M., 7 Motlhabu, M. (2005, July). THE AFRICAN CONCEPT OF UBUNTU/BOTHO AND ITS SOCIO-MORAL SIGNIFICANCE. Black Theology: An International Journal, 3(2), 215-237. Retrieved November 4, 2007, from Academic Search Premier Database.

Tutu, D. (1999). No future without forgiveness. NY: Doubleday.

Van Binsbergen, Wim. (2002). Ubuntu and the globalization of southern African thought and society. http://www.shikanda.net/general/ubuntu.htm

Venter, E. (2004, March) The Notion of Ubuntu and Communalism in African Educational Discourse. Studies in Philosophy & Education, 23 (2/3), 149-160. Retrieved November 4, 2007, from Academic Search Premier Database.

Anne Mungai
Ruth S. Ammon School of Education
Adelphi University

HEALING

MICHAEL O'LOUGHLIN

BEING OTHERWISE, TEACHING OTHERWISE[1]

"And what about your origins? Tell us about them, it must be fascinating!" Blundering fools never fail to ask the question. Their surface kindness hides the sticky clumsiness that so exasperates the foreigner." Kristeva (1991, p. 29)

My father lived all of his life in rural Ireland. Having lost all of his siblings as emigrants to London in the worst of circumstances, he stacked up the economic benefits of exile against the lifelong loss he knew would ensue and it just simply didn't add up. I never could find the words to explain my decision to emigrate to my dad. He wept profusely every time I left. I, in turn, am left perpetually to wonder if Kristeva wasn't correct when, in *Strangers to Ourselves* (1991) she suggested that all of us who choose the path of exile are running away from, and toward, alienation: "Or should one recognize that one becomes a foreigner in another country because one is already a foreigner from within?" (1991, p.14). Speaking of her own parents, Kristeva – an immigrant from Bulgaria to France – captured the violent alienation of this loss as follows:

> And nevertheless, no, I have nothing to say to them, to any parents. Nothing. Nothing and everything, as always. If I tried – out of boldness, through luck, or in distress – to share with them some of the violence that causes me to be so totally on my own, they would not know where I am, who I am, what it is, in others, that rubs me the wrong way. I am henceforth foreign to them. (1991, pp. 22–23).

Philip Noyce's film, *Rabbit-Proof Fence* (Noyce, 2003; see also Pilkington, 2002*)*, tells the story of the flight of three aboriginal girls from Moore River Settlement, a mission school for *half caste* children born as the result of liaisons between white fencers and aboriginal women. They were members of Australia's *stolen generation* of aboriginal and mixed-race children who were forcibly removed from their homes in an attempt at cultural annihilation and forced assimilation.[2]

As I watched this story of the systematic attempt by the Australian government to *whiten* Aboriginal people I was struck by the layers of complexity and complicity in the colonizing enterprise. The three girls are tracked relentlessly by the Australian police, and while they are betrayed by some whites on their twelve hundred mile trek, they are assisted materially by others. Their most formidable opponent is one of their own, Moodoo, an Aboriginal tracker who gives them a run for their money. Yet he, himself, is coerced into working for the government, and his daughter, too, is incarcerated in the school. Like all *good natives*, he has cultivated an inscrutability that makes it impossible to tell if he is working faithfully for the government or secretly subverting the pursuit. The inscrutable native allows us to project onto him whatever we choose.[3] Consistent with the colonial narrative, Christianity and racism are conjoined in the persons of the angelic white nuns who run the mission school, scrubbing the children white, policing their language use, and tutoring them in Kiplingesque ditties for the benefit of their white benefactor, the ironically titled Chief Protector of Aborigines, Mr. Neville, named by the children "Mr. Devil."

As I read postcolonial reconstructions of the history of India, the Caribbean, the Pacific, countries in Africa, histories of indigenous peoples around the world, and of course the history of Ireland itself, I am increasingly struck by the unvarying sameness of the narrative, including economic colonization and military repression in the service of capitalism; racism through processes of inferiorization, dehumanization, and even enslavement; cultural and literal genocide; prohibition on access to schooling and the banning of native language and cultural practices; the development of a planter class, a local bourgeoisie, who through mimicry crudely ape their masters, implement their will, and aspire to inherit their power; the use of Christianization as a tool of subjugation, except in Ireland, where Otherness had to be reinforced through the attempted imposition of Anglican Christianity on a Roman Catholic population; and the elimination of indigenous knowledge-making through installation of a univocal, Eurocentric worldview and master discourse. All of this has ultimately led to participation of the oppressed in their own subjugation, frequently in late capitalist "democracies," in which the colonized people in what are now often called postcolonial societies are taught to believe that they are free. Gramsci (1971), who claimed there was no more powerful form of oppression than that which occurs with the consent of the oppressed, would be proud![4]

I come from Ireland and I spend a great deal of time meditating on the ways in which colonization, class subjugation, and Catholicism have interpellated and split my being. I will begin with some autobiographical meditations that will hopefully help locate myself. I will then introduce a few brief excerpts from writers whose capacity to capture some of the splits in Irish identity I find useful. I will then offer some meditations on history, memory, subjectivity, and the possibility of occupying the pedagogical margin subversively.

But first, a cautionary note from Trinh Minh-ha about the trickiness of this enterprise:

> How do you inscribe difference without bursting into a series of euphoric narcissistic accounts of yourself and your own kind? Without indulging in a marketable romanticism or in a naïve whining about your condition? …Between the twin chasms of navel-gazing and navel-erasing the ground is narrow and slippery. (Trinh, 1989, p. 28)

My God! I'm Split!

In 1940, one of my father's five sisters became pregnant out of wedlock at age sixteen. As was the custom then, as Peter Mullan details in his film *The Magdalene Sisters* (Mullan, 2004), girls who had sinned in this way were essentially ordered into permanent servitude under the auspices of Catholic nuns. They lived out their lives scrubbing floors and operating commercial ventures such as hand laundries on behalf of the nuns, in conditions that were appalling. Many children were physically and sexually abused in these institutions.[5] Their bastard children were either fostered to families in Ireland or sent as adoptees to Catholic families in the U.S. My father's sister was thus consigned to the local workhouse as an indentured-for-life servant. My dad saved enough money from his own meager income for her boat passage to England. He bribed the night watchman, climbed the gate, extracted her from the workhouse, and sent her to England. He never set eyes on her again. Her child, fostered out to a farm family in another abject form of indentured service in the Ireland of the period, died in his teenage years. My father continued to be a devoutly observant Catholic to the very end of his life. His sister's child was fostered to a family less than five miles from my family home…but we were not to learn of this until well after his death.

> *"C'mon. Hurry up. We'll miss our lift to school," my brother urged. I ran furiously. P.J. and Frances, older than I, knew that if we were there he'd let us pile in with all the other kids. What kid wanted to walk the mile to school in the frosty winter of 1958? We arrived at the van out of breath, with thank-yous on the tips of our tongues. We were on the tail end of the group as I scrambled after my brother and sister into the back of the blue Ford van. That was when the hand shot out and Hogan's voice rasped: "Are you an O'Loughlin? Get out. No O'Loughlins or Macs. I don't want to see the likes of you again.*

The story of my early life is in large part a battle against sanctioned inferiorization. I grew up as a member of the working poor in a rigidly class-stratified society. In the Ireland of my youth, local county councils bought plots of land from farmers and built subsidized *council houses*, commonly called laborer's cottages, for the working poor. They put special red tiled clay roofs on the houses so that they were distinctive. *A ghetto of red-roofed houses, scattered across the rural landscape.* I guess they felt that we were not sufficiently marked by poverty, and God forbid we might rise above it and conceal our origins. The red roofs served as a powerful reminder to all of our abject origins. My mother lives in that house to this day. She is still marked as Other by the tyranny of bureaucratic architecture. I can recall returning from the only college visit I ever made, and asking the coach driver to stop a quarter of a mile from my home so that my abject origins would not be evident to my classmates.

I grew up in a society that endured British colonization for over eight hundred years. British colonialism in Ireland continues to this day. Since the British erased our language in a purposeful campaign of cultural genocide, most of us grew up speaking only English. However, as Homi Bhabha reminds us in his discussion of mimicry, while the British forced us to speak their language for purposes of domination, there were limits to how well we should speak it: "[T]o be Anglicized is *emphatically* not to be English" (Bhabha, 1994, p. 87). Our English was actually meant to mark us as inferior, in the same way that Indian English and

Caribbean Englishes mark their speakers as Other. It worked. I can recall attending a conference a few years ago and, by chance, sitting next to a colleague from Oxford University who spoke in the perfect cadences of Oxford English. In spite of my best efforts to carry on a collegial conversation, I became overwhelmed with a sense of inferiority and was tongue-tied throughout the meal.

Growing up working-class, I often feel mystified as I try to live the life of an academic and try to understand the pretensions, aspirations, and mysterious ways of my academic colleagues. Ryan and Sackrey's (1995) *Strangers in Paradise* and Sennett and Cobb's (1993) *Hidden Injuries of Class* comfort me that the class dislocations I experience are not uniquely mine, but are in fact typical of the contradictions and tensions people experience as they try to cross boundaries in a class stratified society. Must we hide? Do we have to become impostors to ourselves? Or can we make room in our society for hybrid identities that allow us to minimize loss as we move across class, gender, race, and national boundaries?

Although I was not conscious of my racial formation, I now realize that the signs of otherness were always present. In our small town people commonly referred to the occasional Nigerian intern at the county hospital as 'the black doctor.' The Catholic Church abetted our racial formation through ubiquitous collection boxes soliciting pennies for 'black babies' in Africa. There was a collection box in every classroom, with a destitute 'black baby' staring vacantly from the photograph pasted on the front. Colonialist images of African blackness as destitute, ignorant, and *other* were promulgated in glossy missionary magazines such as *The Far East* and *Africa*, which we sold door to door to help Irish missionaries in 'darkest Africa' and South America. When television came to Ireland we also received our share of images of exotic black otherness from National Geographic type documentaries. I would go to a neighbor's house on summer evenings to watch television. In a country in which Catholic bishops had the power to suppress all images of sexuality, we were permitted to gaze without shame on the dark nakedness of the African Other in National Geographic specials. As Franz Fanon remarks in his analysis of the effects of colonialism on the black psyche: "In Europe, that is to say, in every civilized and civilizing country, the Negro is the symbol of sin. The Negro represents the archetype of the lowest values" (1967, p. 189).

I sit here, more than forty years later, and wonder what effect these unexamined representations of otherness have on my psyche. When my mom was in New York for her annual visit a few years ago we got to speaking of my sister and her newly adopted child from India. We were discussing how well my sister was prepared for raising an ethnically Indian child in Ireland. My mother acknowledged that the child would have problems, and went on to cite widely publicized incidents of racial harassment involving a family of Indian origin. Then, to my surprise, she said: *"It's just as well your father is not alive. He'd never speak to her again."* She went on: *"The baby's too dark. Dad would never accept him. He was always dead set against blacks."* My father had only a fourth-grade formal education. He had limited access to literacy and no interest in television. He rarely traveled beyond a forty mile radius of home. Living in a racially homogenous society what could be the source of his hatred of 'blacks'? Did his father before him hate 'blacks' too? Did his neighbors and friends? What effect did this unacknowledged hatred have on my racial formation? Are such sentiments handed down unconsciously from one generation to the next through the inferiorization of the psyche and the transmission of historical memory? What does knowing this do to me? As for my nephew, he was beaten up on the first day of kindergarten that fall in his neighborhood school in a small town in Ireland.

Shadows of Memories: Exactly Who Do You/I Think I Am?

History matters. Traumatic events in history and in families matter even more. There is considerable literature in psychoanalysis on the effects of ghosts (Fraiberg, Adelson & Shapiro, 1975; Gordon, 1997) phantoms (Abraham & Torok, 1994), unspoken secrets (Rashkin, 1992; Rogers, 2007), specters (Derrida, 1994; Venn, 2002) and catastrophic histories (Davoine & Gaudillière, 2004) on the psyches of people.[6] Selma Fraiberg, for example, suggests that pathological responses in the present can often be traced back across multiple generations, and Davoine & Gaudillière offer compelling evidence of a relationship between madness in the present and unspoken ancestral trauma. In attempting to understand myself, and particularly the unquiet aspects of my being, I have attempted to reach into my past and retrieve not only individual and familial narratives, but also narratives from the larger sweep of history that may serve to help explain my passions, disquietudes, and inhibitions to myself.

Reading *The Irish Mind* (1985) by Richard Kearney, for example, I cringe anew at the characterization of my ancestors and wonder how this disrespect was internalized by them and whether remnants of it are still lurking in my psyche producing potential for inferiority, rage, and even racism:

> The British historian Charles Kingsley provided further justification for the cultural and military oppression of his Irish neighbours, when he composed this racist portrait in 1860: "I am daunted by the human chimpanzees I saw along that hundred miles of horrible country. I don't believe they are our fault. I believe that there are not only many more of them than of old, but that they are happier, better and more comfortably fed and lodged under our rule than they ever were. But to see white chimpanzees is dreadful; if they were black, one would not feel it so much, but their skins, except where tanned by exposure, are as white as ours." So much for the colonial calibanization of the Irish. (1985, p. 7)

When I was a child a mass grave with a large number of skeletons was discovered a few hundred yards from my home. These were the remains of victims of the Great Famine which overtook Ireland in the mid-1800s. In her epic work on the Irish Famine, *The great hunger* (1962), Cecil Woodham-Smith offers vivid and depressing descriptions of the genocidal famines that yielded over a million deaths in Ireland and forced millions more into exile as indentured servants, while Great Britain exported Irish grain and livestock. Many of those who fled traveled in dreadful conditions in the holds of sailing ships. So many died that the ships became known as *coffin ships*. From a passenger's journal here is how one such voyage was described:

> Most of the passengers were from the South of Ireland; provisions and water were short and of execrable quality, but the captain, Thompson, was kind. Ship fever appeared before the *India* was a week out and Captain Thompson caught it and died; twenty six passengers also died, water ran short and the ration was reduced to a pint a day, three of the passengers became lunatics, and one threw himself overboard. Two ships were hailed and implored for a little water; they replied that they had none to spare – ship fever was raging in their own holds…when, after a voyage of more than eight weeks the *India* arrived at Staten Island he [the journal author] and 122 others were taken to the hospital…the patients were cruelly treated: the beds, grids of iron bars with a little straw laid on the top inflicted torture on the sick, who were reduced by fever to skin and bone; the doctors were negligent and indifferent, the male nurses took a delight in abusing and thwarting the helpless and struck patients for innocent errors; food was uneatable and conditions horribly insanitary. (Woodham-Smith, p. 251)

What phantom might dwell within me from the suffering of my ancestors who evidently survived such wrenching events? At what psychic cost did they survive, and did those psychic scars have an opportunity to heal or are they still haunting contemporary descendants such as I? I do know that I experienced Cecil Woodham-Smith's *The great hunger* as profoundly haunting from the first time I read it at age sixteen.

While there is tragedy aplenty in my Irish heritage, it is possible, nevertheless, to fashion redemptive narratives from Irish history that induce stirrings of patriotism, creativity and pride. Much of the great literary output of Ireland may well be associated with the ready juxtaposition of tragedy, comedy and hope. The story of my encounter with Irish-American history is a much more difficult tale however. Tragically, the Irish who made it to the U.S. were greeted with an onslaught of nativist prejudice and xenophobia.[7] Irish immigrants might have responded to this by making common cause with free Negroes and by supporting the movement for abolition. Instead, they edged out blacks at the bottom of the social ladder, and, on the basis of racial bonding, claimed domestic and laboring jobs as their right by virtue of their whiteness. As Frederick Douglass noted in 1853, "The Irish, who at home readily sympathize with the oppressed everywhere, are instantly taught when they step upon our soil to hate and despise the Negro" (cited in Ignatiev, 1995, frontispiece). Douglass also commented: "Every hour sees us elbowed out of some employment to make room for some newly-arrived emigrant from the Emerald Isle, whose hunger and color entitle him to special favor…" (cited in Ignatiev, 1995, p. 111–12). Ignatiev concludes: "To be acknowledged as white, it was not enough for the Irish to have a competitive advantage over Afro-Americans in the labor market; in order for them to avoid the taint of blackness it was necessary that no Negro be allowed to work in occupations where Irish were to be found" (pp. 111-12).

Scholarship on whiteness (Fine et al, 2004; Frankenberg, 1995; McIntosh, 1988; Roediger, 2006, 2007; Seshadri-Crooks, 2000; Tuckwell, 2002) has established the responsibilities white people bear for historical inequalities and oppression, and for the perpetuation of those inequities through implicit systems of privilege. My awareness of the strategic role Irish Americans played in declaring themselves white troubles further my engagement with my white privilege. It is very difficult for me to square my progressive politics, which are in part a product of the kind of privilege that access to cultural capital such as my advanced education provides, with the historical inequalities on which such privilege is constructed.

As I rummage in my cultural/historical backpack a few other elements are worthy of scrutiny. Growing up in southern Ireland, I was raised in an ultra-Catholic environment, and while it would probably take many years on an analyst's couch to disentangle the intepellative effects of that experience on my being, I will content myself with this brief satirical thumbnail sketch from the pen of Anglo Irish social critic Terry Eagelton. In *The Gatekeeper*, Eagelton, raised in an Irish family in England, summarizes his experience of Catholicism, this way:

> Just as the convent bore only a tenuous relation to reality, so did Catholicism as a whole. Its esoteric doctrines seemed no more applicable to everyday life than trigonometry was applicable to pressing your trousers. Like magic, it was a highly determinate system, but entirely self-confirming, with all the exceptional clarity of an hallucination. Catholicism was less about good deeds than about how to keep the charcoal in your thurible alight or knock about fifty years off your allotted time in purgatory. It was less about charity than candelabras. We were pious and heartless, strict-minded and mean, pure-living and pagan. There was a crazed precision about the Church's doctrinal system…It resembled the insane exactitude of the psychotic whose mathematical calculations are impeccable, but who is carrying them out perched on a window ledge thirty floors up. (2002, pp. 30–31)

Another deeply embedded dimension of Irish culture, one not so removed from the Catholic Puritanism of that era in Ireland, is a certain hardness when it comes to children's emotions. This is evident, for example, in Frank McCourt's widely read *Angela's Ashes* (1996), a work that was received in parts of Ireland with considerable resentment. Writing in 1991, Anthony Clare, one of Ireland's leading psychiatrists, characterized Irish culture as "A culture heavily impregnated by an emphasis on physical control, original sin, cultural inferiority and psychological defensiveness" (p. 14), and he quotes an Irish psychiatrist writing on Irish child-rearing practices in 1976:

> The family home in Ireland is a novitiate for violence. Even from the cradle the child is made to feel rejection, hostility, and open physical pain. The infant is left to cry in his cot because his mother does not want to 'give in to him.' Later he is smacked with the hand or a stick. He is made to go to bed early. He is not allowed to have his tea. He is put in a room by himself… and in

order to invite this morale breaking treatment from his parents, all the Irish child has to do is to be *normal.* It is the normality of childhood that sets parents' teeth on edge. They take no joy in childishness (1996, pp. 15–16).

I am a child therapist, I teach courses on children's emotional well-being, and I consider myself an advocate for children. I spend a large portion of my life working with parents and teachers to create the possibility of healing and caring communities for children at home and at school (e.g., O'Loughlin, 2001, 2006, 2007b, 2009, In press). I am in little doubt that these activities are fueled by a reparative impulse based on the tone-deafness to children's needs in my Irish childhood.

My return to my native Ireland a few summers ago was unsettling. I went home – yes, I still call it "home" - but everywhere I went I felt that people silently coded me as Other. I wandered through Dublin trying fruitlessly to find myself in a sea of Irish faces. At the conference I attended I felt pierced by an Irish gaze. This contemptuous gaze, with which I was all too familiar, was the one that we - oops, "they" - reserve for pathetic Yanks coming back to find their roots. As Eva Hoffman (1990) and others (e.g., Aciman, 1999) have noted, a journey into subjectivity is also a wrenching journey away from subjectivity. Gains come through losses. Voice emerges from muteness. Movement stems from paralysis. As Kristeva (1991) notes, border crossers – and here I include gender, class, and ethnic border crossers as well as migrants and exiles – become strangers to themselves. This painful location, one of displacement, ambiguity, hybridity and loss, is increasingly a feature of the alienated global capitalist world all of us inhabit (cf. Augé, 1995; Cushman, 1995). While alienation structures all of our subjectivities, it is etched in sharpest relief in the migrant's futile search for home.

And Then I Went to School [8]

Although Western societies propagate the myth of the child as innocent, and of child development as a process of unfettered intrapsychic growth, the cynicism behind this view is evident in the ways in which even the most supposedly liberal and democratic societies control the process of schooling. The rhetoric of liberal and progressive education is wedded to a rhetoric of cultural transmission and ideological control that shapes the subjectivity of children in very specific ways. As Jonathan Lear (2006) noted, in discussing the cultural cohesion of the turn-of-the-century Crow nation, membership in the Crow required seeing the world in a particular Crow way. Cultural rituals, rites of initiation, and apprenticeships often serve this function for groups. For post-industrial societies, schooling serves as the major mechanism of cultural socialization and homogenization. There is considerable literature both on how western institutions foster a particular kind of consumer self-hood in people, and on how schools, in particular, socialize children into knowing their place in the particular segment of the social order made available to them.[9] Despite liberal hand-wringing over schooling, governments have continued to develop very specific accountability mechanisms for schools in order to control the aspirations and desires – and hence the subjectivities – of their citizens.

While freedom and desire may be possible, too often the constraints on subjectivity are such that children's horizons are foreshortened. As Gregory Jay noted, schools feature a pedagogy of *consumption* rather than a pedagogy of active *production* (1987, p. 798). This does not surprise me. If society's demand is that citizens become *consumers* (of ideas, goods) then it makes sense to apprenticeship them in consumption. If society wished for children to be *originators* (of ideas, inventions) educational experiences would be structured radically differently so that expansive narratives of self and society could be imagined and lived.

The workings of these processes can best be seen in the language of schooling. Does schooling speak to the unconscious and enable the articulation of desire and curiosity or is school a place where conversations about the subjective possibilities of the child's being are shut down? Too often, schools shut down subjective possibilities for children. Some children are lucky enough, either alone or with assistance, to transcend the palette of available identificatory possibilities so that they do not limit themselves to slots in predetermined narratives. Although subjugated, I made some efforts along those lines as a child.

For the most part, my schooling mirrored the kind of experience described by Charles Dickens (1854/1994) in *Hard Times*. The teacher was not the *subject supposed to know*. The teacher *did* know. The children were ignorant recipients of the teacher's knowledge. As Oliver Goldsmith stated in *The village schoolmaster*, a poem from my childhood, "And still they gaz'd, and still the wonder grew, that one small head could carry all he knew" (Goldsmith, 1770/2003). The environment in which our mastery of skills and facts took place was crafted to maximize anxiety and fear so that we were neurotically focused entirely on the demand of the teacher. At first, avoidance of punishment and the winning of approval was all that mattered. Later, the emphasis deftly shifted to the pursuit of grades and credentials as means of satisfying external demand. Apart from acquiring a high capacity for conformity and a high level of the kind of neurotic personality characteristics described so ably by Karen Horney (1991) and Harry Stack Sullivan (1968), the subjective possibilities were abysmal. *Did you get it done? Did you get it right? How many did you get wrong?* These were the trembling queries we posed to each other. And as for the catastrophic consequences of failure, these came in the form of the daily ritual of *Sín amach do lábh!* (Stretch out your hand) as we waited for the delivery of slaps from the teacher's rod, a switch that one of us had personally been ordered to pluck for him from a nearby ash tree. Anxiety. Fear. Humiliation. Anxiety. Fear. Humiliation. Anxiety. Fear. Humiliation. Annihilation…

The subjective possibilities of schooling ultimately come down to the possibilities of language. If teachers *know* and students are thereby recipients of inert facts, then subjective possibilities are killed off. If teachers recognize that children contain unconscious knowledge, and that this can be brought into conversation so that curiosity and desire are engendered in the child this opens up possibilities for the construction of agentic narratives of their lives. In Lacanian terms,[10] in order for the child to become the *sujet-supposé-savoir* ("the-subject-supposed-to-know") the teacher must relinquish the position of omniscience and allow the student's *lack* to emerge in the form of questions. Recognition of the child's questions and an awareness by the teacher of the need to become a receptor for the child until the child can assume the *sujet-supposé-savoir* position creates an opportunity for the kind of agentic dialogue that allows the child to begin to construct a narrative of possibility for his or her own subjectivity. Judicious selection of literature that opens the possibilities of historical memory, and an invitation to adopt multiple subject positions relating to *difference,* to *knowing,* to *history*, and to *imagination* only serve to expand subjective possibilities further.

Some children appear willing to go to extraordinary lengths to fight *misrecognition* and come to be seen as beings-in-their-own-right. My two favorite examples are Billy Elliot, the main character in the movie of the same title (Daldry, 2003) and Ludo, the main character of *Ma vie en rose* (Berliner, 1997). Billy fights valiantly to become a ballet dancer, despite growing up in a staunchly sexist working-class British community, and Ludo battles gender stereotypes and familial and community prejudice so that he can lay claim to his feminine self. Notably, Billy received powerful affirmative mirroring from his deceased mother, and Ludovic received similar recognition from his oddly vibrant grandmother.

I was not so strong. It was not lack of indignation or imagination that hampered me, so much as sufficient *misrecognition* to cause me to feel that I needed to harbor my hopes and dreams internally. There were three notable exceptions, and each, though small, contributed in important ways to my capacity to claim my place as a *sujet-supposé-savoir.* The first occurred when I was seven. In our three-room schoolhouse we had the same teacher for grades 2-4. She was a young teacher, newly married, and she spent practically every day of the three years I spent in her room creating art and craft projects for her house. The only time she made an effort to teach was when the feared *Cigire* (School Inspector) arrived for his annual visit. Much as children are pressed into service today to do well on standardized tests to save the school's skin, we were pressed into service to save her from the wrath of the feared *Cigire*.

The *Cigire* examined us orally for hours, and then, as he was writing up his observations, he summoned me to the front of the room. Quaking with fear, burning under the anxious gaze of my classmates, I walked forward. He spoke to me kindly. He asked me my name. Then he asked me what my father did in order to assess my economic status. He asked me if I intended to go to secondary school and university, and I was too embarrassed and confused to answer coherently. He told me I was a bright boy, and that I should think about this for the future. Later that evening, when I told my parents about the encounter, I cannot recall mentioning the university part. I think I had already acquired a disposition where the anticipation of that much entitlement was more than I could handle.

Our headmaster taught fifth and sixth grade, and he derived much of his social status from preparing sixth-graders for local exams that allowed top achievers to win scholarships to pay secondary school tuition. As his most promising student I was drilled by rote on all aspects of the test, and we prepared canned compositions so that there would be no surprises on the exam. We also had an Irish oral recitation requirement. In addition to the simple school poems, my mother had acquired from my uncle, a fluent Gaelic speaker, a lengthy mournful elegy to some child who had died in a snowstorm. It began: *"Is cuimhin liom an sneachta mór"* ("I remember the great snowfall"), and descended into misery from there. She insisted I memorize it so as to stand out during the competition. On the day of the recitation, when the examiner scrutinized my list he asked me to pick a poem. Instead of choosing the mournful poem, I said it didn't matter to me and asked him to choose. He picked the simplest poem on the list and I recited it perfectly. During the English exam I ignored the canned composition topic for which I had been so thoroughly prepared. Instead I wrote an essay on "Books," the topic of my choice.

My teacher met with me after the exam and when I told him my topic choice for the essay, and how I had handled the oral exam, he walked off, got in his car, and drove immediately to see my mother to tell her that I had failed. "After all our preparation he wrote about 'Books,'" he said contemptuously. When I arrived home on my bicycle an hour later, my mother was despondent. I explained what I did, though I felt despondent and unsure of myself. Needless to say, I did very well and earned a scholarship, but my teacher never apologized for his behavior.

My entire secondary school experience was forgettable except for Denis Canty. In my junior year, in what must have been a fit of temporary madness, my strait-laced school hired a drama teacher. Denis taught us improvisation, and was the only teacher I ever encountered who began each class with "Well boys, what would you like to do today?" It was an incredible gift.

Teaching Otherwise

In this chapter I have tried to articulate some aspects of the sociohistorical constitutedness of my own subjectivity so that I might better understand how I come to be with my students. In becoming conscious of the predicament of my own marginality I hope I can work to complexify and decolonize my students' understandings of their origins. By becoming sensitive to the exquisite losses involved in my own border crossings I hope to engage my migrant, ethnic, and class border crossing students and my gender bending students in conversations that rupture reality and reveal the socially constructed and hence hegemonic nature of the discursive structures within which our lives are embedded. I may never be able to assure them that they will become comfortable with the predicament of marginality, but at least I can let them know that they are not alone (cf, hooks, 1990; Spitzer, 1989). The margins are actually pretty crowded places – thankfully!

My approach to teaching teachers might be described, therefore, as a critical narrative approach. I assume that all of my students are inserted into narrative processes that have become their ways of seeing. My first step, therefore, is to engender in students an awareness of their own sociohistorical situatedness by inviting them to narrate their lives. Earlier in my career, following a crude critical pedagogical recipe, I attempted to change the worldviews of my students through engaging them directly with more progressive and radical alternatives. This not only failed, but it actually produced deep resistance to change.[11] Now, understanding how deeply embedded all people are in unconscious personal and cultural ideologies – what Freud called "the archive"[12] – I recognize that my first task with my students – as well as my first obligation with respect to myself – is to name the baggage and attendant privileges that accompany each of our individual worldviews. This process occurs partly through communal sharing that allows students to recognize – in their necessary differences – the peculiarities of the archive from which each one's subjectivity is formed. This is a deep process of mutual interrogation of worldviews. In my class on children's emotional lives, for example, this process begins by allocating every participant as much time as they choose to meditate on the saddest moment in their lives to date. In my class on cultural difference, the exploration begins with an opening invitation to all students to meditate on their ethnic and racial origins and positioning by society.[13]

A second goal of my work is to expand the depth and possibilities of the narratives of the lives that students are constructing by exposing them to a rich range of narrative possibilities beyond their own lived experiences, particularly by exposing them to people who have lived their lives otherwise. I accomplish this through use of evocative novels, memoirs, poetry, and films. Exposure to these narrative modes offers a broad range of identificatory possibilities to students. More important, perhaps, carefully chosen novels, memoirs, poems, and films make powerful connections with the unconscious and open up an emotional fissure that then becomes progenitor for the kind of intellectual and political change that may lead them to imagine lives lived otherwise.[14]

Autobiographical and narrative work can readily fall into what Trinh (1989) calls "navel gazing" if a critical edge is not preserved, To avoid this I provide critical theoretical writings that deconstruct the givens of conscious and unconscious experience, and students are encouraged to use these critical tools to deconstruct their own lived experience. This is what I would refer to, perhaps, as a decolonizing approach to pedagogy (cf. O'Loughlin, 2002).

In sum, as I work and rework my own life narrative, I see my project as assisting my students – and my patients in psychotherapy – in weaving and re-weaving their own narrative lives so that they may begin to imagine new possibilities of being otherwise and hence new possibilities of teaching otherwise.

NOTES

[1] Portions of this chapter also appear in Michael O'Loughlin's book *The subject of childhood* (2009).

[2] For the severe consequences of this for contemporary Australian Aboriginal communities see Michael O'Loughlin, (2008), *Radical hope or death by a thousand cuts? The future for Indigenous Australians* and Jon Altman and Melinda Hinkson, (2007), *Coercive reconciliation: Stabilize, normalize and exit aboriginal Australia*. For a similar discussion in a North American context see Ward Churchill's (2004) aptly titled *Kill the Indian, save the man*.

[3] Aboriginal actor David Gulpilil who plays Moodoo in *Rabbit Proof Fence* offers another variation on the *inscrutable native* in Rolf de Heer's (2002) film *The Tracker*.

[4] In *Imaginary maps* (1995), Mashaweta Devi, commenting on oppression of Native American peoples in the U.S. notes: "Only in the names of places the Native American legacy survives.

Otherwise entire tribes have been butchered. Their land has been taken away... But I say to my American readers, see what has been done to them, you will understand what has been done to the Indian tribals [i.e., in India]. Everywhere it is the same story." (1995, p. xi)

[5] See, for example, Frances Finnegan, (2001), *Do penance or perish: Magdalen asylums in Ireland;* Mary Raftery and Eoin O'Sullivan, (1999), *Suffer the little children: The inside story of Ireland's industrial schools;* Patrick Galvin (2002), *The raggy boy trilogy.*

[6] See Michael O'Loughlin, (2007a), *Whereof one cannot speak... thereof one cannot stay silent,* for an overview of this literature

[7] See, example, the depiction of anti-Irish nativist sentiment in Martin Scorsese's (2003) film *The gangs of New York.*

[8] This section is extracted from Michael O'Loughlin, (In press), "The curious subject of childhood."

[9] See David Nasaw, (1981), *Schooled to order: A social history of public schooling in the United States* and Jay MacLeod, (1995), *Ain't no makin' it: Aspirations and attainment in a low-income neighborhood* for discussion of the limiting effects of school discourses. See Barry Richards, (1984), *Capitalism and infancy: Essays on psychoanalysis and politics* and Philip Cushman, (1995), *Constructing the self, constructing America: A cultural history of* psychotherapy for discussion of the effects of contemporary capitalism on the self. For larger discussion of the totalizing effects of social systems on subjectivity see Jacques Donzelot, (1997), *The policing of families* and Erving Goffman, (1961), *Asylums: Essays on the social situation of mental patients and other inmates.*

[10] For an introduction to Lacanian thought see Apollon, Bergeron, & Cantin, (2002), *After Lacan;* Bruce Fink (1995), *The Lacanian subject: Between language and jouissance*; Bruce Fink (1997), *Lacanian Psychoanalysis: Theory and technique*; Danny Nobus, (1998), *Key concepts of Lacanian Psychoanalysis.*

[11] For critical discussion of the impositional qualities of critical pedagogy see Elizabeth Ellsworth, (1989), *Why doesn't this feel empowering?*

[12] See Freud's (1939/1967) *Moses and monotheism.* For further discussion of the archive, see Lisa Farley, (2008), *An unhomely archive: The child in Freud.*

[13] Copies of my syllabi, illustrating my pedagogical approaches, may be requested by emailing me at: oloughli@adelphi.edu

[14] For a discussion of *evocative pedagogy* see Michael O'Loughlin, (2009), *The subject of childhood.*

REFERENCES

Abraham, N., & Torok, M. (1994). *The kernel and the shell* (Vol. 1). Chicago: University of Chicago Press.
Aciman, A. (Ed.). (1999). *Letters of transit.* New York: New Press.
Altman, J., & Hinkson, M. (2007). *Coercive reconciliation: Stabilize, normalize and exit aboriginal Australia.* Fitzroy, Australia: Arena Publications.
Apollon, W., Bergeron, D., & Cantin, L. (2002). *After Lacan.* Albany, NY: SUNY Press.
Augé, M. (1995). *Non-places: Introduction to an anthropology of supermodernity.* London: Verso.
Berliner, A. [Director]. (1997). *Ma vie en rose.* Sony Pictures.
Bhabha, H. (1994). *The location of culture.* London: Routledge.
Churchill, W. (2004). *Kill the Indian, save the man.* San Francisco: City Lights Books.
Clare, A. (1991). The mad Irish? In C. Keane (Ed.), *Mental health in Ireland.* Dublin: Gill & Macmillan and RTE.
Cushman, P. (1995). *Constructing the self: Constructing America.* Reading, MA: Addison Wesley.
Daldry, S. [Director]. (2001). *Billy Elliot.* Universal Studios.
Davoine, F., & Gaudillière, J. (2004). *History beyond trauma.* New York: Other Press.

Derrida, J. (1994). *Specters of Marx: The state of the debt, the work of mourning, and the new international*. New York: Routledge.
de Heer, R. [Director]. (2002). *The tracker* [DVD]. ArtMattan Productions.
Devi, M. (1995). *Imaginary maps* (G. Spivak, Trans.). New York: Routledge.
Dickens, C. (1854/1994). *Hard times*. New York: Penguin Popular Classics.
Donzelot, J. (1997). *The policing of families*. New York: Pantheon.
Eagelton, T. (2002). *The gatekeeper*. London: Penguin.
Ellsworth, E. (1989). Why doesn't this feel empowering? Working through the repressive myths of critical pedagogy. *Harvard Educational Review, 59*(3), 297–324.
Fanon, F. (1967). *Black skin, white masks*. New York: Grove Press.
Farley, L. (2008). *An unhomely archive: The child in Freud*. Presented at annual meeting of American Educational Research Association, New York.
Fine, M., Powell, L., Pruitt, L., & Burns. (2004). *Off White: Readings on power, privilege and resistance*. London & New York: Routledge.
Fink, B. (1995). *The Lacanian subject: Between language and jouissance*. Princeton, NJ: Princeton University Press.
Fink, B. (1997). *Lacanian psychoanalysis: Theory and technique*. Cambridge, MA: Harvard University Press.
Finnegan, F. (2001). *Do penance or perish: Magdalen asylums in Ireland*. London: Oxford University Press.
Fraiberg, S., Adelson, E., & Shapiro, V. (1975). Ghosts in the nursery. *Journal of the American Academy of Child Psychiatry, 14*, 387–421.
Frankenberg, R. (1995). *White women, race matters: The social construction of whiteness*. Minneapolis, MN: University of Minnesota Press.
Freud, S. (1939/1967). *Moses and monotheism*. New York: Vintage.
Galvin. (2002). *The raggy boy trilogy*. Dublin: New Island Books.
Goffman, E. (1961). *Asylums: Essays on the social situation of mental patients and other inmates*. New York: Anchor.
Goldsmith, O. (1770/2003). The village schoolmaster. In T. Hosic (Ed.), *Gray's Elegy and Goldsmith's the deserted village, the traveler, and other poems*. Honolulu, HI: University Press of the Pacific.
Gordon, A. (1997). *Ghostly matters: Haunting and the sociological imagination*. Minneapolis, MN: University of Minnesota Press.
Gramsci. A. (1971). *Selections from the prison notebooks*. New York: International Publishers.
Hoffman, E. (1990). *Lost in translation: A life in a new language*. New York: Penguin Books.
hooks, b. (1990). Choosing the margin as a space of radical openness. In Author (Ed.), *Yearning: Race, gender and cultural politics*. Boston: South End Press.
Horney, K. (1991). *Neurosis and human growth: The struggle toward self-realization*. New York: Norton.
Ignatiev, N. (1995). *How the Irish became white*. New York: Routledge.
Jay, J. (1987). The subject of pedagogy: Lessons in psychoanalysis and politics. *College English, 49*(7), 785–800.
Kearney, R. (1985). Introduction. In Author (Ed.), *The Irish mind*. Dublin: Wolfhound Press.
Kristeva, J. (1991). *Strangers to ourselves* (L. S. Roudiez, Trans.). New York: Columbia University Press.
Lear, J. (2006). *Radical hope: Ethics in the face of cultural devastation*. Cambridge, MA: Harvard University Press.
McCourt, F. (1996). *Angela's ashes*. New York: HarperCollins.
MacLeod, J. (1995). *Ain't no makin' it: Aspirations and attainment in a low-income neighborhood*. Boulder, CO: Westview.

McIntosh, P. (1988). *White privilege: Unpacking the invisible knapsack*. Retrieved from http://seamonkey.ed.asu.edu/~mcisaac/emc598ge/Unpacking.html
Mullan, P. [Director]. (2002). *Magadelene Sisters* (2004), Peter Mullan, Director. [DVD]. Miramax Home Entertainment.
Nasaw, D. (1981). *Schooled to order: A social history of public schooling in the United States*. New York: Oxford.
Nobus, D. (Ed.). (1998). *Key concepts of Lacanian psychoanalysis*. New York: Other Press.
Noyce, P. [Director]. (2003). *Rabbit-proof fence* [DVD]. Miramax Home Entertainment.
O'Loughlin, M. (In press). The curious subject of the child. In M. O'Loughlin & R. Johnson (Eds.), *Exploring childhood subjectivity*. Albany, NY: SUNY Press.
O'Loughlin, M. (2009). *The subject of childhood*. New York: Peter Lang Publishing.
O'Loughlin, M. (2008). Radical hope or death by a thousand cuts? The future for indigenous Australians. *Arena Journal*.
O'Loughlin, M. (2007a). *Whereof one cannot speak... thereof one cannot stay silent*. Presented at meeting of International Society for Theoretical psychology, Toronto, Canada.
O'Loughlin, M. (2007b). On losses that are not easily mourned. In L. Bohm, R. Curtis, & B. Willock (Eds.), *Psychoanalysts' reflections on deaths and endings: Finality, transformations, new beginnings*. New York: Routledge.
O'Loughlin, M. (2006). On knowing and desiring children: The significance of the unthought known. In G. Boldt & P. Salvio (Eds.), *Love's return: Psychoanalytic essays on childhood teaching and learning*. New York: Routledge.
O'Loughlin, M. (2002, October). *A decolonizing pedagogy: Introducing undergraduate students to the psychology of hatred and genocide and the nature of historical memory*. Presented at fourth annual Race, Gender, & Class conference, New Orleans.
O'Loughlin, M. (2001). The development of subjectivity in young children: Theoretical and pedagogical considerations. *Contemporary Issues in Early Childhood*, 2(1), 49–65.
Pilkington, D. (2002). *Rabbit-proof fence*. New York: Hyperion.
Raftery, M., & O'Sullivan, E. (1999). *Suffer the little children: The inside story of Ireland's industrial schools*. Dublin: New Island Books.
Rashkin, E. (1992). *Family secrets and the psychoanalysis of narrative*. Princeton, NJ: Princeton University Press.
Richards, B. (1984). *Capitalism and infancy: Essays on psychoanalysis and politics*. London: Free Association Books.
Roediger, D. (2007). *The wages of whiteness: Race and the making of the American working class: Revised and expanded edition*. London: Verso.
Roediger, D. (2006). *Working toward whiteness: How America's immigrants became white: The strange journey form Ellis island to the suburbs*. New York: Perseus Books.
Rogers, A. (2006). *The unsayable: The hidden language of trauma*. New York: Random House.
Ryan, J., & Sackrey, C. (1995). *Strangers in paradise*. Washington, DC: University Press of America.
Scorsese, M. [Director]. (2003). *The gangs of New York* [DVD]. Miramax Home Entertainment.
Sennett, R., & Cobb, J. (1993). *The hidden injuries of class*. New York: Norton.
Seshadri-Crooks, K. (2000). *Desiring whiteness: A Lacanian analysis of race*. London & New York: Routledge.
Spitzer, L. (1989). *Lives in between: The experience of marginality in a century of emancipation*. New York: Hill & Wang.
Sullivan, H. (1968). *The interpersonal theory of psychiatry*. New York: Norton.
Trinh, M. (1989). *Woman, native, other*. Bloomington, IN: Indiana University Press.
Tuckwell, G. (2002). *Racial identity: White counsellors and therapists*. London: Open University Press.
Venn, C. (2002). Refiguring subjectivity after modernity. In V. Walkerdine (Ed.), *Challenging subjects: Critical psychology for a new millennium*. New York: Palgrave.

Wiesel, E. (1982). *Night*. New York: Bantam.
Woodham-Smith, C. (1962). *The great hunger*. London: New English Library.

Michael O'Loughlin
Ruth S. Ammon School of Education & Derner Institute of Advanced Psychological Studies
Adelphi University

FRANCES V. RAINS, Ph.D.

EVEN WHEN ERASED, WE EXIST:

Native[1] Women Standing Strong for Justice

INTRODUCTION

As native women work for the benefit of future generations, they are embraced by the memory of their ancestors. In the strength of that embrace, the line between the past, present, and future is not as distinct as it is in the larger society. Native women know the sacred places generations of their people have gone for renewal and for ceremony. They know where great battles were once fought and where their people held meetings to discuss momentous decisions about war and peace. They have a special relationship with the land where their ancestors sang their songs, told their stories, and were returned to the earth for burial. This is their homeland. (Wilma Mankiller, 2004, pp. 5-6)

In November, 2007, I attended the Second Annual Indigenous Ways of Knowing Conference, at Lewis and Clark College. At the closing of this conference, in High Plateau Longhouse fashion, we were assembled, women on one side, men on the other, forming a sort of horse shoe around the room. Beginning with the women, each person stood in turn, to share their final words about Indigenous ways of knowing.

I listened as Elder women of the Yakama, Palouse, Warm Springs, Wasco, and Paiute Nations stood, each in their turn, to give voice to their experiences with cultural genocide when they were young mothers. They risked opening up their old wounds, in order for others to understand the significance and meaning of a sacred place that was more than geography, more than a location, it was a place integral to a pattern of life that had existed for ten millennia.

Each of these Native Nations used Indigenous knowledge to sustainably harvest salmon at an extraordinary place known as Celilo Falls on the Columbia River. From both sides of the river, the Native Nations had built scaffolds and fished the falls with hand held nets and gaff poles at particular times. Always each Nation was mindful that others also fished at Celilo Falls, where an unwritten, yet time-honored, rhythm ensured that each Nation received their bounty.

Each year over 5,000 Native people would gather at this place to participate in spiritual ceremonies and to fish, trade and feast. Fish would be preserved for the winter months in the fish camps, as Native women shared news, gossiped, and taught young girls how to prepare the salmon, while young men and women courted. It was not simply a place where water fell over boulders in a thunderous roar that could be heard over a mile away, it was a place of political, cultural and social importance. And so, in 1957, when the Army Corp of Engineers had the Native people forcible removed, many of the young Native women and men resisted, but were bodily removed while their Elders wailed and their children cried. The Army Corp of Engineers proceeded to *kill* the Falls by using dynamite to blast not only all the boulders, but also the small island in the middle of the Columbia known as Celilo Village. This village had been home to more than one of the Elder women who were speaking that day. A place that has been continuously inhabited for over 11,000 years was, in a matter of less than an hour, reduced to mere pebbles under water. It was not a matter of how much the one-time-only payment of money for the loss of the Falls would be, for many Native families refused the pittance offered. It was a matter of respecting Tribal Sovereignty and respecting the lifeblood of many Native Nations, the Salmon, itself.

The Dalles Dam, situated on top of where Celilo Falls had once been, was built to provide cheap electricity for non-Indian[2] communities far from the river itself. This dam is one of 27 major dams on the Columbia and Snake River systems. Along with the 2,900 other smaller dams in the Columbia River Basin, the Dalles Dam had *no means* of preserving the Salmon runs, no way of preserving, honoring, or respecting Indigenous ways of living. And now, at this conference, fifty years later, some of the oldest living witnesses to this death of Celilo Falls were these Native women who were sharing their stories.

I was one of the last to speak, because I was on the Leadership Council and had played a minor role in the conference. I said that I was a "woman warrior" in modern clothes and times. As a Choctaw/Cherokee & Japanese woman, I had been raised to recognize that with education came responsibility. Earning a Ph.D. meant I had a great responsibility to educate so that cultural genocide would not continue to happen in a country that prides itself on liberty and justice for all.

I had been deeply humbled by the testimony of the Elder women and so I didn't want the spotlight to move away from their concerns. I was ready to sit down, when one of the Elder women stood up and walked over to me. She gifted me with a very tiny pair of hand made buckskin gloves in the style of the High Plateau cultures. They were earrings. She said to everyone, as public witnesses in Longhouse tradition, that she was gifting me with these earrings because she wanted me to never forget my responsibility as a warrior.

Therefore, I write this chapter, wearing these earrings, with the stories of these Elder women echoing in my head. I think of their courage to stand strong in the face of injustice, even though the history of Native American women is hardly ever recognized. I think of the persistence of stereotypes and ignorance about Native women and feel that I must stand up. This chapter, then, is a humble effort to provide a different way of knowing about Native women as a backdrop for the actual women's lives I share here. It was very difficult to select only a few stories, as it isn't often that I get a chance to share such stories at all. But the background and context are offered so that the stories will be better understood, and I hope, remembered. Thank you.

A Different Reality

Native American women have been erased from history. It is *not* that they did not exist; it is that they were *made invisible*, omitted from history books and lessons. At the same time, certain stereotypes (e.g., squaw, princess, sexually promiscuous) have plagued Native women since 1492. Aside from the "good Indians"–Pocahontas, Powhatan Confederacy,[3] and Sacajewea, Shoshone Nation–who aided White men in their quest for more land, the erasure of Native women from much of U.S. history, and from much of Women's history, has left the stereotypes very much intact.

Ironically, the history of Native women has reflected an extremely different reality. Many Native women had rights 1,000 years ago that White women would not receive in this country until 1920, after almost a century of serious struggle and protest. These rights–reciprocal voice in important decisions, freedom of speech, territorial rights to food resources, rights within marriage–often historically empowered Native American women and freed them from the struggle for such rights that White women had to work so hard to gain. Such historic differences have granted these women a long time to strengthen and refine their voices.

Native women have been at the forefront of challenges, standing strong for justice. They have stood: to protect their Homelands and the Natural World; to defend Tribal Sovereignty; to protect and maintain the cultures, languages and traditions; and to protect the health and well being of their families. But few people learn about these Native women who have consistently defied the stereotypes to work for justice.

What The Stereotypes Miss

When we study the history of this land, we often begin with 1492. However, from a Native viewpoint, history here did not begin with Columbus.

Native people have been here from between 20,000 to 40,000 years (Jennings, 1993; Nies, 1996), not just Native men, but Native women as well. This may sound like a simple point, that Native women have been here for a long time, but it has direct bearing upon how we understand the positionality of American Indian women in history. That is, when we study the history here and begin with 1492, we neglect the longer history and relationship of the various Native Nations to this land. The traditional roles of Native women and men, their cultures, languages and ways of being and knowing are all connected *to* the land. Cultivated over thousands of years, the history of the Native People *is* the history of the land. However, when a history is narrowly constructed, these relationships are erased. So, the background of this story draws on this longer history to shed light on how Native women not only existed, but existed in ways that were in direct contrast to the stereotypes established by the Colonizers.[4]

Too, we often overlook the fact that European men did not typically bring European women with them until almost a hundred years after Columbus's arrival (Green, 1992; Steer, 1996). Many Native Nations along the eastern seaboard had oral traditions of first encounters with the Europeans. Typically, these reports pointed out that these men were very odd; not only for their skin, which was very hairy and looked sickly, but also for how forgetful these strangers to their shores seemed to be. "'Where are your women?' Outacitty, Cherokee leader, [queried] upon meeting with British representatives, early [in the] eighteenth century." (Steer, 1996, p. 19) After all, to many Native Nations, it seemed a glaring oversight to forget to bring half your people.

In most Native Nations, there was a clear delineation of gender roles and responsibilities, but these roles were "not generally perceived to be hierarchical" (Klein & Ackerman, 1995, p. 14). Women's roles, while differing greatly from the men's, were deemed equally important to the survival of their peoples (Green, 1992; Sonneborn, 1998; Steer, 1996). Rather than being seen as inferior, as often was the case for European women of the times, in most Native Nations, women were seen as indispensable members of their communities (Steer, 1996).

> As mothers, Indian women have given life. As workers, they have farmed fields, built houses, and performed other labor crucial to their tribe's well being. As caregivers and teachers, they have instructed young tribe's people in how to live properly and productively. (Sonneborn, 1998, p. vii.)

Native women, from this perspective, were the very backbone of their Nations. As the ancient Cheyenne proverb reveals, "A nation is not conquered until the hearts of its women are on the ground. Then it is done, no matter how brave its warriors or strong its weapons." As deeply valued members of their societies, in some Native Nations, a woman might earn a leadership role within the band[5] or even earn such a role over the entire nation. This was at a time when their female counterparts in feudal Europe rarely had the opportunity to earn such a position outside of birthright or marriage.

As well, Native women often had women's councils or clans within their village, band or Nation (Green, 1992; Steer, 1996). These women's councils or clans helped maintain the balance between men's power and women's power within their traditional life ways, their spiritual practices and social politics. These women often had the right to divorce their husbands and keep the children with them, something that would have been unheard of in Europe at the beginning of colonization and conquest (Green, 1992).

The early Colonizers brought with them very patriarchal Christian beliefs about women. These beliefs deeply influenced their views of the roles of Native women here. These strange men were often not privy to the Native women's councils or clans (Green, 1992; Sonneborn, 1998; Steer, 1996). As outsiders, and as men, they had no access. Therefore, drawing on their own beliefs about European women as a standard of measure, these men frequently described Native women as "dirty squaws." This was at a time in Europe when bathing was not a popular form of hygiene, and Native women often bathed daily. These men often assumed that Native "squaws"[6] were slave-like drudges, and inaccurately interpreted their role as subservient to the Native men when they saw women working in fields, for example (Green, 1992; Sonneborn, 1998; Steer, 1996). What these Colonizers did not know was that the fields were likely part of the women's property and, thereby, would fall in the women's domain of responsibilities.

Missed, too, by the Colonizing men was how the work Native women did, was not simply necessary, but was a means of instructing the young on Indigenous ways of knowing. Daughters and nieces learned about medicinal plants, their properties, uses, preparation and storage. They learned how to make cradleboards or other means of taking care of the young to ensure that while these working women carried out their daily tasks, their babies would be safe. They learned the ways to prepare and maintain the summer and winter shelters in particular, as these often were part of a woman's personal property. They also learned where, when, and how to harvest and prepare the natural materials important in the making of baskets, pottery, or other needed daily items. As well, they learned skills and techniques regarding dyes and various art forms to add beauty and personalize household items and clothing. These young women learned how to prepare and preserve foods, including where and when seasonal foods like berries or edible roots could be harvested. Additionally, they learned how to make and repair summer and winter clothing, including hats, footwear, and gloves. In short, the work that Native women did, modeled the practices important in becoming contributing adult members of their communities. The Colonizers, however, overlooked this important educating role, when they labeled working Native women as squaws or drudges.

In the hotter climates of the coastal southeast, Native women often went barebreasted. No doubt, for the women-less Colonizers, armed with Euro-Christian constructs of chastity and womanhood, other urges took over, as rape was a common early Native complaint against the Colonizers (Jennings, 1993). As primary reporters of Native life to the news-hungry European kingdoms, these Colonizing men often gave accounts of Native women as sexually promiscuous. It didn't occur to them that in a society where the climate was extremely hot, and limited clothing the norm, partial nudity did not represent sexual promiscuity. Native stories of the first encounters often discussed how Native women comported themselves respectfully. It was the strange, homeless, Colonizing men that were brutish and sexually abusive, to the horror of Native women and men. But armed with the power of the written word, these Colonizing men frequently mis-cast Native women as provocative whores or as sexually promiscuous.

In addition, these women-less Colonizers brought with them a political lens steeped in feudal tradition. The use of "king," and "queen" permeated the early writings that were sent back to Europe. On the one hand, changing the names of Native People and "elevating" particular Native leaders' status to "king" or "queen" seemed harmless enough. On the other hand, the use of such a political lens obscured from view the different political, social, and spiritual leadership structures[7] that varied across the many Native Nations. By perpetuating the euro-feudal patriarchy, the Colonizers could ignore any weight women's voices might carry here.

The label "princess" was another matter. The early Colonizers' designation of "princess" seemed uniquely reserved for the "good" Indian women who gave up their own cultures, to aid in the non-Indian takeover of lands and resources in the "new" world. Such Indian "princesses" were mythologized, their real lives distorted and their stories sanitized (Green, 1975; Klein & Ackerman, 1995; Sonneborn, 1998).

So, over the first 100 years of invasions, the women-less Colonizers generated several stereotypes of Native women. The narrowly constructed images of "squaw," "drudge," "sexually promiscuous," or "princess" were sent back to Europe. There, lacking any evidence to the contrary, the stereotypes returned to these shores intact, etched like tatoos on the psyches of European immigrants for generations to come. Over time, these stereotypes contributed to the struggle of Native women to be heard, obscuring these real women from view.

Circumventing Assimilation

In most Native Nations, even under the most oppressed of circumstances, Native women were raised to think for themselves. While Native women never completely lost their voices, certainly, many efforts were made to ensure their silence.

For example, from the 1600s to the early 1800s, missionary schools focused their recruitment on Indian boys (Bowker, 1993; Reyner & Eder, 2004). However, by the mid-1800s, Indian girls were also targeted. Native girls and boys were taken away from their families, cultures, languages, and Homelands in an effort to force assimilation upon them. By the 1870s, the government supported military-style boarding schools. These boarding schools were typically placed far from the reservation to more completely assimilate the children and minimize cultural contact with their families (Green, 1992; Reyhner & Eder, 2004; Szasz & Ryan, 1988). Still, an amazing thing sometimes occurred.

Native girls who attended such schools were sometimes able to resist the process of complete assimilation hoped for by the Colonizers (Green, 1992). The purpose of the Colonizers' schools had been to "civilize" these young women. They were expected to leave their traditional ways behind and become Indian versions of Christian "Victorian womanhood" (Adams, 1995). For example, during a visit to Hampton Normal and Agricultural Institute in 1898, to oversee the progress of Indian education there, Commissioner Jones noted, "Don't be discouraged, girls, much more depends upon you than upon the boys, and we look to you to carry home the refinement that shall really elevate your people" (Adams, 1995, p. 175). The "elevation" Commissioner Jones referenced was the emulation of white society. Make no mistake, many young Native women did succumb to the heavy pressure to religiously convert and culturally assimilate. However, there were some who used their understanding of non-Indian values, languages, customs and practices to stand up against the injustices Native Nations were experiencing (Green, 1992). These young Native women often spent the better part of their adult lives using their voices against the newest versions of maltreatment perpetrated by the Colonizers.

In the 1870s, one such Native woman was Thocmetony (Shell Flower)–Sarah Winnemucca Hopkins, Northern Paiute Nation. She was born around 1844 near present day Humbolt Lake in northwestern Nevada (Winnemucca Hopkins,

1883/1969). In 1860, she and one of her sisters attended St. Mary's Convent school in San Jose, California. However, the White parents objected so much to the presence of "savages" at the school, that within a month, the two girls were forced to leave (Waldman, 2001; Winnemucca Hopkins, 1883/1969). Although Sarah had limited exposure to written English, she was able to learn spoken English while growing up.

In 1860, the federal government established the Pyramid Lake Reservation, which was sixty miles long and fifteen miles wide. This was a dry land with lush fertile green belts along the rivers and lakes. The government agent overseeing this reservation was corrupt and he turned a blind eye as non-Indians began settling all the lush wooded areas designated by Treaty for the Paiutes (Winnemucca Hopkins, 1883/1969). The Paiutes were left with little access to water, no ability to fish for food, and only the harshest of dry terrain to make their homes. Within a few years, the non-Indians had cut all of the timber in the region, so that the Northern Paiute could not even build a wooden structure on their own Reservation. The Paiute were left parched, starving and destitute by a corrupt government agent, while non-Indians illegally occupied the best of their reservation lands and squandered all the natural resources.

Sarah tried different ways to help her people. She became an interpreter at Fort McDermitt, Nevada and used the money she earned to buy food and support her people as she could. She also created a stage show with her father, Winnemucca, and one of her sisters, but unfortunately, it raised little money (Sonneborn, 1998). By 1870, conditions on the Reservation had worsened, so Sarah "traveled to San Francisco to meet with General John Scholfeld, then to Gold Hill, Nevada, to speak to Senator John Jones concerning the mistreatment of [the] Paiute by Indian agents. Both claimed the problem was not under their jurisdiction" (Waldman, 2001, p. 419).

She became more hopeful when her people were force-relocated to the Malheur Reservation in present day Oregon, in the early 1870s. The government agent there was a good-hearted man, and so conditions for the Northern Paiute improved. Unfortunately, another corrupt government agent replaced the good-hearted agent. Sarah protested and was banished from the Reservation. Around 1878, the Bannock Nation, confined to a reservation in present day Idaho, made a decision to go to war over the horrible treatment they were receiving from their government agents. Some of the Northern Paiute decided to join the Bannocks in their struggle against the Colonizers. While the Bannock War only lasted from June until September of 1878, Sarah was right in the middle of the conflict.

The Northern Paiutes were divided over the war. Some left to support the Bannock Nation, including Sarah's father, brother, and sister-in-law, while others decided to stay neutral. Sarah volunteered to be an interpreter and a scout for the military. During the war, the Paiutes who had sided with the Bannock decided to rejoin the neutral Paiutes. But the Bannock prevented their return by keeping them captive. Sarah raced into the middle of Bannock Territory, freed her people and led them back to safety (Sonneborn, 1998; Winnemucca Hopkins, 1883/1969).

When the war ended Sarah assumed that the government would allow the neutral Paiutes to return to Malheur. The federal government, however, made no distinctions between allies or foes. All Northern Paiutes were considered Prisoners of War and the Malheur Reservation was terminated (Waldman, 2000). To make matters worse, they were to be force-marched in winter to the Yakama Reservation in present day Washington State. It was a week before Christmas in 1878, and they were given less than a week to get ready for the move. Sarah was outraged.

> What! In this cold winter and in all this snow, and my people have so many little children? Why, they will all die. Oh, what can the President be thinking about? Oh, tell me, what is he? Is he man or beast? Yes, he must be a beast; if he has no feeling for my people, surely he ought to have some for the soldiers.
>
> I have never seen a president in my life and I want to know whether he is made of wood or rock, for I cannot once think that he can be a human being. No human being would do such a thing as that–send people across a fearful mountain in midwinter. (Winnemucca Hopkins, 1883/1969, p. 205)

There were few provisions, the journey was arduous and cold, and many did die along the way. The Yakama Nation already occupied the reservation, but Sarah soon learned that Bannock Nation was being force-marched to the same reservation as they were (Green, 1992; Sonneborn, 1998; Winnemucca Hopkins, 1883/1969). Skirmishes between the three groups worsened the situation as space was limited, food and water in short supply, and there was no way to care for the sick and dying (Winnemucca Hopkins, 1883/1969). By June of 1879 even more of her people had died.

That was when she undertook to see the President of the United States. However, with little money on hand, Sarah was forced to give lectures in San Francisco to raise funds for the trip (Sonneborn 1998; Winnemucca Hopkins, 1883/1969). In 1880, Sarah traveled all the way to Washington, D.C. There she briefly met the President, Rutherford B. Hayes. She also met with the Secretary of the Interior, Carl Schurz. Through him, she obtained a letter granting her people the right to return to Malheur, where conditions had been less crowded. She returned to the Yakama Reservation with the letter in hand. However, the government agents and the military officers refused to let her people leave. "The next year, the U.S. government opened Malheur to white settlement, thereby ending any possibility of the area serving as a reservation for the Paiutes" (Sonneborn, 1998, p. 200).

Sarah, again, went on the lecture circuit, this time in the east, to raise her voice in the cause of justice. Trying to bring public attention to the plight of her people she said, "If women could go into your Congress I think justice would soon be done to the Indians" (Jim, 1994, p. 43). She even wrote a book, the first non-fiction book written by a Native woman, to help fund her lecture tour in the east. The book, "Life Among the Piutes [sic.]: Their Wrongs and Claims" was published in 1883 with Mrs. Horace Mann as the editor. Unfortunately, in 1891, at the age of 48, Sarah died without ever seeing justice served.

Native women continued to stand against the aggressions of the Colonizer throughout the late nineteenth and early twentieth centuries. Gertrude Simmons

Bonnin, Nakota Sioux, for example, in 1884 was taken at age eight by Quakers to "White's Indiana Manual Labor Institute in Wabash, Indiana" and later she went to "Earlham College in Richmond, Indiana" (Sonneborn, 1998, p. 12). At the Quaker college, she learned to play the violin and gained a reputation as a great orator, winning many contests. At one speech contest at Earlham, as part of a longer speech, she stated,

> …Unfortunately civilization is not an unmixed blessing. Vices begin to creep into the Indian's life. He learns to crave the European liquid fire. Broken treaties shake his faith in the newcomers. The white man's bullet decimates his tribes and drives him from his home.
>
> What if he [the Indian] fought? His forests were felled; his game frightened away; his streams of finny shoals usurped. He loved his family and defended them. He loved the land of which he was rightful owner. He loved his father's traditions and their graves. Do you wonder that he avenged the loss of his home being ruthlessly driven from his temples of worship? Is patriotism only in white men's hearts? (Rappaport, 1997, pp. 62-63)

Few Indians remained in the state ironically named "Indian-a." Between the "War of 1812" and the Indian Removal Act of 1830 (Josephy, 1994; Waldman, 2000), most Native Nations residing in present day Indiana had either been decimated or forcibly removed. The non-Indians living there were insulated by their 60+ years of "civilization." Now a young Native woman dared to penetrate that insulation with a voice that called for justice. Her speech drew on bleak Native realities in the west and cast non-Indian interactions with Native people in a less than favorable light. Selecting such an Indian focus was a risky endeavor. It might mean the loss of the contest, or worse, potentially racist reactions from her peers.

Surprisingly, her speech won the contest at Earlham College. She was even selected to represent the Quaker school in a statewide college speech competition in Indianapolis, Indiana (Rappaport, 1997; Sonneborn, 1998). There were no other women students representing other colleges and Gertrude was the only Indian at this competition (Rappaport, 1997). For her oration there, she decided to give the same speech she had given at Earlham. She was the last to speak and she remembered,

> …some college rowdies threw out a large white flag with a drawing of a most forlorn Indian girl on it. Under this they had printed in bold black letters words that ridiculed the college which was represented by a 'squaw.' … [after her speech] My teeth were hard set, for the white flag still floated insolently in the air. Anxiously we watched the man carry the envelope with the final decision toward the stage. There were two prizes given that night, and one of them was mine!...and the hands which furled [the flag] hung limp in defeat…. (Rappaport, 1997, p. 65)

In spite of the racist jeers and stereotypes like "squaw," Gertrude's voice against injustice had prevailed. Gertrude learned that the educational skills she acquired could be used to raise her voice on behalf of Native people. She did not forget this lesson.

She graduated from Earlham in 1897, at the age of twenty-one and was recruited as a teacher by Colonel Richard Pratt, the founder of the Carlisle Indian Industrial School (Rappaport, 1997; Sonneborn, 1998). The school occupied abandoned military barracks, in Carlisle, Pennsylvania, and became the home of the famous experimental, military-style boarding school (Witmer, 1993). This school's reputation won over supporters of assimilation, and thus became the model for modern Bureau of Indian Affairs boarding schools across the country (Adams, 1995).

In January of 1899, Gertrude was offered a violin sponsorship by a Quaker benefactor. She left Carlisle and moved to Boston. There, she attended the New England Conservatory of Music (Rappaport, 1997; Sonneborn, 1998). Her sponsorship only lasted five months, however, and that is when Gertrude, once again, took up the pen as a means of using her voice on behalf of her people.

She created the pseudonym "Zitkala-Sa" which meant "Red Bird" in the Lakota language (Rappaport, 1997; Sonneborn, 1998). At the turn of the century, she published articles in *Harper's* and *The Atlantic Monthly* condemning white theories and the hypocrisy of reformers who thought they knew best how to reform Native People (Sonneborn, 1998). Her writings drew fairly swift criticism from the reformers. One criticism of her *Atlantic Monthly* articles was originally published in a Dakota newspaper called *Word Carrier,* and reprinted in the Carlisle Indian School monthly newspaper, *The Red Man.* The reformer attacked her credibility stating she was melodramatic about the stark realities of Native life and that her personal, negative experiences with the boarding school system were basically all lies.

Ironically, reformers often saw themselves as liberating Native Peoples from the shackles of their "primitive" lifestyles. Their intent was to expedite the Indians' transition into "civilization" through such assimilationist practices as the new military-style boarding schools and through the Allotment system[8] of private property ownership. The schools would wipe the Indian children clean from all vestiges of their "archaic," "irrelevant" past and the property ownership would propel Indian adults into the "proper" work ethic, with suitable attire and settler-style homes. So, when a young Native woman dared to use her educated voice to criticize reform efforts as damaging and unhelpful, she was, of course, attacked.

In letters to Carlos Montezuma[9] she was unrepentant, and went even further, claiming that Pratt's model of "civilizing" was under-educating Native children, since they typically only received a few hours of morning classes and spent the rest of the day laboring to keep the school running–from making all their shoes and clothes, to building the buildings, doing the laundry, growing crops and cooking food. In a letter dated only as "Friday A.M. June 1901, page 3," she declared,

> I will never speak of the whites elevating the Indian! I am willing to say higher conceptions of life elevate the whole human family, but not the Indian more than any other. Until Col. Pratt interests himself in giving college education to Indians, I cannot say his making them slaves is the plan [that] is anything other than drudgery! And drudgery is hell, not civilization! If

Carlisle expects the Indian to adapt himself perfectly to 'civilized' life in a century, she must admit that the Indian has powers which entitle him to a better name than Primitive. (B. Landis, personal communication, February 17, 2008)

Clearly, she was not backing down from her strong stance against injustice. In the same year, 1901, she published her first book, *Old Indian Legends*.

In 1916, she became the secretary of the pan-Indian organization, the Society of American Indians (Sonneborn, 1998). This organization was different from other reform groups at the time because educated Indians founded it. It had an all-Native executive board, and the main membership was Native rather than non-Native (Hertzberg, 1971). The organization took on issues of widespread poverty and starvation on Indian reservations; called for the end to the Bureau of Indian Affairs; advocated for self-determination; and called for citizenship for all American Indians (Green, 1992; Sonneborn, 1998).

Later, in 1921, Zitkala-Sa was instrumental in the Indian Welfare Committee, a sub-committee of the General Federation of Women's Clubs (Rappaport, 1997; Sonneborn, 1998). There she spearheaded a study on the "living conditions on reservations and various injustices committed by the U.S. government against Indian peoples. The committee's research pressured the government to begin its own investigation" (Sonneborn, p. 15).

As a consequence, the government hired the Brookings Institute to conduct a study on the success of the Allotment system. In 1928, the Brookings Institute produced a report, often called the "Meriam Report" after the editor, Lewis Meriam. The Meriam Report released a searing indictment of the Bureau of Indian Affairs that included the utter failure of the allotment system and exposed abysmal conditions in many of the government boarding schools. Some of the boarding schools had so little food that Indian children were eating "...a diet of bread, black coffee and syrup for breakfast and bread and boiled potatoes for dinner and supper and a quarter cup of milk with each meal" (Reyhner & Eder, 2004, p. 208). The report also had a series of recommendations including the need to improve the quality of life for Native communities, the need for strong protections for Indian property rights, the need to hire more Native People for reservation jobs, and the need to build day schools in Native communities so that Indian children could be with their families at night (Nies, 1996; Reyhner & Eder, 2004; Sonneborn, 1998). Interestingly, the Meriam Report confirmed many of the long-standing concerns that Zitkala-Sa had raised in her earlier writing and speeches.

Meanwhile, in 1924 Zitkala-Sa co-authored *Oklahoma's Poor Rich Indians, an Orgy of Graft and Exploitation of the Five Civilized Tribes, Legalized Robbery*, an exposé of the murders of Native women and girls during the discovery of oil on Osage Homelands (Sonneborn, 1998). Based on eye-witness accounts that she and other investigators collected, this pamphlet

> ...shocked and horrified even cynical lawmakers. [It] spurred a meeting of 400 Indians in Tulsa, where copies of it were handed out and read... L.T. Hill retaliated and had a warrant issued against Zitkala-Sa for criminal libel. Nine

months later congressional hearings were held in Oklahoma. (Rappaport, 1997, p. 147)

Zitkala-Sa's use of the pen to decry inhumane treatment had been effective. Two of her efforts, her study for the Indian Welfare Committee and her study of the crimes on the Osage Homelands, challenged the federal government to become involved in the issues she helped to bring to the surface.

Finally, in 1926, Gertrude, and her husband, Richard T. Bonnin, Nakota Sioux, helped to create The National Council of American Indians (Rappaport, 1997; Sonneborn, 1998). This organization advocated for Native land and water rights and the importance of protecting treaty rights (Green, 1992; Sonneborn, 1998). Unfortunately, when Gertrude died in 1938, the National Council of American Indians ceased to exist (Sonneborn, 1998).

Sarah Winnemucca and Gertrude Zitkala-Sa Simmons Bonnin were just two of the Native women who circumvented assimilation and used their voices to work for social justice in the late 1800s and early 1900s. They risked racism and sexism to protect human rights in the face of cultural genocide and injustices waged by Colonizers who, in many ways, had changed little from their predecessors of previous centuries.

It was one thing to stand and give voice in a Nation that respected what you had to say and treated you as an equal. It was quite another to bravely stand before the Colonizer and give voice to injustices the Colonizers, themselves, were committing. At a time when Native people were barely recognized *as* people and were treated as if they had no rights, it was an incredible act of courage to take a stand. The stories of their lives, often affected as they were by the context and circumstances of the times, are worth knowing.

Contemporary Activism

When I ask my college students to name some contemporary Native women, they often draw a complete blank. Yet, when I look across the last sixty years or so, I see a well spring of Native women standing firm in their advocacy for justice and what is right. The contemporary Native women are different than Gertrude and Sarah, in that they take a stand not only to protect human rights, but also to protect the importance of place and the connection of Indigenous knowledge, cultures, languages and People *to* the land. Indigenous well being depends on the well being of the elements of life – place, air, water, animals and plants – that sustain traditional ways of living and knowing (S. Wiedenhaupt, Ph.D., personal communication, March 5, 2008). Sometimes, Native women exercise a Treaty right to remind new Colonizers that trampling on such rights is a violation of long standing Treaties. Other times, they give Congressional testimony or develop grassroots organizations to fight the newest Colonizers polluting their waters and lands. No matter how it is carried forth, their voices remain strong in the cause of justice for Native peoples. In order to make visible the efforts of such women, a few brief examples with context are provided here.

In 1953 Congress approved the Termination Resolution, which effectively terminated the "federal relationship of 61 tribes, bands, and communities" (Waldman, 2000, p. 221) over the course of 1954 to 1962. This meant that 61 tribes legally ceased to exist, *not* because all their members had died, *nor* because they had made that decision themselves. Instead, non-Indians in Congress made this determination without even asking the Native leaders or their citizens if they wanted to no longer exist.

> In practice, termination means that the tribes lost trust status and had to start paying taxes, often selling off land to meet tax obligations, and providing their own education and health services. In 1961 the National Congress of American Indians...declared termination to be "the greatest threat to Indian survival since the military campaigns of the 1800s." (Nies, 1996, p. 355)

Without warning or any infrastructure in place, economically strapped "terminated" Nations were suddenly expected to have a cash flow that literally didn't exist due to the Reservation system. There was no way to readily provide the daily needed supportive services that were crucial to their citizens. New Colonizers stood at the ready, waiting to reap the profits from potential timber harvests or from building dams (like at Celilo Falls) on rivers running through newly forfeited Indian lands (Nies, 1996; Waldman, 2000). Meanwhile, entire Native Nations encountered disequilibrium as many of their citizens were forced to relocate to such distant cities as Chicago, San Francisco, Los Angeles, Denver, Seattle, and Phoenix as part of the newest federal assimilation process – this time known as "urbanization."

Ada Deer, Menominee Nation, went before the Senate and House of Representatives in the early 1970s to make a case for a reversal of the terminated status of her Nation. It took great courage to sit in the chair before the people who held the power to deny your very existence. In 1973, President Richard Nixon signed the Menominee Restoration Act. In 1992, President Clinton invited Ada Deer to be the first Native woman to be the Assistant Secretary of the Bureau of Indian Affairs (Sonneborn, 1998).

In the latter half of the twentieth century Native women have been at the forefront of the various movements and protests to protect and promote Native rights. Women like Janet McCloud, Tulalip Nation, mother of eight, who helped create "fish-ins" during the 1960s and 1970s "Fish Wars" in Washington State. She took a stand in order to protect Native Treaty rights to fish in "usual and accustomed places" as spelled out in the Treaty of Medicine Creek, 1854. Many of the northwest's Native Nations rely on fish for their survival; it is a way of living from time immemorial. So, Janet McCloud risked repeated arrests and beatings to protect Tribal Sovereignty, to raise public awareness, and to practice and maintain the time-honored Indigenous way of living here, against local and state forces that wanted to dismiss the Treaty rights as irrelevant in today's world. This world where *commercial fishing* had depleted the fish stocks with their avarice and greed, and, then, wanted to prevent Native fishers from taking fish to feed their families. Her voice and sacrifice helped other Native Nations in Wisconsin, in the

1980s, in their own battles to protect treaty rights to fish. She passed away in 2003 and is remembered for her fierce determination to protect Native rights.

Gail Small, Northern Cheyenne Nation, is director of *Native Action*, a Native environmental justice organization. Since she was a teenager, Gail has worked to protect and preserve the Homelands of the Northern Cheyenne, from the new Colonizers, focused on resource extraction on Indian lands.

> I feel like I have lived a lifetime fighting coal strip-mining, and I long for a better life for my tribe...Since I was in high school, I have been involved in my tribe's fight to protect our reservation and the environment of southeastern Montana. It was during this time, the early 1970s, that the Cheyenne people learned the horrifying news that our federal trustee, the BIA [Bureau of Indian Affairs], had leased over one-half of our reservation to the coal companies for strip-mining. Cheyenne coal was sold for 11 cents a ton, and no environmental safeguards were on the coal leases. The fight was on, and every resource our small tribe had was committed to this battle...The enormity of our situation frightened and angered us. After college, I served on the tribal negotiating committee charged with voiding these coal leases. I was 21 years old, the youngest on my committee, and the only one with a college degree. (La Duke, 1999, p. 85)

It took fifteen long years to finally win concessions and put an end to the strip-mining. Now, *Native Action* has a new charge (Grossman, 2005). A new set of Colonizers want the methane gas that sits below their small Reservation. These Colonizers have begun to surround their Reservation with 75,000 methane gas pumps, each as tall as a one-story building. The pumps already installed are spewing high sodium-laden wastewater, which is currently pumped directly into the Tongue River and its tributaries. This wastewater kills all the plants along that river system, while also polluting the only fresh water supply that the Northern Cheyenne and many non-Indian ranchers have. For over 30 years, the Northern Cheyenne have consistently refused the monetary offer to buy them off, even though the money would make them rich (Grossman, 2005). After all, this is their Homeland, their ancestors are buried here, their sacred places are here, and their culture and language, their stories, and their lives are rooted and bound to this land. As Gail has said, "The fight is on!"

Elouise Cobell, Blackfeet Nation, "is the lead plaintiff in the class-action lawsuit *Cobell v. Kempthorne*, which has successfully challenged the federal government's acknowledged mismanagement of the Indian Trust" (Cobell, 2008, p. 10). First begun as a class action law suit filed in 1996 as *Cobell v. Norton,* the continuing case is an effort to "force the federal government to account for billions of dollars belonging to approximately 500,000 American Indians and their heirs, and held in trust since the late 19th century" (Indian Trust, 2008). In the 1880s, Congress set up "Individual Indian Money Trust Accounts," where the money from the sales of Indian lands were supposed to be collected and saved for Indian beneficiaries. The Federal Government didn't think Native People were capable of managing their own monies, so the Trust was *supposed to protect* these monies. This Trust has continued to this day, only the 13 billion dollars never seemed to reach the Native people it was earmarked for, past or present. In fact, the majority of the Trust monies are gone, with no real record of when, how, or who has taken the monies, that could well serve Native Peoples and ease the poverty and challenges that they now face from the loss of the lands that generated this money; land they didn't want to sell in the first place. Since most of the records for the missing monies have "disappeared," the government has claimed, "[t]he absence of supporting documentation does not imply error" (Cobell, 2008, p. 10). Elouise Cobell is standing up for justice to hold the Federal Government accountable for the loss of these monies. She argues that the government's responses are "…a continuing breach of trust; they've cooked the books and aim to keep it that way…. What I do know is… [t]oo many of our people are suffering from the disgraceful behavior of our trustee: the United States government" (Cobell, 2008, p. 10).

Elouise Cobell, Gail Small, Janet McCloud, and Ada Deer are just a few examples of contemporary activists who have used their voices, roles, and responsibilities as Native women to stand against the newest Colonizers and the legacy of injustice that persists in Indian Country today. The new Colonizers often wear suits, carry brief cases, and represent multi-national corporations, state governments, or even the federal government. These new Colonizers are as insidious and as greed-stricken as those from every century since the Colonizers first landed on these shores. Yet countless contemporary Native women work for justice every day. They are stay-at-home mothers and working women, Elder women and teenagers – all making their voices heard in their own ways, as Native women have since before the Colonizers came.

CONCLUSION

A teacher in Maine said to a Native woman, "What can we call you Native American women if we can't call you 'squaw'?" (D. Reese, Ph.D., personal communication, October 22, 2007)

Native women and their centuries of standing strong for justice is not some minor side story of American history. The invisible story of Native women *is* the invisible story of America. The Colonizers and their practices have had an ongoing major role in this broader history, intertwining our stories together, as they have since 1492. These intertwined stories offer lessons about humanity, and how it works or can break down, contingent on greed, racism, sexism, spiritual arrogance and a heavy dose of the ends justifying the means.

The story we typically learn about "America" is from the Colonizers' vantage point – heroic, victim-less and sanitized. The Colonizers hide behind such value-neutral terms as "Manifest Destiny" and "progress" to justify the consistently inhumane treatment of Native Peoples and the rape of their natural resources, convincing the audience that this is simply a consequence of an unavoidable turn of events.

But the erasure of Native women neither eliminates their voice nor removes the strength of their struggles against injustice. What is at stake is respect for Tribal Sovereignty. What is at stake is the honoring of Treaty obligations and protections, especially when Treaty rights conflict with state or local government mandates, or with some new Colonizer's proposal. What is at stake is the preservation of, and respect for, Indigenous knowledge cultivated over thousands of years, even though damaged by conquest and Colonization. What is at stake is the sacredness and cultural importance of place that has no price. What is at stake is interdependent life and our connections to it – water, trees, fish, birds, four-legged animals, Indigenous plants and herbs, land, and air – disrupting one, disrupts them all. What is at stake, in reality, is the future of our humanity.

Still, when I think of the teacher in Maine, I wonder if she heard such stories of how Native women have stood up against injustice and worked for change, would she be inspired to teach differently? Would she consider helping her Native and non-Native students understand the way stereotypes about Native women have been used to render the women, and their struggles against injustice, invisible?

Ultimately, what is at stake is the future and what that future holds for *all* our children. I hope we will remember the intertwined story of Native women and the Colonizers, and the lessons of [in] humanity. In looking ahead to that future, I hope that acts of greed, privilege, cultural genocide and the sacrifice of place, like at Celilo Falls, will not be perpetuated. For while Native people may be the canaries in the coalmine, the bottom line is, we are all in the same mine. What happens to Native people will happen to the children of your future. It is my hope that in bringing to light what has been erased, we can begin to see the interconnectedness of our lives, and work *together* as allies, so that future generations will not wonder why we had a chance and did nothing.

> When I am dead and gone, I want to leave something. I want my granddaughter to be sitting someday talking like I talk about my grandmother. That's the kind of legacy I want to leave. I want my granddaughters, great-grandsons, too, to say, "My great-grandma was a fighter. She did this and she did that to protect the land, to protect the culture, to protect the language, to maintain what we have left." (Madonna Thunder Hawk, Lakota, quoted in Farley, 1993, p. 34)

NOTES

[1] It is important to clarify that I use "Native," "Native American," "Indian" and "Native Peoples" interchangeably. I also capitalize "Native" and "Native Peoples" to emphasize sovereignty and respect. It is my effort as an "insider" to name, rather than continue to rely on how "outsiders" choose to name us. After 500 years, it only seems fitting.

[2] I respectfully use the terms "non-Indian" and "non-Native" to represent the rich diversity of people that are not tribally affiliated with a Native Nation.

[3] "Confederacy" is more historically accurate with many eastern Native Nations. Many formed short-lived or long-lasting political alliances with each other. Some times this occurred through warfare, other times, it occurred to prevent warfare or prevent takeovers of valuable hunting/ fishing

territories. The name of the Confederacy often denotes which Native Nation had the most political power within any particular Confederacy.

4 Upon hearing the term "colonization," it would be easy to think about the Europeans (Dutch, English, French, Spanish, Swedish) who 'founded' colonies in the proverbial "wilderness" among the "savages." From this perspective, there is a definite beginning and end to colonization, starting with Columbus and wrapping up with the Revolutionary War. However, from a Native viewpoint, the legacy of Colonization initiated in 1492 has changed little in 517 years. The Colonizers' names may have changed, but the policies laced with greed and the implicit beliefs and theories of European racial superiority continue to this day (Blaut, 1993; Deloria, 1997). The forced removals of entire Native Nations for the benefit of non-Indian individuals, corporations, or governments has also continued into recent times (Fixico, 1998; Grinde & Johansen, 1995). The rape of natural resources on Indian lands by the government and large corporations has continued into the 21st century (Farley, 1993; LaDuke, 1999). Finally, the violation of every single Treaty made, often requiring expensive court battles to protect Treaty rights, have continued into the new millennium (Wilkins & Lomawaima, 2001; Wilkinson, 2005). This is enduring Colonizing legacy that Native women have struggled against.

5 The political/social groupings of Native Nations varied greatly across the continent. It was not uncommon, however, within various Nations, to have smaller groupings sometimes known as bands. Others might call them communities, or some other designation of a form of social and or political grouping. A band might be composed of a few families, or could be composed of a much larger grouping, even upwards of 75-100 families or more, depending on a variety of factors and resources.

6 There is discussion among Native scholars of the use of the term "squaws." Typically used as a vulgar, derogatory term, there is discussion that the word actually refers to female genitalia in the Algonkian language.

7 Leadership structures were neither universal nor necessarily hierarchical. Some Nations might have a single political leader, but might also have a spiritual leader. Other Nations might have entire Councils of chiefs or leaders. Other Nations might have a peace leader or leaders and a war leader or leaders, depending on the situation that faced their respective Nation. And still other Nations might have a single leader from a hereditary chief clan or family.

8 By the 1880s, reformers in their effort to assimilate Native people saw private ownership of land by Indians as a means to bring them into civilization. "In 1887, the United States Congress passed the General Allotment Act (or the Dawes Severalty Act), sponsored by Senator Dawes, under which Indian reservations were to be broken up and allotted to the heads of Indian families in 160-acre pieces…any surplus territory would be distributed to non-Indians…" (Waldman, 2000, p. 218). In 1890, Oklahoma Territory was formed from [the sale of such] lands" (Waldman, 2000, pp. 206–207).

9 Carlos Montezuma was a founding member of the Society of American Indians.

REFERENCES

Adams, D. W. (1995). *Education for extinction: American Indians and the boarding school experience, 1875–1928.* Lawrence, KS: University Press of Kansas.

Blaut, J. M. (1993). *The colonizer's model of the world: Geographical diffusionism and Eurocentric history.* New York: The Guilford Press.

Bowker, A. (1993). *Sisters in the blood: The education of women in Native America.* Newton, MA: WEEA Publishing Center.

Cobell, E. (2008, Mar/Apr). Uncooking the books: The fed's trust fund mess [Viewpoint]. *Native Peoples: Arts & Lifeways,* p. 10.

Deloria, V., Jr. (1997). *Red Earth, white lies: Native Americans and the myth of scientific fact.* Golden, CO: Fulcrum Publishing.

Farley, R. (1993). *Women of the native struggle: Portraits & testimony of Native American women.* New York: Orion Books.

Fixico, D. L. (1998). *The invasion of Indian country in the twentieth century: American capitalism and tribal natural resources.* Niwot, CO: University Press of Colorado.

Green, R. (1975, Autumn). Pocahontas perplex. *Massachusetts Review, 16,* 698–714.

Green, R. (1992). *Women in American Indian society.* New York: Chelsea House Publishers.

Grinde, D. A., & Johansen, B. E. (1995). *Ecocide of native America: Environmental destruction of Indian lands and peoples.* Santa Fe, NM: Clear Light Publishers.

Grossman, R. (Producer/Writer/Director). (2005). *Homeland: Four portraits of native action* [DVD]. (Available from Bullfrog Films, P.O. Box 149, Oley, PA 19547; www.bullfrogfilms.com)

Hertzberg, H. W. (1971). *The search for an American Indian identity: Modern pan-Indian movements.* Syracuse, NY: Syracuse University Press.

Indian Trust: Cobell v. Kempthorne. (2008). Cobell v. Norton: An overview. Retrieved February 23, 2008, from http://www.indiantrust.com/index.cfm?FuseAction=Overview.Home

Jackson, H. H. (1880/1993). *A century of dishonor: A sketch of the United States government's dealings with some of the Indian tribes.* New York: Indian Head Books.

Jennings, F. (1993). *The founders of America: From the earliest migrations to the present.* New York: W.W. Norton & Company.

Jim, R. L. (1994). *Dancing voices: Wisdom of the American Indians.* White Plains, NY: Peter Pauper Press, Inc.

Josephy, A. M., Jr. (1994). *500 nations: An illustrated history of North American Indians.* New York: Alfred A. Knopf.

Klein, L. F., & Ackerman, L. A. (1995). Introduction. In L. F. Klein & L. A. Ackerman (Eds.), *Women and power in native North America* (pp. 3–16). Norman, OK: University of Oklahoma Press.

LaDuke, W. (1999). *All our relations: Native struggles for land and life.* Cambridge, MA: South End Press.

Mankiller, W. (2004). *Every day is a good day: Reflections by contemporary indigenous women.* Golden, CO: Fulcrum Publishing.

Nies, J. (1996). *Native American history: A chronology of a culture's vast achievements and their links to world events.* New York: Ballentine Books.

Rappaport, D. (1997). *The flight of red bird: The life of Zitkala-Sa.* New York: Dial Books.

Reyner, J., & Eder, J. (2004). *American Indian education: A history.* Norman, OK: University of Oklahoma Press.

Sonneborn, L. (1998). *A to Z of Native American women–Encyclopedia of women.* New York: Facts on File, Inc.

Steer, D. (1996). *Native American women.* New York: Barnes & Noble Books.

Szasz, M. C., & Ryan, C. S. (1988). American Indian education. In W. E. Washburn (Ed.), *History of Indian-White relations: Handbook of North American Indians* (Vol. 4, pp. 284–300). Washington, DC: Smithsonian Institution.

Utley, R. M., & Washburn, W. E. (2002). *Indian wars.* Boston: Mariner Books.

Waldman, C. (2000). *Atlas of the North American Indian* (Rev. ed.). New York: Checkmark Books.

Waldman, C. (2001). *Biographical dictionary of American Indian history to 1900* (Rev. ed.). New York: Checkmark Books.

Winnemucca Hopkins, S. (1883/1969). *Life among the Piutes: Their wrongs and claims.* Bishop, CA: Sierra Media, Inc.

Wilkins, D. E., & Lomawaima, K. T. (2001). *Uneven ground: American Indian sovereignty and federal law.* Norman, OK: University of Oklahoma Press.

Wilkinson, C. (2005). *Blood struggle: The rise of modern Indian nations.* New York: W.W. Norton & Company.
Witmer, L. F. (1993). *The Indian industrial school: Carlisle, Pennsylvania, 1879–1918.* Carlisle, PA: Cumberland County Historical Society.

Frances V. Rains, Ph.D.
Native American & World Indigenous Peoples Studies
Evergreen State College.

ROB LINNE'

GROWING UP GAY DEEP IN THE HEART OF TEXAS

Javier and Me

We were walking home from the corner store with snow cones. Javier was eight; I was seven. He had purple syrup all around his mouth from the grape cone he always got; my tongue was a bright florescent orange and red mix. It was Texas hot that day, with no hope of a Gulf Coast breeze, so the cool syrup running together with sweat and dirt, forming little rivers in the wrinkles of our necks, did not bother us. We each had one hand on our cone and the other entwined together over our best buddy's shoulder. He and I loudly sang our favorite song from the summer of '74: *The Loco-motion* by Grand Funk Railroad. "Everybody's doing a brand new dance now/Come on baby do the loco-motion/A little bit of rhythm plus a lot of soul now/Come on baby..."

Despite the heat, I do not think I could have been happier.

Suddenly a voice interrupted our song and called to us from the shadows of an open garage door from one of the larger houses in the neighborhood. "Hey, come here." A tall red-headed boy motioned us over. He was older than us, probably in high school, so following one of the unwritten rules of boys, we did what he commanded and walked up into the garage. I remember being scared by his tone of voice, but also because he had a hammer in his hand. Javier and I released our embrace as we moved toward the boy not knowing what this was about. As we did, the boy who seemed so tall and menacing, thrust the handle of the hammer within inches of Javier's chest and said, "What's the matter with you?"

At this point I did not know what kind of bullying game we were up against—there were so many to keep up with — so I just wanted to run, but my body would not react. "Nothing," Javier quietly replied. "Then why are you walking around like a couple of faggots, holding each other like that?" We had no answer. We knew not to look at each other. "You two make me sick. Don't ever walk around here all faggoty like that again or I will kick both of your asses." With that warning he threw the hammer over our heads, against the oak tree at the side of the driveway. After the hammer bounced off the tree, he glared at us. "You two pussies get out of my sight and don't ever act like that again."

Javier and I took off running, threw our snow cones in the street, and went our separate ways, into our own houses, behind our own closed bedroom doors. I remember jumping into my bed and crying, not really understanding what I had done to deserve being threatened with a hammer. Even though I was scared that someday the older boy would really hurt me and I wanted to tell my parents, I did not. Another unwritten rule of boy culture is that you do not snitch on other boys when they bully you; it only makes things worse. I was just relieved to be alone with my thoughts and figure out what the warning meant.

Javier and I never did "act like that again," and we certainly never walked down the street arm in arm again. I do not remember if we ever sang songs again like we used to enjoy so much. I do know that I had to bury a part of myself deep down and inside where it would never be seen. We had to learn not to act "all faggoty."

Spear the Queer

Homo. Girl. Faggot. Bitch. The boy code was policed relentlessly. To physically reinforce the verbal strictures, the boys in the neighborhood often played "spear the queer." In this game, we would all wait in a large circle while one player would throw a football as far as he could and call another boy out. If your name was called you had to retrieve the football and run back with it as long as you could evade being tackled by the others. The object was to tackle the target as violently as possible and try to make him show signs of pain or emotion. If he betrayed any sign of fear or weakness when being tackled the players would yell "queer" and all would pile on top, with the object being to inflict real pain to punish the perceived weakness.

During one game, I was running with the ball when I was tackled especially hard and had the wind knocked out of me. As I gasped for breath one boy yelled "queer" and the others jumped on top of me—one by one—grinding my face into the grass. I couldn't breathe under the weight of so many boys.

Got AIDS Yet?

The evening news announced a dreaded new disease and showed horrific pictures of very sickly young men who were afflicted. Mostly they showed young white men in New York, but they told us it seemed that black Haitians were also catching it. Some saw in this a sign from above.

A group of college kids visited my Christian high school one week during the initial hysteria to participate in our classes, pray with us, and act as "hip" role models. We spent most of the week separated from the girls, talking about "guy things." They told us about this new curse for homosexuals, warned us about being preyed upon by twisted men, and reminded us that even though Jesus or the Ten Commandments never mentioned homosexuality there is a verse in Leviticus (18:22) that condemned men lying with men. (Years later I found out Leviticus also condemns the eating of pork or shellfish, wearing clothing that has more than one kind of fabric, or sowing a field with mixed seeds. The Old Testament code forbids men to cut their hair or beards, but encourages polygamy and slaves to obey their masters.)

Friday we finished our work in Coach Schneider's History class early so we could have the last fifteen minutes for one of our Friday afternoon comedy clubs. I felt my heart speed up when the line of jokes turned to the latest AIDS riddles.

What does 'gay' stand for? Got AIDS Yet?
What do you call a group of gay musicians? Band AIDS.
What is the definition of AIDS? A disease that turns fruits into vegetables.

I kind of laughed along with the others and discreetly looked around the room—at my friends and my football coach—while questions raced through my head. Is anybody looking at me to gauge any reaction to the jokes? Did I have AIDS yet? Would I become a vegetable for all to laugh at? Would anybody go to my funeral? What did all those sores on the men in the news feel like? The cancers I saw on the sick men on the news seemed to me a kind of scarlet letter that would eventually reveal my secret.

Sometime after that class I remember getting into a fistfight with a friend of mine from theater class. I do not remember what, if anything, started it. I knocked him down, and it ended as quickly as it began. A couple other friends from my football team patted me on the back. "Dude, I hate that faggot." "I am so glad you dropped him like that. He's such an annoying girl."

For hours I prayed for forgiveness, often staying up until early in the morning. I prayed for change, begged for release from all this confusion and anger. Mostly I prayed that I would wake up and suddenly my desires would be straight. I envisioned a blinding light as if I were on the road to Damascus. I thought often of Martin Luther's tortured nights, whipping himself unconscious. He pleaded with the Lord for redemption or a vision that would lead to change. He prayed night after night until the spirit finally moved him. If young Martin Luther could pray his way to a re-birth, perhaps there was some way for me to start over and become somebody completely new. "Lord, please hear my prayer. I am trying so hard. I am nice to everybody, so why this punishment?"

In frustration I began bargaining for a different deal, maybe hoping God would see how serious I really was about this. "Ok then, if I am only going to live life as the most vile of reprobate, please take me out of this world with a car crash so at least I do not feel any more."

I drank ungodly amounts of Jim Beam on the weekends and enjoyed speeding around Garden Oaks with the radio blasting.

The Beauty of Coral Snakes

That summer you taught me
the markings of the deadly coral snake
as distinguished from the harmless king snake.
The old folks say—Do not be mesmerized, but look closely at the stripes.
Red and Yellow—Kill a Fellow
Red and Black—Poison Lack.

And we witnessed
down at Galveston Bay
what a body looks like
waterlogged after two days.

LINNE´

The boy, pulled out of Laguna Madre,
the mother lagoon,
with blue crabs all over him,
each one hanging on for dear life.

Where is his mother?
Does anyone care that he is dead?
Maybe he deserved this
punishment for not following the signs.

That summer you showed me
the danger in the eyes of those
lounging on the rusted mustang
just around the corner.
"Walk on by."
And for some reason holler back something
about one of their sisters.
But do not turn or think about running.
For if you take off
some instinct sets in
and it will be like the hyenas we watched on TV.
You said–Never, ever run.

And now this summer.
In my air conditioned condo
I'm watching more nature shows than ever
and I'm remembering
that animals have tricks to scare each other,
to keep the pecking in order.
And that caution
is not always the surest way to stay alive.

I'm not so afraid now.
I would love to see you again.
And maybe even get close enough to a coral snake
to make out the red and yellow
that just might kill a fellow.

Would Jesus Wear a Rolex on His Television Show?

I found salvation at a run-down bar on Austin's East Side.

    A rotund, black drag queen named Denesha Del Valley hosted a different party every Saturday at probably the only punk/blues/gay club in the world. Sometimes an elderly blues singer named Miss Molly would open the show. She had a bullwhip she would snap at the crowd. Young punk bands, just getting their start, would play deep into the mornings, working everybody up into a sweat. Occasionally, a country band would even play and the punk kids with red Mohawks would do their interpretation of a country line dance. There were usually drag performances, and sometimes just a jukebox. Everyone was welcome at this dance.

Many nights Ms. Del Valley hosted benefits for AIDS Services of Austin, the OutYouth gay youth center which offered services for many homeless young people, or for bus tickets for somebody who needed to get back to Mexico for a funeral. Once a regular was sick and could not afford the medical bills, so there was a fundraiser. Even though the night would only bring in $200 or $300, it made a difference because those in need at least knew there were others trying to look out for them. The Flamingo even hosted Thanksgiving Dinner each year out on the back patio—good turkey, cornbread and pecan pie—for those who did not have a place to go. When I first heard about this I thought surely very few people would go to a *bar* for Thanksgiving, but I was told that each year dozens would show up for the festivity. It seems there were plenty of people in Austin who did not have a big family to go home to, or were not welcome at home, so Denesha Del Valley made sure they had a seat at a Thanksgiving table.

The code I learned at this community seemed to purposefully flip what I learned earlier in life from church and school. Many from this group of outsiders and misfits knew first hand what it was like to be abandoned or vulnerable, so helping the down and out was expected. Many had been pressured to conform all their lives, so the personal deconstruction of gender, race, or class was not only tolerated but congratulated. "Girl, you can walk like a man, or walk like a woman; just look good." Most had been judged by the self-righteous, so deflating the high and mighty became a most valued skill.

We would turn our pent up anger from years of being laughed at onto the bullies and make their ridiculous bigotry look even more ridiculous.

So humor and satire were not simply entertainment. Comedy was political. Every day was to be a Bakhtinian carnival. Everyone of us could play a role in a grand satire skewering the racist, the sexist, and the homophobic. The Bible Belt would no longer constrain us because it could be made into a daring fashion accessory. Anybody in the public eye who was greedy, bigoted, or holier-than-thou was a target.

Austin political writer Molly Ivins (1991) always said that "satire is traditionally the weapon of the powerless against the powerful." This may be especially so in Texas where there have always been many poor and oppressed while a few with power play all the marginalized against one another. It seems the more painful Texas politics is to watch, the more we have to laugh at the whole mess. Our take on politics is much like our take on funerals. I think many visitors to a Southern funeral would be surprised to see how much the mourning is leavened with laughter and jokes about the departed.

One night the Flamingo hosted a P.T.L. party that included Jim and Tammy Faye Baker singing old time religion and disco. That was a classic, but my favorite night was any night the Austin Baptist Women—led by Ophelia Faith and The Widow Modine Murphy—would perform. This gospel drag choir (has to date) raised over 7 million dollars for charity by dressing up in their best Sunday-go-to-meeting clothes—usually floral print cotton dresses and old church lady hats. The high-haired women would get their congregation up on their feet, singing hosannas, often with some of the most unique gospel tunes to ever get radio play across the South. Some of the most inspiring songs from their hymnal included *Would Jesus Wear a Rolex on His Television Show? Oh Operator, Information, Give Me Jesus on the Line*, and my personal favorite, *Jesus Put a Yodel in My Soul*.

My life was empty, without a goal
Then I let Jesus into my soul
Now I'm so happy, never feel low
Jesus put a yodel in my soul

Jesus, Jesus, Jesus set me free
Yodel-ay-ee, yodel-ay-ee
Yodel-ay-ee-dee

Jesus set me free!

By the time the Baptist Women finished the last chorus on that one, everyone was up, waving handkerchiefs, shouting 'amen's,' and filling the collection plate to overflowing for that night's charity. Love filled the room.

Gay Bashed in Brooklyn

Shortly after completing my dissertation defense at the University of Texas at Austin, I moved to Brooklyn and took a job teaching at a leafy East Coast liberal arts college. I found an apartment in a hip Brooklyn neighborhood, close to Harry Ward Beecher's church, known as Grand Central Station of the Underground Railroad. I was giddy with the thought of having intellectual conversations in radical coffee houses, and not having to look over my back all the time in fear of being gay bashed. I had made it to the center of the American Left.

Two weeks later I had my first-ever brush with a gay bashing. I was leaving a gay bar late at night when a car filled with young men drove by, yelled "fag," and threw batteries at me. They circled the block and I ran down a one-way street, scared for my life, so they could not follow me.

A short time after that, a black kid was beaten apparently for the crime of walking through one of the white "Italian" areas of Brooklyn.

I found out that the Long Island town where my university is located originally had deed provisions prohibiting the sale of homes to Jewish families. The county where my university is located is arguably the most segregated area in the United States. So much so that you can easily discern when you drive across the borders of a "white" village and into a "black" town on Long Island. Students tell me real estate agents still "red line" certain areas and will not take black buyers into many white areas.

When Hillary Clinton ran for Senator I found out that New York had never had a female governor or senator, and New York City had never had a female mayor.

This struck me as very odd because I grew up during a time when Texas cities were most often governed by women and Texans had elected female governors and senators long ago.

It did not take me long to learn that although there are differences in degree and kind, prejudice and reactionary politics are not only the providence of the South.

But that does not stop New Yorkers, many of whom really do live in glass highrise houses, from throwing rocks at anybody or anything reeking of the South. I was invited to meet a group for cocktails at a new restaurant and club in Manhattan called Trailer Park Lounge and Grill. I was excited because I was told they actually served fried catfish and because I have always had an affinity for Southern camp. They did not know how to fry catfish and the greasy mess I tried to eat made me feel a bit nauseous. However, the whole experience made me more than a little sick at my stomach. The waitress came over in a tube-top and spoke to us in a cartoonish Southern accent, her syntax confused and her vocabulary riddled with slang. She told us that one of the best cocktails on the menu was called "Billy Bob's I.Q." and that all dinners came with tater tots. As I looked around the room, filled with velvet paintings and old family photos of poor, white Southerners, I read disdain and a most hateful version of the working-class South. They were making fun of my family and me, not laughing with us.

I felt embarrassed and culturally bullied. I have often been made to feel this way while living in New York. Good liberals who rail against any kind of stereotyping or prejudice feel very comfortable stereotyping and prejudging anybody white and working-class who lives in a "red state." It made me think about my love of Southern camp. It was one thing for those of us back in Austin to poke fun at the foibles of our home culture; it is something else altogether for outsiders to laugh at your family and friends with mean-spirited jokes and tirades. It reminds me of how many travelers complain that when they visit Europe they are condescended to and made to feel like they have to explain the conservative craziness of the U.S. I have witnessed liberals and radicals, who back in the states rail against US hegemony, but abroad feel backed into defending American values and arguing that the European view of the states is often too simplistic and monolithic.

All of these experiences have made me more reflective regarding my appreciation for Southern camp. I do not like the way sophisticated "liberals" in New York make fun of working-class people in the rest of the country, people like my family back home. I do not want to do the same. I love my family and many of the people I grew up with so I do not want to dismiss them out of hand as "dumb rednecks." I see the blind spots in the accepted cosmopolitan discourse, a discourse that may do more to maintain a "red state/blue state" divide than to bring people together around the idea of change. I still believe that satire can be extremely powerful in helping people challenge the status quo and work for change. People do not tolerate serious lectures as easily as they do a good laugh at the silliness of cultural hang-ups. We do, however, need to recognize that there is a fine line separating satire and disdain. Camp and satire can either help nudge people along a path of greater acceptance or it can just incite defensiveness that leads people to retreat back into their own corners and cling to old ways of thinking.

On a personal level, I have learned over the years not to dismiss anyone out of hand as a hopeless conservative or a reactionary. People have surprised me time and time again. Sometimes people I assume for one reason or another will be prejudiced toward me, end up being anything but, while other individuals I assume will share my values end up disappointing me with a blind spot to bigotry. A colleague of mine at the university was a devout Mormon and we ended up discovering we had more in common than differences. We actually worked together quite well after we stopped judging one another. Open discussion is the only way I can learn where another person is coming from, and more often than not I learn something valuable from folks who may be coming from a completely different worldview from my own.

So the question that I have been struggling with is where can I draw the line between social satire and protest and social stereotyping and hate. I find that satire and humor is infinitely fascinating because there never is an easy answer to this question. A single joke may function as social satire in one environment while serving to belittle folks in another environment. I watch Black comics and satirists poke fun at Black home life and I wonder how is that different from a racist telling a joke about Blacks? My students often have difficulties attempting to discern humor that shines a light on our foibles from cheap laughter that reinforces stereotypes. How can one tell the difference between hate and protest?

I find that when trying to answer this question that the answers are not as easy as many would have us believe. Laughter may release us from past slights, but if the catharsis does not allow us to let go of the anger we may only be redirecting derision onto others. I have been laughed at out of hate and I have shared laughter out of love. There is a tremendous difference.

Love Makes a Family

> Returning hate for hate multiplies hate, adding deeper darkness to a night already devoid of stars. Darkness cannot drive out darkness: only light can do that. Hate cannot drive out hate: only love can do that. Hate multiplies hate, violence multiplies violence, and toughness multiplies toughness in a descending spiral of destruction. So when Jesus says, "Love your enemies," he is setting forth a profound and ultimately inescapable admonition.
> —Martin Luther King Jr.

In his sermon *Strength to Love* (1963, p. 42), King argues that the social justice activist must cultivate both a tough mind and a soft heart. We must always be tough-minded in interrogating our prejudices and finding our myriad blind spots. Changing a culture is extremely difficult so we must be firm in our commitments and willing to stand up to those who will stop at nothing to maintain the status quo. But at the same time we must not allow our hearts to harden against those who would oppress us or our brothers and sisters. We should allow ourselves to feel anger about any injustice we see in order that we are compelled to act, but we cannot allow that anger to turn to hate against another.

The only way to ethically and effectively attack hate is with love. As I have studied the lives and philosophies of those who have lead great social justice movements over the years, this message has been repeated again and again. Henry Ward Beecher, Mohandas Gandhi, Francis Perkins, Nelson Mandela, Elie Wiesel, James Baldwin, Bayard Rustin, Dolores Huerta, Myles Horton, Paulo Freire, Sister Helen Prejean, Kevin Jennings, Ann Richards, Barbara Jordan, Wangari Maathai. All of these inspiring leaders had witnessed horrific human violence, oppression, and degradation. Each could easily have slipped into nihilism and pessimism regarding the possibility for reconciliation and redemption. However, their experiences only strengthened their resolve. Each leader turned her or his anger about injustices into relentless, creative, and effective drives for change. Love, not revenge, was the driving force for all.

I worry that King or Horton would be disappointed in what has become of much of the discourse from the Left if they were here today to witness the shrill shouting that goes on between "blue" and "red" states. I believe these leaders might argue that part of the reason progressive movements have stalled in so many ways of late is this absence of respect and love. If we do not respect those who oppose us, we effectively shut off discussion and implicitly make the decision that change is not possible. When we lose hope on the idea of change we forget all the social justice work people before us have sacrificed so much for. When I was born, schools in the South were segregated by law and neighborhoods in the North were segregated by violence and "redlining." Gay Rights was not yet even a concept and folks could still be arrested for going to a gay bar. As I write this a Black man is running for president, Ellen Degeneres is the most popular daytime t.v. star, and gay marriage is on the verge of becoming the law of the land.

When love drives the discourse, progress seems to move faster. Angry protests were an important part of the Gay Rights Movement, in part because the protestors made mainstream America open their eyes to an invisible part of the population. However, other forms of protest often did more to open people's hearts. When the AIDS quilt, with thousands of panels handmade for victims of the virus, was stretched the length of the Washington monument, many Americans had to take notice. When mourners of Mathew Shepard lit up our cities with candle light marches, our neighbors could no longer look away from violence against gays and lesbians. And when Massachusetts legalized gay marriage and couples flocked to the courthouses, the entire nation was able to witness why so many gay people continue to fight for the right to love who they choose.

The personal stories I shared above about my youth were quite painful, so I have to work hard not to let the pain overwhelm me with bitterness. I have to reflect often on where my motivations are coming from—love or revenge. I never want to lose my sense of humor and become a dreary old academic who cannot laugh at the ridiculous, but I am looking very carefully at the ways in which smart, cosmopolitan people make fun of those in America's heartland. I know how it feels to be laughed at and dismissed, so I do not want to simply avenge the way I was laughed at by laughing at others. As hard as it is to achieve, I want my way of being to be driven by love.

South Carolina, North

Many of the faculty at my university live in the city and commute out to campus on the Long Island Rail Road. I usually enjoy the train rides with my colleagues. We are not fighting freeway traffic and we have time to sit back and discuss issues of the day. However, when the conversations descend into complaining about students, the commute is not as enjoyable. I find that professors everywhere love to point out the most ridiculous error in student writing or go on incredulously that students no longer thoroughly study all of the assigned readings. But one complaint in particular interests me.

During one commute a professor was complaining about how conservative our students are and how they will not open their minds to progressive or radical ideas. She then went on to say, "I am looking for a job in the city, because out here on Long Island we are basically teaching in the South Carolina of the North. I cannot take these students much longer." Some colleagues laughed and shook their heads in recognition. It seems that calling our students a bunch of Southerners was an acceptable way to put them down. Usually, professors in our region feel free to belittle students if they are "too" Long Island or New Jersey.

I have heard this kind of lament from colleagues all over the country. I have heard academics complain if they have to work in the Midwest, the South, Up-State New York, anywhere other than the most liberal or radical urban enclaves. Professors seem to delight in comparing horror stories of White, sexist, homophobic male student ignorance. The examples of redneck thinking from students are many.

This kind of condescension is especially ironic when it comes, as it often does, from education professors who preach multiculturalism and respecting the local communities we find ourselves teaching within. It seems that the multicultural ideal of respecting all our students only applies if our students come to us already with the belief systems we want to see in them.

I think many of us in academe need to reflect on what this kind of laughter at the expense of our students says. We all want our students to grow into open-minded, caring individuals who value human rights and fight for social justice. But condescending to young people because they may not yet live up to our ideals is surely counterproductive. I have come to believe that some teachers almost dare their students to prove how reactionary they can be. This lets the professor off the hook for doing the hard work of teaching for social justice, because "these students" will never change.

I have also been fortunate enough to observe some very effective teachers who do not condescend to their students. (Some of whom are participating in this collection.) These professors are tough minded and demand that their students question their assumptions and examine their beliefs. But they also approach teaching with a soft heart and begin where the students are and see how far they can progress from there. These professors are the ones who are able to enact a social justice education because they approach their students with respect while always understanding that none of us are without prejudice. It is something we each have to work at everyday so it is a bit hypocritical for us to expect our students to come to us as without their own prejudices. And how meaningless would the call to teach be for us if we only had to preach to the choir. The best teachers I know embrace the challenge. Some of the more "radical" professors who viscerally hate our students, in contrast, give up on the challenge and inevitably fail to make real connections with their students that might lead to authentic conversation.

I think perhaps this is the most important lesson I have learned as an educator in my journey from deep in the heart of Texas to the chaotic streets of New York City. Like many educators I know, I took the call to become a teacher in part because I have felt the sting of injustice and so I want to take part in education that opens minds and lays the foundation for a better society for the next generation. I need to constantly remind myself of this end when I am tempted to give up fighting a losing battle against reactionary culture in a conservative age. All of my talk of educating for social justice is only talk if I close myself off from most of the people in this country, in this world, simply because they do not hold my political worldview. I teach that dialog is everything in education, so I need to live that principle by not shouting down or shutting out people who do not automatically recognize the wisdom in my beliefs. Every great educator and leader I have studied or observed always keeps their hand outstretched in hopes that one person, and then another, will take their hand and begin the conversation. We have to be open to that moment.

REFERENCES

Ivins, M. (1991). Molly Ivins can't say that, can she? New York: Random House.
King, M. L. (1963). Strength to love.

Rob Linné
Ruth S. Ammon School of Education
Adelphi University

RESPECT

DIANE CARACCIOLO

CLOSING THE DISTANCE

Partnering with the Indigenous Peoples on Whose Lands We Earn Our Living[1]

Long Island Absences

I can still remember the mountain of dirt silhouetted against the few remaining tall trees at the bottom of our yard. On top of it my brother stands, tossing handfuls of soil that explode in dusty sprays in all directions—"dirt bombs." Growing up in Suffolk County in the 1960s where new suburban housing developments were spreading eastward from Nassau County meant that building lots became our early playgrounds. In those days, there were still some woods left that were not yet torn down for houses—woods that became the borderland of our childhood wanderings, the places where stray dogs roamed, tree forts were built, and a legendary tiny shrine to the Virgin Mary lay shrouded in vines and mystery. Sunday morning church services were held in the local movie theater, and farm stands and riding stables bordered the emerging neighborhood, which was permeated by their rich, earthy smells when the breeze blew in. Today all but the housing developments have disappeared, replaced by odorless industrial "parks" and strip malls. Of all these early memories, however, there is one remarkable absence: I have no memory of seeing in my neighborhood or in public school classrooms, or in local stores or church services, a child that looked different from my family or neighbors, a child of color. Driving through my old neighborhood decades later, this impression has not changed.

I grew up in a town called *Hauppauge,* surrounded by segregated communities bearing the place names of an invisible history. *Massapequa, Setauket, Nissequogue, Ronkonkoma*—these names appear before the typical public school-educated Long Islander's eyes without context, without history, the disembodied signifiers for collections of strip malls, parking lots, and the rapidly constructed housing developments of a post-World War II United States.

Although divided into four counties, Long Island is most typically associated with its two easternmost—Nassau and Suffolk, as Kings County (Brooklyn) and Queens County are within the jurisdiction of the City of New York. Despite its proximity to New York and the growing ethnic diversity of its populace, there remains an insular quality about community life the farther east one travels. Long Island is one of the most racially segregated suburbs in the United States, and this extends to its school districts as well. And of the many underrepresented peoples of Long Island, Native peoples remain the most unseen and unacknowledged.

But what of that other island, whose natural presence can be felt more strongly the farther east one travels? Placed between mild inland waters to the north and the rougher Atlantic Ocean to the south, Long Island begins at the mouth of the

Hudson River and eventually narrows into two remote and wild points, like the tail of a fish, extending over 100 miles in both physical and psychic distance from Manhattan. Geologically ancient, Long Island was left here by one of the last glaciers on its journey southward down the coast over 12 millennia ago. And when the ice receded, the Island's first peoples began a way of life that lasted for over 10,000 years until the arrival of Henry Hudson in 1609. During several hundred years of contact with Europeans, Indigenous Long Islanders, much like those in other Native communities, have struggled against an often brutal adversary to defend their claims to ancestral lands as well as to their Native identities. Battle lines have been drawn not only along the Island's shores and woodlands and within its colonial and modern courtrooms, but more elusively upon the fields of Western epistemology, with its control over definitions of culture and identity.[2]

Educationally, the experiences of Native peoples have been rendered relatively invisible to the dominant non-Native culture through their absence or inaccurate representation in school textbooks, print and film media, and general racial stereotyping. Many Long Islanders are unaware that Suffolk County is home to two state-recognized Indian reservations—Poospatuck and Shinnecock—as well as to other Native peoples living contemporary lives throughout Long Island's communities. The lack of understanding about Native peoples among the dominant Long Island population, has an educational impact, for often local students enroll in our teacher preparation programs with the desire to continue living on Long Island as educators.

Many of Long Island's suburbs are peopled by the children and grandchildren of working class European immigrants, for whom inclusion in the dominant culture was an important goal, leaving them little understanding of or patience for a perspective that resists assimilation. As the granddaughter of working class European immigrants and the first in my family to attend college, navigating the corporate power structures of academe can sometimes feel like an alien and alienating experience. A more troubling aspect of this journey, however, as I attempt to write myself into a secure place within that privileged structure, is my position as a non-indigenous person whose academic work involves engagement with an Indigenous community. Troubling, because as a non-indigenous, white academic, I represent the face of the colonizer who stands to gain, yet again, from the lives of those colonized. Admitting to our own "inescapable self-interest," according to Findlay (2000, p. x), is a necessary step toward discovering ways in which to engage honestly with Indigenous communities. Rather than being paralysed by guilt or complacency, non-indigenous academics can use our positions to rethink the research and educational systems that continue to oppress colonized peoples. Most importantly, we can share our institutional resources with the Indigenous peoples on whose lands we earn our livings. For me this journey toward community and collaboration began with a simple yet unsettling question.

"Do you know anything about your own Indigenous peoples?"

"You're very interested in learning about Australian Aboriginal art, but do you know anything about your own Indigenous peoples?" Sitting in a circle during a small breakout session, these words spoken by Badtjala artist Fiona Foley, one of the conference presenters, stayed with me long after that midwinter weekend at Teachers College, with its numerous talks, panel discussions and exhibitions was over. That one disquieting question, spoken gently but with power by a contemporary Aboriginal artist, worked its way through my system demanding to be answered. It eventually grew beyond a question, becoming both a challenge and admonition as I confronted the simple answer—that after every possible advantage offered by my suburban public school education and three degrees (and counting) of higher education, I knew relatively nothing about the Indigenous peoples on whose lands I had been raised and for most of my life had earned my living.

I left that weekend with Fiona's admonition toward our ignorance of Indigenous peoples reverberating in my Long Island ears. Filled with unexamined assumptions regarding Indigenous people and research, I chose this question as the focus of my dissertation journey (Caracciolo, 2006).

First Steps and Missteps

What do graduate students studying in the Western academic tradition associate with the word "research"? Words such as *inquiry, evidence, data collection, questioning,* even *search for truth* come to mind. On a more visceral level, the term may invoke feelings of anxiety, stress, challenge, and doubt as to their capacity to walk the rigorous path toward acknowledgement by disciplinary peers. But unless they are members of a colonized people, it is likely that associations remain at heart positive. The pursuit of research questions, although difficult and at times seemingly impossible, remains ultimately noble, filled with cultural value and significance.

It was with such unexamined associations that my research began one autumn afternoon several years ago at the Shinnecock Nation Cultural Center and Museum. The following was written shortly after my first visit there:

> *Outwardly modest, the Shinnecock Museum can be easy to miss speeding east along the main road that runs the length of the South Fork bisecting the upscale villages of the Hamptons. On the inside, however, the Museum's very structure felt alive. Built of white pine by the Oneida Construction Company, a Native American business from upstate New York, the building was designed to awaken the senses and remind us of its natural origins. One of the Museum's educators told me that there were no nails used in the joining of the beams. She also related that the construction of the banister leading to the lower level was made all from one tree. At that point I felt that I had found more than a museum, but a place that in its very construction reaffirmed Native respect for the unity of the human and natural worlds.*

The above description is excerpted from an early doctoral seminar paper. But upon re-reading it, I realize I was already editing, selecting only one aspect of this initial encounter—the theme of an open-minded researcher encountering the living expressions of a Native people. What is missing from this description is the way in which I entered that space at first, with pen and pad in hand, eager to record experiences useful for my research task. Introducing myself as a doctoral student in art education, I was left to explore the Museum on my own. Taking notes at each exhibit, I was approached several times by a museum educator, who encouraged me to ask questions. At one point she inquired whether I had "gotten all I needed." At another stage, while listening to her describe the life stories of some of the individuals whose vibrant portraits appear on the walls, I stumbled across an important cultural boundary by asking whether I could come back with a tape recorder to document some of these rich histories. Such a task was never my intention, but looking back, I realize it came out of both the enthusiasm of the moment and an unexamined sense that claiming this activity would be welcomed. Her response was my first lesson in examining the research act, as she made it clear that the Museum was created for the Shinnecock people to tell their own stories, and not to have outsiders come and "take" them away. Although the entire exchange was mild and friendly, I was taken aback by my own insensitivity toward Shinnecock cultural knowledge. As I reflect on this encounter, I realize it was one of those moments of awakening that helped reshape my understanding of cross-cultural study, forcing me to step back and examine the research act itself.

The following spring, I enrolled in a class on ethnographic inquiry. In my notes for February 18, 2002, I have quoted the professor, "Being a 'professional stranger' is the beauty of ethnography." According to Bernard (2002), in the textbook used extensively for this class:

> *Participant observation is about stalking culture in the wild*—establishing rapport and learning to act so that people go about their business as usual when you show up. If you are a successful participant observer, you will know when to laugh at what people think is funny; and when people laugh at what you say, it will be because you meant it to be a joke....*When it's done right, participant observation turns field workers into instruments of data collection and data analysis.* (emphasis added) (p. 324)

Writing in the 21st century, Bernard's notion of cultural researchers turned to "instruments of data collection and data analysis" points to the tenacity of a Eurocentric and mechanistic paradigm as theoretical foundation for the social sciences over a hundred years after their emergence. Although I acknowledge the contemporary struggle of many ethnographers to come to terms with insider/ outsider status, objectivism and power asymmetries, after one semester in a traditional ethnography course, I was becoming adept at objectifying and distancing culture into a few handy research questions.[3] None of my early questions arose from conversations with Native peoples themselves, but instead from conversations with the professor and his teaching assistant. On re-reading my early ideas, I understand why many people at Shinnecock still view any researcher, no matter how well intended, as interested in them only as *objects* of study leading to professional gain. Trying to frame my desire to learn about the Native peoples on whose land I was born and live into an acceptable ethnographic problem statement bypassed an important quality of a decolonizing research methodology—namely, asking Native peoples themselves for their ideas and what they see as problem areas worthy to address rather than imposing my own agenda.

Dialoguing About Research

Shortly after completing the ethnography class, I initiated encounters with Native artists and educators for advice regarding my original research question, which focused on the role of the arts in Shinnecock culture. One artist from Shinnecock shared his hesitancy to participate in research as the result of bad experiences in the past. He described how his mother had given many stories to non-Native researchers and received neither payment nor a promised copy of the final manuscript. Another phone conversation with a Laguna Pueblo man, who is a tribal council member and retired social worker, reinforced the need to seek insider information. This gentleman related the many misrepresentations of his culture in written form. He said that focusing on respect was a good idea. "You want the truth." As my initial conversations progressed, I began to realize that I was not hearing from Native peoples themselves a need for more non-indigenous peoples to "study" their lifeways and artistic practices, but rather a need for us to *learn to listen* to Indigenous peoples' concerns and to respect their cultural authority.

The responses I received shifted my focus away from Native cultural practices and toward my own. The stories that eventually unfolded revealed the silencing of Indigenous perspectives within K-12 and university institutions and how this miseducation harms both Indigenous and non-indigenous children alike. The main story begins with Shinnecock.

Shinnecock

The modern day Shinnecock Reservation consists of approximately 1,200 acres of land in Shinnecock Neck and West Woods, located on the south shore of eastern Long Island, near the village of Southampton. Approximately 600 residents live on the reservation, which is governed by the Shinnecock Nation Board of Trustees, who handle all membership claims. The Shinnecock people are recognized by the state of New York, and they are currently engaged in efforts to gain federal recognition. Such a dry statement of facts, however, does not do justice to the cultural richness, natural beauty, and social engagement of the reservation, which is home to the Shinnecock Nation Cultural Center and Museum, the first Native owned and operated museum on Long Island. The Museum opened its doors in June 2001, dedicated to their Ancestors with a strong educational mission to preserve and teach the living culture of the Shinnecock people, who have been part of life on the east end of Long Island for over 10,000 years.[4]

Many Indigenous scholars point to a spiritual connection to place as the foundation on which Indigenous knowledge systems rest. Grande (2000), for instance, speaks of the Earth as the "spiritual center" of a "new Red Pedagogy (p. 355). Many Shinnecock people feel deeply connected to their low-lying lands and gentle hills, encircled by the bays and inlets of the Atlantic Ocean. The close connection between the people and their land is inscribed in the place names surrounding the reservation: *Shinnecock* Bay, *Shinnecock* Inlet, *Shinnecock* Hills. In describing a mural in the Shinnecock Museum, Elizabeth Thunder Bird Haile speaks of the Shinnecock Hills, a sacred place taken from the tribe during one of many waves of colonial encroachment:

> This picture depicts the burial customs in the Shinnecock Hills, where our people are still buried, whether people regard them or not. We have to remind them of that all the time. Here's a scene from up there. There's a certain spot. You can still go up that road and go up to the top of that hill and look out. (E. Haile, personal communication, August 12, 2004)

Stark power imbalances resulting from colonial oppression can be seen in the socioeconomic contrasts of the Hamptons, where the elite Shinnecock Hills Golf Club now sits on ancient tribal burial grounds, and the picture windows of multi-million dollar mansions look out upon the reservation from across the rounded sweep of Shinnecock Bay. Despite huge asymmetries of power and wealth between the Shinnecock and their incalculably rich neighbors, the Shinnecock Tribal Trustees have continued to engage in legal battles to reclaim lands and rights, gain federal recognition and build economic self-sufficiency.[5]

As a child growing up in the working class suburbs of Suffolk County, the Hamptons with its private beaches and unknown reservation were destinations passed through unconsciously during family trips to the Montauk Point lighthouse at the remote southern tip of the Island.[6] As a doctoral student my visit to the Shinnecock Museum was my first time on a Long Island reservation. Later that year, I attended my first powwow.

Powwow 2002

Coming as it does on that special threshold that separates the freedom of summer from the start of the new school year, the annual Shinnecock Labor Day weekend powwow formed a natural marker for each phase of my educational journey. Although I grew up on Long Island, my first powwow experience was the Shinnecock's 56th, an event almost completely rained out that particular weekend in late August 2002.

Most years when the weather holds, the powwow, which is open to the public, attracts thousands of visitors to Shinnecock territory. Rainouts are economically devastating for the Shinnecock Nation, which prepare the entire year for this event, their primary means to generate income for the community and its many projects, such as the Senior Nutrition and Indian Education programs. To have such an important source of economic development be dependent on the weather is one reason the Shinnecock trustees are seeking additional means of self-support, such as gaming.

I wandered around the wet grounds waiting for the official grand entry, a formal processional that opens each major segment of the long weekend event. Still somewhat stuck in my "researcher," role, I was searching for some means of interpreting this disarming cross-cultural mix of the modern and traditional, the white Long Islander having an outing with the kids overlapping with the economic, cultural, and spiritual importance of this event for a Shinnecock person. Neither an insider nor a tourist, I remember feeling completely out of place—an alien in search of meaning with paper and pad rather than the more practical folding chair and blanket. Impressions such as the smell of burning sage and fry bread, the taste of *samp*—the traditional mix of white beans, salt pork, and corn—combined with the sound of many voices, both Native and non-Native, on the damp sea air.

How about a bow and arrow, Jack? Lookit, a bow and arrow!

Five minutes to drum roll call.

Do you need a map for a school project? They're two dollars.

Daddy, look at that one. That's a big one [indicating dream catcher hanging in stall].

Singers, dancers, come this way, we're almost ready for Grand Entry.

All singers report to your drums. Singers, report to your drums!

Everything was punctuated by the continual beating of the powerful powwow drums leading up to the official grand entry of the Shinnecock and U.S. flags accompanied by tribal trustees, elders, veterans and an intergenerational community of dancers.

During the grand entry, Elizabeth Thunder Bird Haile, with rain clouds threatening overhead, performed her original interpretive dance to an Indigenous version of the "Lord's Prayer" accompanied by the music of Malotte. I later learned that Mrs. Haile has been opening the Shinnecock powwow with this dance since its inception over 50 years ago, and she has taught the dance to her granddaughters, who now perform it with her, as they did on this day. The powwow, which had at first appeared to me as a mix of open-air market and performing arts festival, began to feel like a great and wonderful family reunion, one that lasts far into the night, long after the public has left the grounds.

That October, I called Mrs. Haile to share ideas about my dissertation, and since that time she has remained my primary guide from Shinnecock. Mrs. Haile is a recognized elder of the Nation and serves as Vice President of the Executive Board of the Museum. She is a dance educator, filmmaker, storyteller, and the eldest daughter of Chief Thunder Bird, who helped to reinstate the annual Labor Day Powwow.[7] Her life long work in Native Studies has been recognized by Southampton College of Long Island University, which awarded her an Honorary Doctor of Humane Letters in 2002. In one of our first conversations, Mrs. Haile framed our work together as a potential "partnership." While writing, I frequently hear echoes of her pointed question asked of academics in general, "Why do you always quote someone else?" This observation led me to shape the dissertation and subsequent academic writing into a predominantly narrative format.

Educational Narratives

Between August 2004 and February 2005, I met with 14 educators, artists, and lawyers who live on the Shinnecock Reservation. They talked with me about their memories of schooling and their insights about education today. Apart from a general focus on education, there were no pre-conceived categories, and my purpose was not "data collection" but to listen and learn. A majority of these conversations took place on the Shinnecock Reservation at locations filled with meaning, such as the Family Preservation Center, which houses the after school Indian Education program for the children and youth of Shinnecock in one wing and the Senior Nutrition Program, which provides hot lunches for Shinnecock senior citizens in an adjoining wing. One conversation took place in early evening sitting in the front pew of the Shinnecock Presbyterian Church, the "oldest continuous reformed Indian Church in the United States" (http://www.shinnecocknation.com/culture.asp). My conversation with Mrs. Haile unfolded at her kitchen table while the sun went down and her husband patiently waited to cook dinner. Not all conversations happened indoors. I can still hear the chirping birds and hum of the wind off Shinnecock Bay in the background of the recording of a conversation with Mrs. Haile and her niece Tonya Bess Hodges, which began inside the Shinnecock Museum and ended outdoors at the Nation's sacred burial grounds. I mention these locales here because they are essential parts of this story, as the land base of Shinnecock itself centers and grounds these narratives.

From the start, Mrs. Haile agreed that documenting the memories and current thinking of non-indigenous educators as well as Shinnecock people would help us prepare for the Museum's work at creating an initial educational workshop for public school teachers. Additionally, I was interested to see if teachers today expressed the same silences and absences I remember from my own schooling. I started in Levittown. Perhaps in the back of my mind was Levittown's iconic stature as a prototypical, white suburban community, infamous for its early discriminatory real estate and rental practices fostering racial segregation.

In April 2004, I met with four social studies chairs and their Assistant Superintendent of Curriculum, who had arranged a lunchtime meeting with his colleagues. As I approached the well-kept school building, surrounded by rows of Levitt houses, I wondered how these educators and curriculum leaders would respond to my inquiry into the absence of the Native perspective in education today. My apprehension dissolved, for in the midst of this predominantly white suburban school district, I found educators eager to grapple honestly with the issue of curricular exclusion as well as the gaps in their own educational histories.

After completing the Levittown focus group I was curious to hear the perspectives of elementary teachers on the topic of teaching and learning about Native peoples. That autumn I drove out to Cutchogue East Elementary School, whose Principal had arranged a focus group with six of her teachers.

The drive out to Cutchogue took me through Suffolk County's North Fork, not far from Orient Point and the ferry to Connecticut. The views couldn't have been more different than the trip to Levittown. Whereas Levittown lies off Hempstead Turnpike, a dense industrial corridor, the journey to Cutchogue passed through picturesque farm stands and vineyards, all framed by the mild waters of Long Island Sound. Perhaps this is how Hempstead Plain looked before the potato harvests failed and Levitt and Sons ushered in their new age of mass production. Although the external appearance of each school is very different, however, both the Mattituck-Cutchogue and Levittown districts, like most of the school districts on Long Island, have predominantly white student bodies and faculties.[8]

CLOSING THE DISTANCE

Reading the Narrative Threads[9]

Listening to the voices of the Shinnecock and non-indigenous educators who shared their educational stories with me brought to light the pervasive, long standing, and malignant power of racial stereotyping regarding the Indigenous peoples of Long Island and elsewhere. On Long Island, stereotyping first takes root in our segregated communities and is later reinforced in our schools, where ignorance regarding Indigenous peoples is the rule rather than the exception. Unfortunately, many in-service and prospective teachers are simply unaware of the curricular bias that relegates Native peoples to the past, and that through such biases, as well as a multitude of unexamined "fun" activities, such as dressing in feathers, they are sanctioning stereotyping and racism.[10]

With few exceptions, the non-indigenous teachers' memories were filled with Hollywood's pervasive "Cowboys and Indians" stereotypes and a few token references to some vaguely remembered injustice somewhere in time. As contemporary teachers, many of them confessed to their own lack of education in this area. Most frequently, time pressure to "cover" required topics in the New York State core curriculum and assessments was given as a major reason for not addressing a more authentic account of Native peoples.

> Our high school mascot [was] the "Chieftains," and of course it was the typical 1950s version of the Indian. My total educational experience in elementary school had to come from television. I watched every Western that there was. I was in elementary school in the 1950s, and I finished high school in '68, so—it's embarrassing to say—it was strictly "Cowboys and Indians." (Cutchogue Elementary focus group)

> But throughout American history, throughout the rest of the book [and] in high school, they tend to have [a] 'token' paragraph in each unit [about] what happened at that time period to Native Americans—which is always the fact that they were 'in the way' and that the American government did terrible things and moved them off their land. (Levittown social studies 7-12 focus group)

Negative stereotyping, according to Henderson (2000), is a strategy that positions differences as inferior in order to justify the privileges and aggression of the colonizer. Until diagnosed, stereotypes are barely conscious habits of thought that permeate public schooling, both in the classroom as well as after school in sporting events. To sense how deeply ingrained such stereotypes have become in the non-indigenous consciousness, we need only take into account the hurt feeling and sense of 'oppression' expressed by University of Illinois students when finally denied their stereotypical sports mascot—Chief Illinewek.[11]

In addition to stereotypes, both Shinnecock and non-indigenous educators described their own memories of schooling as bereft of any genuine content regarding Indigenous cultures and histories.

> I have no memories of Native Americans. None. From 4th grade—none. And then thinking back to high school, it was a lot of world history—a lot of European history. I took a lot of AP *[advanced placement]* courses and a lot of

> 'man's inhumanity to man,' but nothing of Native cultures—nothing that I can recall at least—no books being read, nothing. (Cutchogue Elementary education focus group)

> The only time I studied Long Island Indians was in the 7th grade, I think, in the intermediate school. It was just a very cursory kind of description of the so-called thirteen tribes of Long Island, and it was the basic simplified academic approach. I thought it was too simplified. (David Bunn Martine, Director and Curator of Shinnecock Museum)

Such responses reinforce Cook-Lynn's (2001) notion of "Anti-Indianism" as "that which treats Indians and their tribes as if they do not exist" (p. x). About this problem, civil rights activist Bob Zellner says,

> The first way that Native peoples in this area are perceived is that there are no Native peoples in this area. Because it's out of sight, out of mind. So unless there are a few Shinnecocks or Montauketts or other groups represented in a school or in a community, there's almost no perception that 'there are still Indians here.' Even in our diversity teaching and training, we're still stuck in the Black/White paradigm, rather than seeing Black/White/Native American/Asian/Latino and so forth.... So they're really the victims of both invisibility and active discrimination. (personal communication, January 23, 2005)[12]

What for non-indigenous teachers is an emotionally neutral absence, becomes for Indigenous peoples the strongly felt anger, pain, and for some, resignation, of having their histories and experiences disregarded by school and community.

Among the Shinnecock people who shared their experiences of schooling, the painful sense of isolation and disregard of their cultural identities resulting from curricular bias within K-12 schooling was a recurrent theme. Particularly disturbing was the role teachers played in reinforcing stereotypes.

> The teachers knew where I was from, but they never asked me any of my experiences on the reservation. It was understood that once we got off the bus and walked into the school, we were no longer Indians because we didn't look like the Indians that the teacher was teaching about. (Lucille Bosley, English teacher, member of Shinnecock Museum Executive Board)

> No, never. Never learned [about Native peoples.] Only thing was Thanksgiving— the Pilgrims and that was about it. (Dennis King Bird, artist, Shinnecock)

When such stereotypes become ingrained in the dominant culture, they lead to structural racism, such as the reduced educational expectations encountered by Shinnecock children in public schools.

> They've [Shinnecock children] been tracked in school all these years, for non-Regents—no college—"Do the best you can; if you quit, we won't worry about that." At the age of sixteen, you finish school and become a truck driver. (Elizabeth Haile, Vice-President, Shinnecock Museum)

Despite the lowered expectations of public school teachers, the Shinnecock people who shared their stories grew to become innovative professionals in their fields of art, education, and the law. Many of them related how the cultural knowledge within their strong family networks provided the identity affirming support lacking in public schooling.

> Besides what my family taught me, I didn't learn anything in school about my culture. At home on Shinnecock, I did learn a great deal of information, history, love of this land and spirit of my people. We pass this on to our children, knowing this is the only place they will learn this concept. But in school, no. Wasn't presented to me. Native Americans, who are they? They don't even exist. (Tonya Bess Hodges, English teacher, Shinnecock)

The presence of a sovereign Native institution such as the Shinnecock Museum presents a unique opportunity for Long Island's universities and public schools to begin to responsibly address the erasure of Native identities that permeates curriculum and instruction here.

Building Bridges Across the Institutional Divide: Implications for Practice

At this writing I have collaborated with Mrs. Haile on two professional development workshops at the Museum, one for in-service teachers and a second for pre-service teachers and university teacher education faculty. The workshops brought non-indigenous teachers to Shinnecock territory to learn directly from Shinnecock educators about their history, culture, educational concerns and resources. Each workshop was funded by a non-Native academic institution (Teachers College, Columbia and Adelphi University, respectively.) Such collaborations benefit the Museum by supporting its mission as an authentic educational resource for the Long Island community as well as a vital centre for the preservation and renewal of Shinnecock cultural values and knowledges. They benefit non-indigenous teachers by offering valuable support in a curricular area greatly in need of reform.

In one of our conversations, Elizabeth Haile asserted that much of what is authentic within schooling "hasn't got four walls around it, but it has your grandmother's knowledge." Unlike paternalistic notions of schooling and knowledge construction, where a single authority controls a normalized narrative, this "grandmotherly" vision of education points to respect for the knowledge to be gained from all of the members of our communities, regardless of whether or not they have letters after their names. In reviewing the changes taking place in the academy as a result of the work of Indigenous scholars, Rains and Deyhle (2000) speak of the importance of recognizing "indigenous epistemologies and paradigms developed over thousands of years of sustained living on this Land" (p. 337) as well as the necessary shift in the role of Elders from "informants" to sovereign and respected research guides and teachers (see also Battiste et al., 2002). Future projects can take shape in several ways:

> Collaboratively design credit-bearing university courses and workshops that can be integrated into educational degree programs. Such courses would be taught or co-taught by Indigenous educators.

Make available Native approved films and curricular materials via a resource library and website focused on Indigenous issues and concerns.

Through grant writing provide support for collaborative educational research projects among local university faculty, classroom teachers and members of the Native community.

Create a collective base from which to work to reform the content area regarding Native peoples in the New York State core curriculum and assessments.

Standing at the Western Door

In her Introduction to *Reclaiming Indigenous Voice and Vision*, Battiste (2000) offers the image of the sacred Medicine Wheel of the northern Plains as a tool for both the colonized and the colonizer to confront the essential questions of colonization and its impact on Indigenous peoples' lives and systems of knowledge. She speaks of four doors: The Western/autumn door from which we can map the ideas that have shaped and continue to maintain colonialism; the Southern/winter door from which we diagnose colonialism, exposing the roots of oppressive relationships, and in the evocation of darkness and cold, bear witness to the struggle of Indigenous peoples to survive and also to endure; the Eastern/spring door that offers healing, recovery and the creation of new knowledge; and the Southern/ summer door from which an Indigenous renaissance will spring.

As a non-indigenous scholar, I stand at the Western door, a representative of those forces that have shaped colonialism and continue its dominance despite the word "post" in our literatures. Looking across the Wheel I see Elizabeth Haile and other Shinnecock people whom I have met, standing before the Eastern Door, working hard for the healing and recovery of their people.

Indigenous concepts such as the Medicine Wheel challenge those of us in academic communities to engage in a form of *living* thinking—thinking that transcends the dominance of privileged roles and the reification of "expertism." As scholars, they challenge us to 'be present' in our listening and in the art of inquiry and to reorient our work outward toward what benefits the community rather than for professional gain alone. They urge us to bring warmth to our thinking through the forces of a compassionate heart. Perhaps the very notion of *presence* itself embodies the conceptual tides through which this inquiry has traveled and continues to travel. For it is in the very act of *being present*, as scholars, educators and artists, that we can forge a relational *space between* where listening, respecting, and bearing witness become our new research tools—a space where we are no longer professional strangers, but partners and friends.

NOTES

[1] Portions of this chapter are reproduced from D. Caracciolo (2009), By their very presence: Rethinking research and partnering for change with educators and artists from Long Island's

Shinnecock Nation Cultural Center and Museum. International Journal of Qualitative Studies in Education, 22 (2), 177-200. The journal's website is http://www.informaworld.com.

2. John Strong (2000), The Algonquian peoples of Long Island from earliest times to 1700, recounts some of the violent encounters between Long Island's Native peoples and early colonists.
3. For a discussion of collaborative ethnography that seeks to decenter power relations and close the distance between ethnographer and participants, see L.E.Lassiter (1998), The power of Kiowa song: A collaborative ethnography.
4. For more detailed descriptions of Indigenous Long Island, see E. T. Pritchard (2002), Native New Yorkers: The legacy of the Algonquin people of New York.
5. The Shinnecock Nation is currently state recognized. An application for federal recognition had been sitting unexamined in the Department of the Interior since 1978. The application was moved to "ready for active" status in 2003.The Shinnecock successfully petitioned a federal judge for recognition, and the positive ruling was granted on November 7, 2005. At the time of the ruling the tribal trustees published the following statement: "Today, the Federal Court issued a historic ruling acknowledging the Shinnecock Indian Nation as an Indian Tribe describing the facts of the case as, 'for the most part, undisputed' and ruling that 'the Shinnecocks clearly meet the criteria for tribal status.' Given U.S. District Court Judge Thomas C. Platt's decision, we believe it's time for the State of New York and the Town of Southampton to stop fighting the Nation and work with us to reach a comprehensive, and just solution to our claims. It is time for justice." (http://www.shinnecocknation.com/news/ news157.asp, accessed 06/02/07). Despite this ruling, the Senior U.S. Senator from New York, Charles Schumer, urged the Bureau of Indian Affairs to ignore the judge's decision, and the Shinnecock are still waiting for the BIA to act on their petition.
6. In school we never learned that the easternmost part of Long Island once belonged to the Montaukett people, who have no land base today. See John Strong (2001), The Montaukett Indians of Eastern Long Island, for a detailed historical account of the unsuccessful struggle of this Long Island tribe to reclaim their ancestral lands and gain federal recognition.
7. Mrs. Haile's father, Henry F. Bess, Chief Thunder Bird, ceremonial chief of the Shinnecock, founded the modern Labor Day powwow in 1946. According to Mrs. Haile, prior to this time, the Shinnecock powwows were private gatherings. The first public powwow was held in her backyard, and she and her sisters sold hotdogs from the casement window. The annual event now takes place on the Shinnecock Reservation powwow grounds and hosts thousands of visitors each year.
8. Results from two surveys of school districts and preservice teachers, respectively, as well as excerpts from six additional in-depth interviews with non-Native professionals living on Long Island, whose work demonstrates advocacy for Native peoples and/or an academic specialty in local Native history and culture, were also included in the final dissertation. See further D.M. Caracciolo (2006) By their very presence: Rethinking research and partnering for change with artists and educators from Long Island's Shinnecock Nation for a detailed description of participants and methodology.
9. Discussion of additional narrative threads appear in the article that forms the basis of this chapter: as well as in the dissertation study.
10. For further discussion of the misrepresentation of Native peoples in K-12 teaching, see D. Caracciolo, (2008), Addressing anti-Indianism in the mainstream curriculum: A partnership model.
11. The following text appears on fightingillini.com, the website of University of Illinois athletics: "One of the most dramatic and dignified traditions in college athletics is the performance of Chief Illiniwek at the University of Illinois. Since 1926, this symbol has stirred pride and respect in audiences at Memorial Stadium, the Assembly Hall and Huff Hall." (http: //fightingillini.cstv.com/trads/ill-trads-thechief.html, accessed 06/01/07). On March 13, 2007, after years of resisting pressure from Native rights activists, most notably, Charlene Teeters, the University Board of Trustees, after unsuccessfully appealing removal of NCAA sanctions for continuing to use an offensive mascot, disbanded its use, to the dismay of many in the University community.

[12] I first met Bob Zellner at the Shinnecock Thanksgiving festival on November 20, 2003. Shinnecock Thanksgiving usually takes place the week before the national holiday because, according to Mrs. Haile, Shinnecock people often had to work on Thanksgiving Day cooking holiday turkeys for their wealthy employers. This is one of several times for giving thanks in the Shinnecock year. At this event several non-Natives who are considered "friends of the Nation" are invited and publicly acknowledged. Bob Zellner was one of these special people. Having spent most of his life as a civil rights activist—the first white southerner to serve as a field secretary for a major civil rights organization, the Student Non-Violent Coordinating Committee (SNCC)—Bob was recruited as a young man by Dr. Martin Luther King, Jr. He now lives in Southampton and has been active in support of the civil rights of the Shinnecock people.

REFERENCES

Battiste, M. (2000). Introduction: Unfolding the lessons of colonization. In M. Battiste (Ed.), *Reclaiming indigenous voice and vision* (pp. xvi–xxx). Vancouver: UBC Press.

Battiste, M., Bell, L., & Findlay, L. M. (2002). Decolonizing education in Canadian universities: An interdisciplinary, international, indigenous research project. *Canadian Journal of Native Education, 262*(2), 82–95.

Bernard, H. R. (2002). *Research methods in anthropology: Qualitative and quantitative approaches* (3rd ed.). Walnut Creek, CA: Alta Mira Press.

Caracciolo, D. (2009). By their very presence: Rethinking research and partnering for change with educators and artists from Long Island's Shinnecock Nation Cultural Center and Museum. *International Journal of Qualitative Studies in Education, 22*(2), 177-200.

Caracciolo, D. (2008). Addressing anti-Indianism in the mainstream curriculum: A partnership model. *Multicultural Perspectives.* 22 (4), 224-228.

Caracciolo, D. M. (2006). *By their very presence: Rethinking research and partnering for change with artists and educators from Long Island's Shinnecock Nation.* Doctoral Dissertation, Teachers College, Columbia, 2006. ProQuest, AAT 3205328.

Cook-Lynn, E. (2001). *Anti-Indianism in North America: A voice from Tatekeya's Earth.* Urbana, IL: University of Illinois Press.

Findlay, L. M. (2000). Forward. In M. Battiste (Ed.), *Reclaiming indigenous voice and vision* (pp. ix–xiii). Vancouver: UBC Press.

Grande, S. (2000). American Indian identity and intellectualism: The quest for a new red pedagogy. *Qualitative Studies in Education, 13*(4), 343–359.

Henderson, S. (2000). Postcolonial ghost dancing: Diagnosing European colonialism. In M. Battiste (Ed.), *Reclaiming indigenous voice and vision* (pp. xvi–xxx, pp. 57–76). Vancouver: UBC Press.

Pritchard, E. T. (2002). *Native New Yorkers: The legacy of the Algonquin people of New York.* San Francisco: Council Oak Books.

Rains, F. V., Archibald, J., & Deyhle, D. (2000, July/August). Introduction: Through our eyes and in our own words. *International Journal of Qualitative Studies in Education, 13*(4), 337–342.

Shinnecock Indian Nation religion and culture. (n.d.). Retrieved June 12, 2007, from http://www.shinnecocknation.com/culture.asp

Strong, J. A. (2001). *The Montaukett Indians of Eastern Long Island.* New York: Syracuse University Press.

Diane Caracciolo
Ruth S. Ammon School of Education
Adelphi University

KRYSSI STAIKIDIS

PATHS IN

Transformations of a Painter

Figure 1. Abduction of the Rooster Domingo Garcia Criado 1999

THE ABSENCE OF PRESENCE IN ART EDUCATION

My childhood and high school years were full of art that I made and created on my own, which could perhaps be considered an only child's musings. I was accustomed to working with stories and creating my own worlds through painting. My family's response was always positive because they saw my art as a part of who I was. What I made mattered as I discovered new things to do, novel ways to explore with different materials and visual ways to communicate my personal experiences. As the ongoing pain of my parent's divorce nudged me to paint, my art became the vehicle to express narratives of sadness and longing – a child longing for parental unity, an immigrant child's longing to go back to the abstract homeland, a child and dog, best friends on a journey to search for their family. My art described a lone world that became a safe place full of disquieting color that expressed feelings unutterable in traditional conversation. Art was my safe haven, not rooted in actual community, but rooted in the child's imagination of a community, a family, a place to belong where concrete events could not disrupt or harm.

When thinking about what I would do when I grew up, there was no question that I would become an artist. As I applied to colleges, it was clear that at least some of the schools I looked into would be art schools. When I heard back from colleges, I found that I had been accepted to a school in the Midwest, halfway around, what seemed to a New Yorker, the world. I went, excited to "study art" for the first time. But if I thought that this academic setting would provide me with a path into myself, or a means to reach out to talk with others, I was sorely wrong. What I found instead in each introductory foundations class was a set of rules for rendering from observation. Rather than speaking through paint and line, through gesture, through form, presenting silences and sadnesses, I was being asked to draw cubes, spheres, and pyramids. I was required to construct relationships with objects through drawing their contours and shadows, through studying their surfaces to reproduce them. My response to such exercises was to feel clumsy, to feel inadequate, to feel small and insignificant. These were not paths in or out; they were cold sterile rooms.

Art had gone from a safe community of one to a series of bland exercises in which the potential community sat in seats of isolation connecting with inanimate objects only through attempts to emulate them. If this was art, then I had chosen wrong. Panic overwhelmed me and I realized that I did not feel at home or want to be found in these classrooms where no part of who I was mattered or even entered the picture. There was no dialogue, no community, no caring. There was critique of the form of drawing and painting, but no attention paid to the heart of it. I understood that there were a series of hurdles that I needed to pass through, the music scales of visual art, but there were no classes where narrative or meaning mattered. This was too much for a young artist, and I withdrew after one semester. I reasoned that if I stayed, it would destroy the creator in me and forever obscure my image of what an artistic community was or could be.

The Journey Begins: Looking for Community

From that time on, as a young person, I wanted to know what art making could mean in a community. I also wondered who might teach me in a way that felt comfortable, familiar and caring. Although I wondered about all of this, I couldn't really put these thoughts into words. Nevertheless, due to the absence of my own presence in the history of my art education, I wanted to retrieve that which was not allowed to be – namely me. After studying anthropology and art history in college, and continuing to paint on my own, I traveled to South America in search of a mentoring experience. Perhaps if I found a mentor in a community of artists, I could redefine art on my own terms. Clearly the academy had an entirely different definition. In Ecuador, I found a Chilean painter, Carmen Silva, who taught me drawing and painting.

It was during this time, the years of my early twenties, that I traveled the highlands of Bolivia, Chile and Peru and observed highland Bolivian indigenous Aymara traditions of weaving. In the Aymara communities, art and life were not treated as separate entities. Traveling on buses, looking out of the windows I saw women in traditional woven skirts and blouses spinning alpaca wool on wooden spools, with their children doing homework and their husbands working in the field. Women wove on back strap looms, while food simmered on the stove and children played. Here, I observed traditions that integrated art with daily living. Observing such indigenous traditions, I became interested in exploring the possibilities for teaching and learning art informally. I thought about what it might mean to make art in a community context where feedback was instant and those who watched on became involved in the process. This would be a new experience for me, to study in the midst of community and daily life. But how could I do this in my own culture where art was taught in formal classroom settings? These images of indigenous highland communities and the making of weavings within community settings stayed with me as possibilities for teaching and learning art in the future.

With the images of the Aymara women weaving in mind, embarking upon my doctoral research fifteen years later, I decided that I would look for an indigenous community of painters where I might learn in a setting away from Euro-American traditions. During that fifteen year period, I had also become a teacher of art and was interested in observing teaching that took place outside of classrooms. For this reason, I sought teaching outside of a formal context and decided to apprentice myself to Guatemalan Maya painters Paula Nicho Cúmez and Pedro Rafael González Chavajay who taught me to paint in their art studios.

Pedro Rafael, a Maya Tz'utuhil artist, lives in San Pedro La Laguna, a small town tucked into the side of a volcano on Lake Atitlan. His grandfather was the first painter in San Pedro, a Maya Tz'uthuhil community, and Pedro Rafael is the father of the Pedrano painting school. Paula, a Maya Kaqchikel artist, lives in San Juan de Comalapa, an arid town in the highlands. She is the leader of the Maya Kaqchikel indigenous women's painting movement, made up of some of the first Maya female painters in the entire country. Each town is home to a regional painting movement with a unique style. I traveled to meet both painters before beginning my studies with them. Each decided to take me on, Pedro after meeting me, and Paula after meeting me and seeing my work. I have now been their student for seven years, studying with each over the course of several summers in their studios. Their teachings were nothing like the sterile exercises that I had previously experienced in traditional academic art classes. They were full of family laughter, children eating and playing, friends dropping in for chats, meals and community activities such as parades, outings, markets and night walks in a bustling town with my mentors. I had finally found what I was looking for – a community of artists who did not separate art from lived experiences.[1]

The Journey Rewinds: Biases I Brought

Before leaving for study in Guatemala, I began to think about teaching art in communities. Was teaching passed down from generation to generation? Was learning one-to-one? Were teaching and learning peer centered, or teacher centered, or both? How did whole families learn about symbols and colors and carry on weaving or painting traditions with no formal schooling? My prejudices informed my thinking about teaching which had up until then been isolated in buildings apart from daily life and lived experiences. Could lessons in Maya painting studios help me to teach in classroom communities in my own culture? I realized that as an educator, I was seeking ways to reform pedagogy so that a quest for meaning naturally became part of the educational experience. If I went to indigenous cultures to learn about artistic traditions taking place in communities, might I transfer knowledge to the classrooms of my own educational cultures?

These were the many thoughts I had as I embarked upon this learning exchange with Maya painters. However, my thoughts themselves were depersonalized, colored by my own perspectives as both a doctoral student and teacher within a system that had taught me to see my studies as experiences taking place outside of myself. Therefore, as I began my work with Pedro Rafael and Paula, I was thinking broadly and only about contributing to a more holistic approach to teaching art at the college level. In other words, just like a traditional Eurocentric ethnographer, I thought that I might be able to "take" what I learned from my Maya mentors and "bring it back" to my own culture. What I hadn't contemplated yet were the effects that this experience would have upon me as an artist, as a student, as a researcher and as a teacher. How would I change as a result of this experience? Reflecting back, I can see that at the onset of this study, I was still bridled in my thinking – the residue of having been brought up in an era of the traditional ethnographic study where the "subject" provides information and the investigator illuminates the academy.

Shamed by my own naiveté, and simultaneously fascinated by exciting new possibilities, I began to read ethnographic studies that questioned such unilateral forms of investigation.[2] As I began work with Paula and Pedro Rafael, my perspectives slowly shifted. I say slowly because it was not easy to disengage from the cultural privilege that I both embodied and had grown accustomed to. Over time, I realized that transformations within me as the researcher were an important part of the research process and perhaps the true subject under investigation. The biases that I brought to the table also surprised me and I found that learning outside of my culture enabled me to begin to dismantle such long-held Eurocentric beliefs. This study was just as much about me as it was about my teachers. I also began to realize that the potential for deconstructing traditional power exchanges inherent in ethnography lay in my examination of self.[3]

The Journey Continues: Fostering Relationships

I started by observing my learning process as a student of art in this new context. Although I had long felt like an outsider in my own art schooling, I had internalized most of the beliefs about the "proper" ways to teach art: what determined quality was mastery of skills. As an art student, if I delved into my interior, then I was "cheating" and would not become a good artist. The conceptual, the visceral, the idea played a lesser part in making art than did technique. Ironically, I thought I had already rejected these conventions when I dropped out of art school, but I soon understood that they comprised a large part of how I judged myself and others.

Maya painters had much to teach me. Studying art in a new context fostered a pathway into the lives of artists who had been schooled differently from me. As I began to paint side by side with my Maya mentors, I was able to recognize some of my own biases and struggled to do battle with them on more than an intellectual level. Maya artists did not render from observation and infused their paintings with stories about their lives and their cultures. They viewed making work as a visual form of storytelling and transmitting cultural knowledge. They loved their work for what it meant and what it represented rather than for how they made it. The techniques were important, but they served the narrative in an organic way, rather then being disconnected. As a painter I was not at all perplexed by the idea of story in painting since that was very much the way I worked. As an educator, however, understanding was more complicated. I sought to realize how I might bring the personal and cultural narratives so much a part of my teachers' paintings into my own teaching and into the lives of the students whom I would teach in the future. I also thought about how I might look at informal learning in the home, among family and community, and transfer some of the relational aspects of being mentored caringly into formal classroom settings, not generally connected to heart, home, or a sense of community.

Mentoring as a process within community becomes an informed, loving, cultural and spiritual act as well as a bridge of friendship for crossing cultures. Teaching and learning in Maya communities are dual parts of what often feels like a kind of parenting. The relationships that I formed with Pedro Rafael and Paula were the essence of teaching and I often visualized the relationship within the teaching-learning process as a conduit through which knowledge flowed. And all the while, as I sat in those studios filled with the ongoings of daily life – children, customers, callers, marimba music – I wondered how this work with my mentors could serve as a pathway into lived experiences that might be brought home to classrooms.

In this narrative, I hope to convey the deep impact that this collaboration had on the three of us. Seven years later, we are working on a book together about our collaborative experiences. The memories that hold us together went well beyond teaching, learning and painting. They are rooted in love that has transpired over time and repeated discovery. There is recognition that is greatly gratified by the realization that there is a commonality in all. We became a family through the shared language of art and community.

Multiple Journeys: The Teachings of Maya Mentors

Pedro Rafael and Paula taught me from inside their cultures. They did not separate their lives from their art in any way. One day while talking about both of his grandfathers, one, the first painter in San Pedro and the other, aged 102 and the first person to practice Catholicism in San Pedro, Pedro Rafael said,

> When I began painting, I engraved my grandfather's themes in my mind. He always worked in customs, traditions and rituals. I carried all of his ideas inside of me in addition to my own. So when I began, I already felt the theme of customs through him. And the triptych that I just finished came from my other grandfather who told it to me through story; it was related to him and so I *had* to paint it. As an artist, I feel, analyze, and engrave all that I will create in my mind. My creation is then transmitted to the canvas...I feel a tremendous sense of relief spiritually and I think to myself this is what I wanted it to be. I have captured what I thought I would, what I felt, what I imagined. I have taken my insides, all that I hold inside, as well as what my ancestors held, and fused them to the canvas. (Personal Communication, July 15, 2007)

Pedro Rafael makes it clear that painting is a spiritual act, an act imagined and then transmitted to canvas. Figure 2 shows an image of the ceremony that Pedro Rafael's grandfather described to him. When Pedro Rafael talked about the process of painting, he said that as his grandfather spoke, he remembered having seen this ceremony vaguely as a small child. He added that it was through his listening and imagining as his grandfather narrated the story that he was able to "see and capture" all of the characters involved as if he were projecting a movie on a large screen.

I was intrigued by the idea of having all of the images, landscapes, colors and clothing planned out in one's mind before the actual execution of the painting. The process Pedro Rafael described was unfamiliar to me. His was a cultural memorizing that was transmitted from one generation to the next through visual text. I named the process for this in Maya painting *Imagined Realism*.[4] Pedro Rafael said that he wanted to leave the image of this ceremony for his children because they would not have any opportunity to remember this on their own, except through his painting, which became a witness to a moment frozen in time.

Figure 2. Maya Ceremony Pedro Rafael González Chavajay 2003

PATHS IN: TRANSFORMATIONS OF A PAINTER

Artists who do not separate their lived experiences from their painting inspire me. I began to see and think in new ways. Often times I observed myself making comparisons between ways that I had been previously taught while being presented with new ways of teaching. In so doing, I pondered whether I could authentically take part in an artistic activity, even briefly, from a cultural perspective that was not mine. I was used to thinking in categories; not thinking in such ways presented a constant challenge. But Pedro Rafael and Paula did not think of culture, life experiences, painting, or teaching as separate categories. The reality of culture was essential to all three. As I worked with my mentors, I realized that not only were their lived experiences at the center of their teaching, but so were mine.

TRANSFORMATIONS: PATHS IN AS LIVED EXPERIENCE

Transformations: Sites for Learning

What was most intriguing to me about this study was that it took place in artists' studios, where I learned and transformed knowledge through art making processes (Sullivan, 2006).[5] Both Pedro Rafael and Paula attempted to transmit their artistic knowledge to me, a non-Maya painter. I feel there is great potential for inter-cultural learning within artists' studios - intimate places that foster artistic dialogues where familiarity with artistic materials and a common artistic language become cultural bridges. Below is a painting made by Paula that is part of a thematic series related to the success of women. In her series, Paula paints multiple images related to one theme that speak to the values and beliefs she holds closest to her heart such as protection of her culture, the power of women, and discrimination against the Maya.

Figure 3. Woman Flying Paula Nicho Cúmez 2000

In her painting "Woman Flying" Paula remembers a dream in which she saw herself in flight and which represented her future successes in painting. In Kaqchikel cultures, women are often perceived as caretakers of the home and family and Paula's painting is significant as she is one of few women painters in her town. She has great faith in her talent as a painter and her unique role as a woman artist.

Studio as Site

Teaching in Maya studios provided me with insights into both pedagogical and conceptual processes for making art in Tz'utuhil and Kaqchikel cultures. I was asked to conceptualize the creation of paintings in an unfamiliar way that involved recording of images in the mind to communicate them later to canvas. This required me to work with my mind in a way that was different from all prior experiences. I was awakened to seeing in new ways because this process involved concentrated looking and feeling of natural surroundings that I was not accustomed to. Additionally, although personal narrative had always been the basis of my own painting, I was now asked to see and think of cultural customs as ideas for paintings. Because these cultural customs were not my own, I had to imagine them from stories told to me by my teachers, and conceive according to oratory and observation of surroundings and existing traditions. This was both new and a challenge for me, I am sure not unlike the challenge for young Maya painters who imagined memories of elders into being, fusing them with the canvas. But in this process what became apparent was that, unlike Maya painters, I was unfamiliar with cultural customs on a visceral level that made it very hard for me to capture them "realistically" or with the *knowing* of the artists from Maya cultures. This brought into question the idea of recognition, or *knowing* something well enough to paint it, very much a part of Maya cosmovision and not much a part of my experience.[6] One day while painting with Luciano, a fellow student, he commented:

> Fishermen still exist, but the way fish were sold in the market differed, so I would have to imagine that, and *remember* how it was done with the ancestors. I would have to use my mind because you cannot see it now. (Sitan Sicay, Personal Communication, July 30, 2005)

When I returned to my studio after such experiences in the field with Maya mentors, I realized that my own artistic ways of knowing were both comparable and different. I had been educated to draw from life and rarely to rely on cultural memory. The idea of rendering from nature is not part of Maya artistic processes and although I never liked rendering from nature, I realized that it was definitely part of my conceptual framework. But I had never consciously encountered the Maya concept of ancestors passing down iconography viscerally. Yet, when I thought about it I realized that in many ways I did feel that the Greek side of my family had passed its grief down through me, which most definitely appeared in my paintings. Studies with Maya mentors enabled me to view my own work with fresh perspectives.

PATHS IN: TRANSFORMATIONS OF A PAINTER

Self as Site

Along with the *Studio* as a site for transformative knowledge, I felt I must consider the *Self* as a site for knowledge transformation as well. As a result of this work, I had changed in many ways. The first was artistic practice: I transformed my self-concept and my art works. The second was learning practice: I became more confident as a student in Maya artists' studios. The third was teaching practice: I would teach differently in the future after having experienced the teachings of Maya mentors.

Sketches: Glimpses In

As an artist I must always think about what's in the painting and how it relates to human life, the "I" of the painting (Pedro Rafael Gonzalez Chavajay, 2005)

In the past, I had art educational experiences in school that made me feel awkward because I was not a realist. In contrast, I gained confidence from the Maya mentorship partnerships where my mentors appreciated my color sense, drawing, and painting ability. I also received more attention on an individualized basis, which was a new experience for me. I became emotionally stronger because of my teachers' investment of time and energy in me. I felt confident as an artist in ways that had nothing to do with the actual skills learned from lessons, but rather from my mentors' beliefs in my abilities and talent.

Additionally, the integration of culture with art making that I was exposed to in Maya cultures enabled me to begin to overcome my feelings of shyness and shame over the cultural hybridity that had haunted me growing up in North America. I envied the surety that Maya teachers and peers felt about who they were. I had been hiding my separated cultural heritages in the classrooms of my childhood, adolescence, and adulthood. For many years growing up in a relatively small town with a Greek last name (my father, born and raised in Greece, my mother Russian Jewish, born and raised in Brooklyn, New York), it was easy for me to hide behind my Greek last name when people made deriding jokes about Jewish people. I always felt that I was two halves of a whole with neither part being quite intact. We had lived in Greece when I was little so I never felt completely American. The Greek culture traditionally felt antagonism toward the Jewish culture, and so it went, the inner conflict ensued. For example, when we moved to Greece, my father told his family that my mother was Christian. When living in the States, however, my mother told her Jewish family that my father was Jewish. Both changed their last names, my mother from Bronstein to Brown, my father from Staikidis to Stack. I therefore grew up Kryssi Stack. At adult age, I went back. Literally. I went back to the original - Staikidis - a desire to be somebody real.

Additionally, growing up in U.S. classrooms, I was never given a feeling of freedom to express who I was or what cultures belonged to me. Living with Maya families who took such pride in their Maya cultures, who actually defined themselves by their cultures, affected me in positive ways. I began to consciously contemplate my cultural make-ups, which my paintings also had subconsciously been trying to do for a long time. I decided to address the feelings associated with my cultural hybridity: feelings of loss, longing, confusion, and mystery. I wondered seriously if I could feel pride about my cultures of origin. I also contemplated what it meant to embrace the white American cultures to which I belonged.

Prior to study with Pedro Rafael and Paula, I had painted autobiographies that portrayed vignettes from my childhood when I had lived in Greece. The painting in Figure 4 is based on a photograph taken of my father and me when we lived in Greece. I always paint the sea and moon in my paintings, which signify the desire to travel back to my father's country so as to know him and my own ancestry more thoroughly. However, it was not until my return from Guatemala and my studies with Pedro Rafael the first summer that I decided I would explore the Russian Jewish side of myself through painting.

This painting is part of an autobiographical series tracing birth to adulthood. Each painting captures one episode in time. This painting is called *In His Arms* and emerges from a memory of a photo of my grandmother, my uncle, my father, and me in his arms, as we stood together and posed outside on the terrace on a sunny Sunday afternoon in Greece. I was about three years old and I saw this vividly in my mind as I painted.

Figure 4. In His Arms Kryssi Staikidis 2001

As a result of my studies with Paula and Pedro Rafael, personal and cultural narratives that had not appeared before were revealed in my paintings; I began to create narrative themes related to exploring my cultural heritages. I felt the need to view my life with pride and develop my sense of self through representing my cultural identities in new ways. I started to ask my mother about the migration of her grandparents and parents in the early 1900's. They were Russian Jews who had come, one at a time, out of a family of fourteen children from Odessa, Russia to the shores of New York City on a ship landing at Ellis Island. I began a series of crossover paintings that took place two and three generations before me. I simultaneously became interested in the ways my experiences in Greece as a child had affected my iconography as a painter. I interviewed my father about both sides of our family coming from Crete and Constantinople, now Istanbul to Athens, as well as his migration to the United States from Greece.

In addition to changes in narrative contents of paintings, transformation of formal knowledge took place as a direct result of the pedagogical experiences with Maya painters. My color palette changed as I applied what Pedro Rafael had taught me about mixing color. He had a technique for mixing colors that involved repeating colors in different combinations on the palette so that monochromatic paintings appeared luminous. My colors simplified as I contemplated portraying cultural narratives originating in Greece with its widows wearing black, walking the islands alongside whitewashed homes and tomato gardens by the sea. I learned from my studies in Guatemala that there was nothing too literal or too banal to paint if it mattered to me and if it contributed to my life story. I looked back on my father's paintings riddled with black lines and grief. I realized that for years I had been using black lines in my work and that the formalist teachers in my MFA program had systematically attempted to "rid" my paintings of the black lines because "line was for drawing, and painting was about form." After my studies with Pedro Rafael and Paula, I let the floodgates open and the black lines back in, to strangle the subjects if they wanted, to tie them up, to wash them onto shore. My works after my first study experience with Pedro Rafael finally allowed the black lines to rule, as they communicated my father's lineage and my own. This narrative theme, although seemingly formal, a black line, had been repressed for so long but it still managed to intermittently creep back into my works. Now, I just owned it as part of me, disregarding the previously critical commentaries lodged in my mind from teachers of the past. Monochromatic reds replete with sensations of extreme emotion also came into my new pieces as a result of my studies. Thematic shifts as well as formal explorations were transformed as I applied my studio experiences from Guatemala to my paintings in New York.

The desire to go back and interview my family through oratory was based upon approaches to painting learned from my studies with Maya mentors. The paintings in Figure 5 are the results of these interviews. The first painting was a story told to me about my grandmother giving birth. In it, one sees the wild exploration of the black line on the red ground as the pregnant belly comes front with birds that symbolize the unleashing of my repressed identities through the act of painting.

The painting of the large face and hand refers to a story that my father told me about his past. He was a child looking out of his house in Athens through shutters during World War Two, when German tanks occupied the streets. The painting also tells my story as the only child of divorce, looking out with my father's hand upon my head, our united destiny pulling me back towards family unity, a lost hope.

This painting is part of the black line series made after studies with Pedro Rafael. The black line finally takes over. It represents aspects of the parts of me that are tied to Greece. In the past, when the lines appeared, I would push them away. For the first time I allow them in.

Labor on a Warm Summer Night 2003

This painting was also part of a series done after studies with Pedro Rafael. I was interested in exploring color in a different way after seeing how he mixed the same colors and used them in different ways in each painting. I was interested in color as emotion as he had made it clear to me that color reveals the spirit of the artist.

My Father's Hand: Looking Back at the Occupation 2003

Figure 5. Two Paintings by Kryssi Staikidis

As well as going back into family histories and making sense of them through iconography, I had also learned that the way I talked about my paintings was nothing to be ashamed of. As part of my studies, Paula asked me to make a painting for her in my own style and she watched me work the way I had watched her. When I described the story of the painting I made for Paula to her, she understood what I meant. She probed me about the narrative and looked for symbols that represented parts of the story. The way that I describe my works always returns to their stories. This was accepted by my Maya teachers as the norm, not the aberration. Therefore, I found a place to exist as a visual artist within an explanatory framework that felt comfortable and familiar to me, instead of unfamiliar as it so often had in critiques amongst groups of peers in formal studio settings, where I was always encouraged to talk about form as if it were disassociated from meaning. The experience of narrative storytelling associated with art making after its completion, which is part of the Maya painting process, was pleasing to me because I recognized it. As a result, I have begun to describe my storied paintings without restraint upon returning to the States. Maya mentors taught me that our lives are the essences from which we paint, and our cultural pasts inform our lives at their deepest levels.

Sketches: Glimpses In

Then, I came up with an idea. "The woman springs out of the water, the circles of water about her feet." Paula loved that and said, "You see?" "You're learning!" We're thinking and drawing directly on canvas. (Staikidis, 2003, Fieldnotes)

As a student, I absorbed new information during the fieldwork process as well. Artists' studios, sites where informal learning occurs, become places that integrate artists' lived experiences and art making. In this way, the learning context allows for an intimacy between student and teacher that is rarely experienced in a formal classroom setting. Teaching becomes highly personalized. This kind of intimacy between student and teacher, along with the guided participation approach to teaching, coupled by the intensity and length of the lessons, enabled me to learn at a quicker pace than previously experienced. I felt cared for and attended to and became a part of the family and community. Such teaching approaches broke down walls that could have gone up due to cultural misunderstandings. I realized that the relationship with my teacher was most important as it was the vehicle for learning. As Pedro Rafael stated,

> When I have a student, I like to give them food and want them to be part of the family. And this is because I want them to feel trust. Otherwise it becomes like a school where you're given the class and you leave and you forget everything. (Personal Communication, August 2, 2003)

Pedro Rafael's comment may seem naïve to most educators whose teaching is located in schools within classrooms where leaving students with information is the method for teaching. But drawing a distinction between the act of accumulating information versus constructing knowledge becomes necessary. Pedro Rafael refers to "information" as forgettable whereas "knowledge" is retained. His meaning is clear. He implies that when relationship is not at the core of teaching, information is forgotten and knowledge construction does not take place. Relationship and trust are essential aspects of teaching, the means through which forgettable information is transformed into knowledge that is valued.

Relationship may be likened to a meeting ground that holds understandings. It might be visualized as a space created between intersecting entities with a door for entry and exit forming a common area. Trust within the relationship becomes the invisible yet powerful force which is hand built by repeated actions such as showing up, responding predictably, telling the truth, being present, and finally, embracing. It is not easy to create relationships that are instilled with trust, yet these were the converging spaces that existed between Maya mentors and me. Studying in an informal setting for the first time, I reflected upon my reactions to being cared for and how these affected my learning and self-esteem, and on a deeper level, how they affected my happiness as a learner within a community.

CONCLUSION: THE JOURNEY ACROSS CULTURES

My painting life, my ideas about teaching painting, and my ideas of what teaching can be were completely transformed as a result of learning in two Maya communities. Teaching in the home and the studio, young painters become part of the family and the fiber of a non-linear learning. As Pedro Rafael notes, only knowledge is worthy of safekeeping. Through the mentoring experience as a student, I became a teacher who thought of humanity first and teaching as part of a humanity emerging from and through community. I had associated the teaching of craft alone with formal classroom settings, isolated and apart from daily experiences. In a sense, I was alone in my learning. In contrast, the concept of community runs throughout the fabric of Maya cultures, where study becomes part of the home and the mentoring experience is not separated from caring.

My own experience teaches me that there is great potential for crossing cultures through collaborative artistic mentoring. As Paula observed one day near the end of our studies together: "Our teaching collaboration has resulted in a great friendship. We have taken part in an important interchange as women painters who have come to know and learn from each other" (Personal Communication, 2007). Artistic language in some ways transcends lines of separation when crossing cultures – artistic language can be a bridge that reaches across and through cultures. The opportunity to study with Maya painters changed my life as an artist, a student, and a teacher. This work shed light on the possibilities of artistic mentoring collaborations in communities, even for people who do not belong to those communities. Such artistic intercultural exchanges have the potential to become life changing. The painting studies that comprised this work, along with the two Maya families that I have grown to love, have been the greatest influences upon my life.

NOTES

[1] I wish to explore what might be called a *living tradition* as a process of making art that involves many aspects of community. Guillermo Gomez-Pena (1996) notes, "The indigenous philosophies of the Americas remind us that everything is interconnected" (p. 221). Art is derived from the traditional beliefs and values of the culture (Pio, 1997). An artistic living tradition involves the passing on of art that is alive in that it plays a substantial role in maintaining the group's cultural identity. Thus, art solidifies and reinforces identity (Myers, 1999).

[2] Tedlock (1991) and Lassiter (1998) have developed ethnographic models that fully embrace dialogue with "consultants" (Lassiter, p. 8), a term used to replace informants during ethnographic practice and ethnographic writing. Lassiter terms his approach "collaborative ethnography" (p. 10). Lassiter states that collaborative ethnography "with its focus on developing interpretations that are collaboratively derived and writing descriptions that are multivocal, begins to depart from traditional ethnographic practice" (p.11). Also included in his approach is the shift away from "participant observation" to the critical "observation of participation" (p. 13), so that both Self and Other are presented together within a multivocal text focused on the process and character of the human encounter.

Linda Tuhiwai-Smith (1999) advocates specific appropriate approaches for ethnographic research that can be ethically employed for non-indigenous researchers. Tuhiwai-Smith presents the mentoring model (*tiaki*) as one in which the authoritative indigenous person guides the research. The adoption model (*whangai*) posits that researchers are incorporated into the daily life of the indigenous people which eventually enables them to "sustain a lifelong relationship which extends far beyond the realms of research" (p. 177).

[3] In *The Ethnographic I*, Carolyn Ellis (2004) questions the role of the 'I' in ethnography. Is the 'I' only that of the researcher as she who stands apart and looks, or is the 'I' the part that not only looks back but is looked back at, "that not only acts but is acted upon by those in her focus" (p.xix). When the self is examined as part of the ethnographic process, work becomes relational and is about the other as well as the 'I' of the researcher in interaction (p.xix). The researcher is a subject who looks inward and outward. Ellis defines autoethnography as ethnographic inquiry that combines research, writing, story, and method, while connecting autobiographical and personal to the cultural, social, and political.

[4] *Imagined Realism* is a descriptor for the style of Mayan Tz'utuhil painting that I observed. The artists see themselves as cultural historians whose responsibility it is to create art works that will serve as accurate cultural referents for future generations who are seeking to understand the lost ways of their ancestors. Therefore, the painter is a realist – one who captures nature, people, community, tradition, customs, and ceremonies as true to tale as he can. Reality must be depicted with as little distortion as possible. However, to rely on observation, defined as rendering from nature, is not part of the Tzutuhil artistic conceptual framework. Pedro Rafael González Chavajay notes, "When one draws, one must capture the movement like a still. One must look and engrave and capture the scene in one's mind. Only then when it is engraved in the imagination is it possible to draw. Like a recorded tape, one does not have to observe over and over" (Pedro Rafael González Chavajay, Personal Communication, 2005). The realism that is depicted is imagined for it comes through prior observation, or narrative from an elder then translated from the artist's mental concept to the canvas. The intermediary is the artist's capacity to imagine, or the artist's capacity to educate his mind. The artist emphasizes the ability to engrave and retain what one observes for later use. The artist relies on his stored visual knowledge, which is readily accessed when needed to conceive of the themes of new paintings. The most challenging moment is the "thinking" out of the work before its execution. In its execution, there exists the necessity for altering the painting to fit the pre-

imagined scene. The process involved in *Imagined Realism* is the capacity to create, imagine and embellish reality based on each artist's spirituality and intuition, combined with verifiable facts generated by oral or visual narrative passed down through the generations.

[5] Sullivan (2006) believes that painting as studio practice is both a means of creative and critical investigation. He observes that art practice is a "robust form of human engagement that has the potential to reveal new insights and understandings" (p. 30). Ultimately, Sullivan proposes that art practice can be conceptualized as research, which might be directed towards both personal and public ends. Studio practice as a site for research becomes a "...*transformative* act that has an impact on the researcher and the researched" (p. 22).

[6] Sullivan (2004) notes: "During modernist times the prevailing construct was: 'to see is to know.' This was grounded in an empirical understanding based on direct experience and was mostly achieved by participation in the grand tradition of cultural tourism. During postmodern times, if we understand the constructions that shape what we see, then 'to know is to see' (Rose, 2001). Therefore there are different ways of seeing and knowing the world. The critical task is to determine the social impact of these different visions" (p. 809).

In the *Handbook of Critical and Indigenous Methodologies,* Meyer (2008) observes that the act of sensing is culturally shaped. Such differences at these fundamental levels influence epistemologies. Meyer states, "This fundamental idea that our senses are culturally shaped seems almost obvious, but it must be understood deeply if you are to proceed into what many may not understand" (p. 220). Meyer posits seven categories that help to organize systems of consciousness needed to "enliven what knowing means in today's rampage called modernity" (p. 218): Spirituality and Knowing; Physical Place and Knowing; The Cultural Nature of the Senses; Relationship and Knowledge: Self Through Other; Utility and Knowledge; Words and Knowledge; and the Body/Mind Question.

REFERENCES

Ellis, C. (2004). *The ethnographic I: A methodological novel about autoethnography.* New York: Altamira Press.

Gomez-Pena, G. (1996). *The new world border: Prophecies, poems, loqueras for the end of the century.* New York: New Museum of Contemporary Art.

Lassiter, L. E. (1998). *The power of Kiowa song: A collaborative ethnography.* Tucson, AZ: University of Arizona Press.

Meyer, M. A. (2008). Indigenous and authentic: Hawaiian epistemology and the triangulation of meaning. In N. K. Denzin, Y. S. Lincoln, & L. T. Smith (Eds.), *Handbook of critical and indigenous methodologies* (pp. 217–232). Los Angeles: Sage Publications.

Myers, F. (1999). Aesthetic function and practice: A local history of pintupi painting. In H. Morphy & M. Boles (Eds.), *Art from the land.* Charlottesville, VA: University of Virginia Press.

Pio, F. (1997). *The creation and development of a program of study derived from Ojibwe philosophy for a proposed center of learning and research in the arts.* Dissertation Abstracts International, New York University.

Rose, G. (2001). *Visual methodologies: An introduction to the interpretation of visual methods.* Thousand Oaks, CA: Sage Publications.

Smith, L. T. (1999). *Decolonizing methodologies: Research and indigenous peoples.* New York: Zed Books Ltd.

Sullivan, G. (2004). Studio art as research practice. In E. W. Eisner & M. D. Day (Eds.), *Handbook of research and policy in art education* (pp. 795–814). Mahwah, NJ: Lawrence Erlbaum Associates.

Sullivan, G. (2006). Research arts in art practice. *Studies in Art Education, 48*(1), 19–35. Reston, VA: National Art Education Association.
Tedlock, B. (1991). From participant observation to the participation of observation: The emergence of narrative ethnography. *Journal of Anthropological Research, 47*, 69–94.

Kryssi Staikidis
School of Art
Northern Illinois University

JENNY RITCHIE

BICULTURAL JOURNEYING IN AOTEAROA

INTRODUCTION

This chapter reflects on my personal journey as a Pākehā, a citizen of Aotearoa/ New Zealand of European ancestry, committed to social justice and cultural equity, particularly within education. Aotearoa is a country with two main 'peoples,' the Indigenous Māori, comprising many different tribes and sub-tribes, and the mainly Pākehā majority culture, which has also subsumed many diverse immigrant cultures. Aotearoa's history of colonisation resonates with other colonisation narratives. Māori have been resoundingly and systematically marginalised from decision-making, dispossessed of lands, and excluded from educational achievement (Jackson, 1992, 2007). Despite this onslaught, there have been countering voices from Pākehā who have protested injustices, valued Māori world views, supported Māori endeavours, and who have collaborated in generating alternatives to colonising processes (King, 1999; J. E. Ritchie, 1992).

Within early childhood education in this country, our distance from the compulsory education sectors, and our connection to grass-roots community needs, has enabled the promulgation of a curriculum committed to honouring the Māori language and culture (May, 2001). Yet the huge majority of teachers are not Māori, and our education system has not equipped them to deliver anything beyond a monocultural worldview. In my subsequent service as a kindergarten teacher, I experienced tension and distress as I sensed a huge mismatch between what was offered by well-intentioned teachers (Simon, 1996) and the lives and values of the Māori families and children who attended the kindergarten. These experiences set in place a core of critical resistance which has underpinned my subsequent academic career. As an academic I have supported teachers who have also sought alternative pathways, and have worked collaboratively with Māori and other colleagues in my research endeavours. As a mother of six I have witnessed and supported my bicultural children's educational journeys.

Positionality

During my doctoral work my supervisor, Barbara Harrison, whose lifelong experience as a non-Indigenous ally within Indigenous communities proved to be a source of invaluable wisdom, suggested that I write a section outlining my positionality as a researcher (Harrison, 2001; J. Ritchie, 2002). Despite my awareness "of post-modern concerns with authenticity and positionality," I struggled "to unravel the complexity of strands that are woven together in such an indeterminate pattern as the fabric of my life" (J. Ritchie, 2002, p. 146). I nevertheless persisted, reflecting on my privileged middle-class Pākehā background as a child of academic parents, my feelings of being an outsider in the narrow, grey world of New Zealand suburbia in the 1960s and 70s, and my career comprising two interwoven strands, those of a commitment to early childhood care and education, and decolonisation.

My choice of career as a kindergarten teacher reflected an idealistic sense that whilst working with young children the regular contact with their families would not only reinforce the learning that we were offering their children, but provide opportunities to proactively work towards social change. During my years qualifying to be a kindergarten teacher I chose additional university courses in Māori language, culture and politics. After being arrested whilst protesting against the apartheid South African Springbok Tour I was indignant that my political stance was redefined by the justice system as 'disorderly behaviour,' when from my perspective, it was the New Zealand government that was out of order in implicating our country in playing sport with representatives of a racist regime.

My initial optimism was tempered by the reality of teaching experiences in kindergartens in the 1980s. Although most of the kindergartens in which I taught had 60-65% Māori rolls, the monocultural, middle-class Pākehā teachers made absolutely no concessions to this very visible ethnic presence in terms of culturally relevant content within their programmes. Neither did they appear to attempt to connect with the Māori families, instead problematising them and their children. I often felt very uncomfortable with the comments and actions of these teachers, and sensed huge misunderstandings in their perceptions of Māori families. At one kindergarten, in an economically depressed community where many people were unemployed and workers were mostly in low-paid labouring jobs, the kindergarten head teacher made comments about the fact that "these people are never up early in the morning." She also expressed her annoyance when Māori mothers or grandmothers would come in person to see her to confirm details about the written notice she had previously sent home detailing the annual trip by bus to a zoo. She would repeatedly remark, "Why don't these people ever read their notices? It's all written down there for them." She seemed unaware of the sub-text of these parents' purposes in approaching her "kanohi ki te kanohi" (face-to-face) as the organiser of the trip, in order to form a relationship; to check her out; to see if she could be entrusted with the responsibility of caring for their treasured mokopuna (grandchild) during the planned out-of-town excursion.

At this kindergarten, the other teachers found the behaviour of one of the Māori boys very difficult. He was seen as a 'ringleader,' who would quite often initiate an impromptu haka (a chant and action performance) as a teacher was trying to settle the children for a mat-time. It was not until later, when the family invited me (and not the other teachers) to their son's fifth birthday party, that I realised that this child's mother had perceived the negativity of those teachers towards her son. My visit to his home also provided me with insight into his whānau (family) role as a demonstrator of haka to visiting tour parties. Despite these kinds of tensions,

Māori parents in this community still brought their children to the kindergarten, wanting their children to have a good start to their education.

After the 1981 Springbok tour, Māori activists had challenged the middle-class Pākehā who had protested alongside them to address the racism in our own country. When I later resumed academic studies I explored my interest in my work as a facilitator of anti-racism workshops and in the critical pedagogy of Paulo Freire (Freire, 1972; Freire & Shor, 1987). In 1990 I began lecturing in early childhood teacher education, integrating my commitment to social justice and anti-racism within this new role. In 1994 Rita Walker, my Ngāti Porou colleague, and I were contracted by Te Puni Kōkiri, the Ministry of Māori Development, to design a Māori immersion early childhood teacher education qualification. Valuable learning came from being closely involved in a project that was Māori-driven and involved wide consultation with iwi (tribes) and in te reo Māori (the Māori language). I recall the challenge from an elder that we bring our teacher education qualification out to his rural community, rather than expecting them to send their prospective teachers to reside for several years in the university town some distance away.[1]

Research Journeys: "It's becoming part of their knowing"

In 1996 I settled on a doctoral project that I hoped would support our work as early childhood teacher educators. I chose to focus on exploring ways in which our teacher education programme was addressing its stated intention of honouring Te Tiriti o Waitangi, the 1840 agreement that having assured Māori that their land, and other less tangible valuables would be protected, resulted in the colonisation of Aotearoa (Orange, 1987, 2004; Walker, 2004).

Early childhood education in Aotearoa has a progressive history (May, 1992, 1997, 2001). Despite this context of community responsiveness and rhetoric supportive of Tiriti-based commitment, my colleagues and I were very aware of the challenges we faced in preparing our teacher education students, who were primarily monocultural Pākehā, to deliver on the obligations that our early childhood sector aimed to uphold. The promulgation of our first national early childhood education curriculum, Te Whāriki (Ministry of Education, 1996), with a strong bicultural emphasis in recognition of Te Tiriti, coincided with the commencement of my doctoral research.

Whilst Māori and other Indigenous scholars are justifiably concerned about the historical track-record of the colonising nature of non-Indigenous research into Indigenous matters, there has been acknowledgement of a role for non-Indigenous allies in supporting research aspirations of Indigenous people (Bishop & Glynn, 1999; L. T. Smith, 1999). It can also be seen as an ethical responsibility for non-Indigenous people to seek pathways beyond colonisation, rather than leaving this struggle to Indigenous people alone. According to Lynne Davis, "Although insiders and outsiders may have different paths to negotiate in efforts to decolonize research, both have serious responsibilities with respect to decolonizing their own thinking, methods, and quality of relationships established with Indigenous communities and organizations" (Davis, 2004, p. 17).

In approaching my doctorate, my intention was somewhat problematic in that I needed to demonstrate the required independent, autonomous research integrity of the individualistic Western academy, and yet I also wanted to ensure that my research served the aspirations of Māori, particularly with regard to the right of Māori to early childhood education that honours their language and culture. The narrative research approach I employed relied on quality of relationships and such ingredients as mutual regard and trust, honesty, and a sense that people are cared for and about (Schulz, Schroeder, & Brody, 1997). I considered that an "ethic of care applied within a research context means that the researcher honours her relationships with participants and knows that to misrepresent their meanings would damage the integrity of both data and relationships" (J. Ritchie, 2002, p. 251).

All the participants were people with whom I had longstanding pre-existing relationships. I invited participation from a range of colleagues, Māori and Pākehā in equal numbers, whose experience I knew would inform an exploration of how our early childhood teacher education programme implemented a commitment to Te Tiriti o Waitangi, in terms of reflecting self-determination for Māori, and the sustenance of Māori values, knowledge and language. These included early childhood teacher education colleagues within the university, providers of professional development to early childhood teachers, graduates from our programme who were now practicing as early childhood educators, and students within the early childhood degree programme. In interviews I sought their stories of their journeys as people committed to both early childhood education and to Te Tiriti. In order to anchor these narratives in the realities of early childhood education contexts, I also spent time observing 13 different early childhood programmes.

A methodological response to issues of accountability, legitimacy and representation was to invite participants to be involved in co-theorising the data that they had initially contributed via interviews (Bishop, 2005; Connelly & Clandinin, 1990). It was at a final co-theorising hui (research discussion) with six Māori participants that some ideas emerged that have carried forward into our subsequent research. One was the articulation of examples of pedagogies in which the Māori language and cultural practices were 'becoming part of the knowing' and enactment of both educators and children in early childhood centres, through for example, the inclusion of Māori legends. In the following excerpt, colleagues discuss the ways in which dramatising Māori legends in the early childhood centre programme carries the deeper significance of representing Māori genealogies connecting contemporary Māori with their ancestral histories. Ariana,[2] a facilitator of professional development opportunities for in-service early childhood teachers, had described how her work supporting Pākehā teachers in an early childhood centre to include Māori legends within the programme, had led parents to request copies of these legends to read to their children at home, and how she had observed Pākehā children enacting the legend spontaneously in the playground. Ariana's colleague, Kiri, connects the use of these legends to deeper Māori constructs, manifestations of genealogical ties (whakapapa) with ancestors (tūpuna) providing sources of identity and spiritual interconnectedness (wairua).

Kiri: And it's also like seeing the face of Māori through their tūpuna, through Rangi and Papa (The Sky Father and Earth Mother who were the ancestral parents of all living creatures including people).

Ariana: The connection to that was to that whole whakapapa (genealogy). *But the thing that also came out alongside of whakapapa and understanding that wairua* (spiritual interconnectedness) *is something that you carry anyway and that that wairua is all about connecting and the connections that you make in those relationships are whanaungatanga* (family connectedness). *That's just so awesome, and the important thing is that they are actually articulating it and they are talking about moving it out beyond the staff and into their whānau.*

Kiri: Bringing Te Whāriki together.

Ariana: An indicator of that is the child role-modelling Maui (an ancestral demi-god) *out in the playground. So something really great is happening, eh. It's becoming part of their knowing. It's a natural part of it.*

Emergent from this co-theorising hui was the notion of a 'whanaungatanga approach', which prioritises welcoming and valuing of families (and in particular, Māori families), through modelling of core Māori values such as manaakitanga (caring, sharing, generosity) as an intrinsic part of the early childhood education programme. This was offered as an alternative to the individualistic, impersonal Western models that Māori participants in my research had experienced as forbidding.

Moana: Non-Māori may take the stance of "Okay, I've got this checklist of things to do – A,B,C, and keep within the timeframe," while Māori may go off and work within a collaborative whanaungatanga approach, where they achieve the same outcome, but come through different processes of getting there.

JR: Maybe we need to be helping our students look at a whanaungatanga approach?

Kiri: So it's an understanding of that philosophical base then of Māori, then isn't it? It's actually inter-weaving it alongside our practice.

Rina: It's about relationships, eh.

These Māori colleagues articulated their understanding of the centrality of relationships to their construct of early childhood education. Relationships, or whanaungatanga are an integral feature of Māori child-rearing and pedagogy. (Durie, 1997; Pere, 1982; G. H. Smith, 1995). Explaining her model of traditional Tuhoe (a North Island tribe) whanaungatanga, Rangimarie Rose Pere (1982) emphasised the components of aroha, which she defines as the commitment of people related though common ancestry; loyalty; obligation; an inbuilt support system; stability; self-sufficiency; and spiritual protection. Graham Hinangaroa Smith (1995) has observed that contemporary Māori constructions of whānau, although not necessarily kinship-based, retain traditional values such as manaakitanga (sharing and caring); aroha (respect); whakaiti (humility); and tuakana/teina (older children caring for younger).

Responsiveness, respectfulness, and reciprocity are words used within early childhood discourse to describe characteristics of effective teacher interactions (Anning, Cullen, & Fleer, 2004; Goodfellow, 2003), and which could equally be applied to a process of whakawhanaungatanga, with regard to building relationships with Maori (and other) families. Despite rhetorical best intentions, the legacy of white supremacist colonialism may continue to impinge on Pākehā teachers' willingness and facility to enact whanaungatanga. Dilemmas arising from considerations of our colonial context, its ongoing residual power effects and the racism that remains an undercurrent in our teaching and wider society are matters requiring ongoing attention. Many questions arise in consideration of how effectively Pākehā and other non-Māori early childhood educators might be supported to develop an understanding of a Māori world view, and concepts as integral as whanaungatanga, in order to apply them within their work in early childhood education settings. To what extent can (and should) non-Māori emulate qualities of 'Māoriness'? Can (and should) non-Māori early childhood educators learn to act as Māori do, in situations such as urban kōhanga reo, where modern non-kinship-based whānau have been created and operate from a kaupapa (philosophy) of aroha, manaakitanga, and whakaiti?[3]

Postmodern and sociocultural understandings around pedagogies are challenging the Western reliance on dominant discourses of developmentalism, critiquing notions of universal truths and canonical bodies of knowledge (Canella, 1997; Mac Naughton, 2005). Karen Martin (2007), an Indigenous Australian academic, has called for the decolonisation of pedagogical paradigms. She sees Indigenous paradigms as having the potential "to decolonise existing systems through processes of critiquing and reframing to provide the necessary spaces for the harmonisation of Aboriginal ways of knowing, ways of being and ways of doing" (p. 17).

A whanaungatanga approach can be seen as one such pedagogical reconceptualisation which is validating of Māori ways of being, knowing and doing. Such an approach also problematises the construct of teacher as 'expert.' As Lisa Delpit (1995) reminds us, we cannot be experts in another person's culture if we do not share that cultural background. Humility and openness are dispositions that may enable those from the dominant culture to avoid pitfalls that can easily befall those who come from an uncritiqued paradigm of 'expert.' Māori have expressed concern about appropriation of their language and culture (Mead, 1996; G. H. Smith, 1990; L. T. Smith, 1999). A genuinely respectful, humble demeanour is a counter-approach to the arrogance that has characterised the assumption of an un-critiqued right to misrepresent Māori cultural symbols and meanings (J. Ritchie, 2007). It is also a salient quality for Pākehā educators to emulate, working as we do in a context shadowed by its colonial legacy and ongoing undercurrents of racism.

Through embodying such a demeanour, Pākehā educators may sustain and maintain relationships with Māori colleagues in which colonial power effects are identified and challenged, and where space is created that enables Māori to enact advocacy and leadership in educational and research processes (Rau & Ritchie, 2003).

Whakawhanaungatanga Study

In 2004, I began co-researching with my colleague Cheryl Rau whose Masters dissertation (2002) had demonstrated the continuity of Māori values within an intergenerational whānau context. We were fortunate to receive funding[4] to further explore the notion of whanaungatanga as an approach for early childhood educators. In the Whakawhanaungatanga project we worked with a wide range of Māori and Pākehā early childhood educators, teacher educators, and providers of specialist education and professional learning services (J. Ritchie & Rau, 2006).

Our research process was a hybrid of narrative enquiry, informed by Kaupapa Māori and decolonising research and theoretical perspectives (Bishop, 2003; Clandinin & Connelly, 2000; L. T. Smith, 1999). This enabled us to give voice to the experiences of educators' enactment of practices reflective of their commitment to honouring Māori ways of knowing, being and doing. Throughout our research and writing, Cheryl's advocacy continues to ensure that Māori voices are privileged in our work (Rau, 2007). Partners in the study, again evenly Māori and Pākehā, included co-researchers from two tertiary institutions that provide early childhood education qualifications, an iwi education initiative, a Kindergarten Association, and an organisation that delivers professional learning to the early childhood sector. These co-researchers shared a commitment to what we have begun to call 'Tiriti-based early childhood practice,' that is, practice that reflects a commitment to honouring the ways of being, knowing, and doing of Māori as the Indigenous people of this land, alongside the dominant Western, Pākehā culture, as well as those of other immigrants.

Respectful relationships with the partner researchers were again intrinsic to our research journeying. Marcelle Townsend-Cross, an Indigenous Australian educator, explains that respect is grounded in connectivity: "True respect cannot occur between strangers. True respect is a deep and emotional relationship developed through understanding and connectivity" (2004, p. 5). Our co-researchers' willingness to take part in the project reflected their trust in our integrity as colleagues and researchers. Riana, a Māori kindergarten head teacher, explained to Cheryl the reasons for her willingness to join our project:

> *I don't often become involved in research project. I'm very particular about who I choose to research with and for. I've really got to believe in the kaupapa of the research and know that the input that I can have, coming from our centre is going to be put to really good use. I'm not just in there as the token Māori — quite often that's why we get offered to go into research projects. Probably one reason is because you and Jenny are both doing it. I think one of the other reasons is that I really believe in the kaupapa and I see*

huge gaps in terms of how our Māori tamariki and their whānau, but I have concerns about how Te Whāriki is actually delivered for the tamariki and for those whānau.

Penny is a Pākehā kindergarten head teacher for whom Tiriti-based practice has been a life-long commitment and journey. Penny's enactment of whanaungatanga embodies a sincere reverence in welcoming those families who choose to share their children with her. Rather than asking Māori families to contribute their knowledge to the programme, Penny explained that:

I have no expectations of what a family should or should not give us because they have gifts and taonga (treasures) *that are not mine, and there's no way that I can make them give them to us, so all we can do is make this place as warm a place as possible where they would like to spend time, and if anything comes because they're here, then that's an absolute blessing and a real treasure that they've shared. So we share what we have with them. Our joy is just that their children are here and that they're prepared to share their greatest treasure with us.*

Penny, whilst deeply appreciative of those Māori mentors who have supported her learning over the years, is mindful of the Pākehā tendency to grasp at Māori people and things in their zealousness to address the lack of Māori content in their programmes. Penny is intuitively aware of the uneven power effects Levinas describes: "If one could possess, grasp and know the other, it would not be the other. Possessing, knowing, and grasping are synonyms of power" (1987, p. 90). As part of our co-theorising process, I shared Penny's thoughts with a team of teacher educator colleagues. The immediate reflection of a Māori teacher educator was to describe Penny's orientation as one of manaakitanga – a generosity that is reflective of the obligation to care for others. This revealed the potential for Pākehā educators to enact Māori values, an enactment that is profoundly deeper than formulaic delivery of curriculum requirements. Consequently, I reframed my understandings around a whanaungatanga approach, to emphasise this generosity on the part of educators, rather than seeing the building of relationships with Māori as instrumental to gaining their input into the early childhood programme in service of Māori self-determination.

Final Thoughts

Our co-researchers have continued their journeys, and as Cheryl and I have worked alongside them we have become aware that voyage of Tiriti-based early childhood practice is not about arriving at any possible pre-determined destination. It is about the journey itself. As Lao Tzu said, "A good traveller has no fixed plans, and is not intent on arriving" (1995, p. 27). Our waka is fuelled by a shared commitment to an ethic of social justice, and our destination is the continuing project of decolonisation, rather than any conceivable point of arrival. Nor do we have the option to disembark. Lynne Davis implores us to acknowledge in our ways of being, knowing, and doing, the spiritual dimension that underlies our relationships with others, as an ethical force. "Ethics has spirit. It is this spirit of ethics that needs to break free to create ethical research relationships that escape colonization's bonds" (2004, p. 17).

For me this has meant a deepening self-conscious awareness of how I work as a researcher, a reconceptualising of my Western individualistic frameworks towards collaborative processes. These processes involve listening, hearing, and responding from an ethical stance of openness to negotiation of power relations around issues of decision-making and control (Davis, 2004). I have been mindful, as I juggle the demands of the research with my other lecturing responsibilities, along with parenting six children, of taking time to regenerate my energy in order to deliver the concentration, compassion, understanding, love, and sense of peace that will sustain me. I constantly remind myself, as Thich Nhat Hanh has written, that "patience is the mark of true love" (2001, p. 85).

As we re-story the shared narratives in our research work, we are aware of the transformative possibilities inherent in the reframing of individual narratives within the collective research waka (vehicle). We are also conscious of our power as researchers in the privileging of knowledges through selectively highlighting excerpts from the shared narratives. As Linda Tuhiwai Smith (1999) reminds us, discourse "is never innocent" (p. 36). Respect for our colleagues commits us to honouring their intent as educators and co-researchers, as we share our learning from these metaphoric narratives of wayfinding journeys. It may be possible that by re-contextualizing and re-legitimizing Indigenous knowledges as central to their ways of being, knowing, and giving voice, these educators are demonstrating a de-colonization of their hearts and minds.

GLOSSARY

Haka is an expressive, active, performance of chant and movement.
Hui are gatherings or meetings.
Iwi are tribes.
Maui is a legendary demi-god.
Mokopuna are children or grandchildren.
Rangi and Papa are the Sky father and Earth Mother.
Taonga are treasures – both tangible and intangible.
Te reo Māori is the Māori language.
Te Tiriti o Waitangi was the 1840 agreement that having assured Māori that their land, and other less tangible valuables would be protected, resulted in the colonisation of Aotearoa
Tiriti or treaty, refers to Te Tiriti o Waitangi.
Tuhoe are an iwi, a tribe, of the Urewera area in the North Island.
Tūpuna are ancestors.
Wairua is spiritual interconnectedness.
Waka are canoes or vehicles.
Whakapapa is genealogy.
Whānau are families.
Whanaungatanga is the inter-connectedness of kin relationships, and the active maintenance of these relationships.

NOTES

[1] Papers were written outlining the Māori immersion diploma (J. Ritchie, 1994a) and anti-racism with the early childhood education programme (J. Ritchie, 1994b, 1996).
[2] Throughout this chapter the names of research participants have been changed.
[3] Papers have been written on racism and other post-colonial dilemmas facing early childhood teacher education (J. Ritchie, 2003, 2005a).
[4] We wish to acknowledge the Teaching Learning Research Initiative, administered by the New Zealand Council for Educational Research for funding our study, Whakawhanaungatanga – Partnerships in bicultural development in early childhood education (Ritchie & Rau, 2006).

REFERENCES

Anning, A., Cullen, J., & Fleer, M. (2004). *Early childhood education. Society and culture*. London: Sage.
Bishop, R. (2003). Changing power relations in education: Kaupapa Māori messages for 'mainstream' education in Aotearoa/New Zealand. *Comparative Education, 39*(2), 221–238.
Bishop, R. (2005). Freeing ourselves from neocolonial domination in research: A Kaupapa Māori approach to creating knowledge. In N. K. Denzin & Y. S. Lincoln (Eds.), *The sage handbook of qualitative research* (3rd ed., pp. 109–164). Thousand Oaks, CA: Sage.
Bishop, R., & Glynn, T. (1999). *Culture counts: Changing power relations in education*. Palmerston North: Dunmore.
Canella, G. (1997). *Deconstructing early childhood education: Social justice and revolution*. New York: Peter Lang.
Clandinin, D. J., & Connelly, F. M. (2000). *Narrative inquiry: Experience and story in qualitative research*. San Francisco: Jossey Bass.
Connelly, F. M., & Clandinin, D. J. (1990). Stories of experience and narrative inquiry. *Educational Researcher, 19*(5), 2–14.
Davis, L. (2004). Risky stories: Speaking and writing in colonial spaces. *Native Studies Review, 15*(1), 1–20.
Delpit, L. (1995). *Other people's children: Cultural conflict in the classroom*. New York: The New Press.
Durie, M. H. (1997). Whānau, Whanaungatanga and healthy Māori development. In P. Te Whāiti, M. McCarthy, & A. Durie (Eds.), *Mai i Rangiātea. Māori Wellbeing and development* (pp. 1–24). Auckland: Auckland University Press with Bridget Williams Books.
Florio-Ruane. (2001). *Teacher education and the cultural imagination*. Mahwah, NJ: Lawrence Erlbaum.
Freire, P. (1972). *Pedagogy of the oppressed*. London: Penguin.
Freire, P., & Shor, I. (1987). *A pedagogy for liberation: Dialogues on transforming education*. Houndmills: Macmillan.
Goodfellow, J. (2003). Practical wisdom in professional practice: The person in the process. *Contemporary Issues in Early Childhood, 4*(1), 48–63.
Hanh, T. N. (2001). *Anger*. New York: Riverhead Books.
Harrison, B. (2001). *Collaborative programs in indigenous communities*. Walnut Creek, CA: Altamira.
Jackson, M. (1992). The treaty and the word: The colonisation of Māori philosophy. In G. Oddie & R. Perrett (Eds.), *Justice, ethics, and New Zealand society* (pp. 1–10). Auckland: Oxford University Press.

Jackson, M. (2007). Globalisation and the colonising state of mind. In M. Bargh (Ed.), *Resistance: an indigenous response to neoliberalism* (pp. 167–182). Wellington: Huia.
King, M. (1999). *Being Pākehā now. Reflections and recollections of a white native.* Auckland: Penguin.
Lao-Tzu. (1995). *Tao Te Ching* (S. Mitchell, Trans.). New York. Retrieved May 2, 2008, from http://academic.brooklyn.cuny.edu/core9/phalsall/texts/taote-v3.html#2
Levinas, E. (1987). *Time and the other [and additional essays]* (R. A. Cohen, Trans.). Pittsburgh, PA: Duquesne University Press.
Mac Naughton, G. (2005). *Doing Foucault in early childhood studies. Applying poststructural ideas.* London and New York: Routledge.
Martin, K. (2005). Childhood, lifehood and relatedness: Aboriginal ways of being, knowing and doing. In J. Phillips & J. Lampert (Eds.), *Introductory indigenous studies in education: The importance of knowing* (pp. 27–40). French Forest: New South Wales Pearson.
Martin, K. (2007). Making tracks and reconceptualising aboriginal early childhood education: An aboriginal Australian perspective. *Children's Issues, 11*(1), 15–20.
May, H. (1992). Learning through play: Women, progressivism and early childhood education 1920s-1950s. In S. Middleton & A. Jones (Eds.), *Women and education in Aotearoa 2* (pp. 83–101). Wellington: Bridget Williams Books.
May, H. (1997). *The discovery of early childhood.* Auckland: Bridget Williams Books, Auckland University Press.
May, H. (2001). *Politics in the playground. The world of early childhood in postwar New Zealand.* Wellington: Bridget Williams Books and New Zealand Council for Educational Research.
Mead, L. T. T. R. (1996). *Nga Aho o te Kakahu Matauranga: The multiple layers of struggle by Maori in education.* Unpublished PhD Thesis, University of Auckland, Auckland.
Ministry of Education. (1996). *Te Whāriki. He Whāriki Mātauranga mō ngā Mokopuna o Aotearoa: Early childhood curriculum.* Wellington: Learning Media.
Orange, C. (1987). *The treaty of Waitangi.* Wellington: Allen and Unwin/Port Nicholson Press.
Orange, C. (2004). *An illustrated history of the treaty of Waitangi.* Wellington: Bridget Williams Books.
Pere, R. R. (1982). *AKO. Concepts and learning in the Māori tradition.* Working Paper No 17. Hamilton: Department of Sociology, University of Waikato.
Rau, C. (2002). *Te Ahutanga Atu o Toku Whanau.* Unpublished Masters Dissertation, University of Waikato.
Rau, C. (2007). Shifting paradigms: Māori women at the interface of Te Tiriti (Treaty) based early childhood education in Aotearoa. *Children's Issues, 11*(1), 33–36.
Rau, C., & Ritchie, J. (2003). *Māori led partnership. A model for Tiriti implementation.* Paper presented at the 8th Early Childhood Convention, Palmerston North.
Ritchie, J. (1994a). Development of a Maori immersion early childhood education diploma of teaching. *ERIC Clearinghouse on Languages and Linguistics, ERIC Document Reproduction Service NO. ED393 291.*
Ritchie, J. (1994b). Implementing a commitment to biculturalism in early childhood training. *Australian Journal of Research in Early Childhood, 1*, 122–132.
Ritchie, J. (1996). Anti-racism education within an early childhood education diploma programme. *International Journal of Early Years Education, 4*(1), 65–84.
Ritchie, J. (2002). *"It's becoming part of their knowing": A study of bicultural development in an early childhood teacher education setting in Aotearoa/New Zealand.* Unpublished PhD Thesis, University of Waikato, Hamilton.
Ritchie, J. (2003). *Whakawhanaungatanga: Dilemmas for mainstream New Zealand early childhood education of a commitment to bicultural pedagogy.* Paper presented at the 11th Reconceptualizing Early Childhood conference, Tempe, Arizona. Retrieved March 26, 2008, from http://www.reconece.org/proceedings/ritchie_az2003.pdf

Ritchie, J. (2005a). *"It's the controlling still". Power effects in the implementation of the bicultural/bilingual early childhood curriculum in Aotearoa/New Zealand*. Refereed conference proceedings of the 1st international conference on Language, Education and Diversity. Hamilton, Wilf Malcolm Institute of Educational Research, University of Waikato.

Ritchie, J. (2005b). *Mixing our metaphors*. Paper presented in panel: Counterstories and Reconstructed Metaphors: Indigenous/Pacific Perspectives on Language, Discourse and Power in the Pacific. The 13th Reconceptualizing Early Childhood conference, University of Wisconsin Madison, WI, October 16–20.

Ritchie, J. (2007). *Honouring Māori subjectivities within early childhood education in Aotearoa*. Paper presented at a plenary session of 15th international conference of Reconceptualizing Early Childhood, Hong Kong Institute of Education, Hong Kong, December 13–17.

Ritchie, J., & Rau, C. (2006). *Whakawhanaungatanga. Partnerships in bicultural development in early childhood education*. Final Report from the Teaching & Learning Research Initiative Project. Wellington: Teaching Learning Research Initiative. Retrieved March 26, 2008, from http://www.tlri.org.nz/pdfs/9207_finalreport.pdf

Ritchie, J. E. (1992). *Becoming bicultural*. Wellington: Huia Publications.

Schulz, R., Schroeder, D., & Brody, C. M. (1997). Collaborative narrative inquiry: Fidelity and the ethics of caring in teacher research. *Qualitative Studies in Education, 10*(4), 473–485.

Simon, J. (1996). Good intentions, but... In R. Steele (Ed.), *Whakamana Tangata* (pp. 38–42). Wellington: Quest Rapuara.

Smith, G. H. (1990). Taha Mäori: Pakeha capture. In J. Codd, R. Harker, & R. Nash (Eds.), *Political issues in New Zealand education* (2nd ed., pp. 183–197). Palmerston North: Dunmore.

Smith, G. H. (1995). Whakaoho Whānau. New formations of Whānau as an innovative intervention into Māori cultural and educational crises. *He Pukenga Kōrero, 1*(1), 18–36.

Smith, L. T. (1999). *Decolonizing methodologies. Research and indigenous peoples*. London and Dunedin: Zed Books Ltd and University of Otago Press.

Townsend-Cross, M. (2004). *Respect in education - healing and cultural expression*. Keynote presentation to the Pacific Early Childhood Education Research Association 5th annual international conference and meeting, Identities and innovations: Shaping better worlds through early childhood education, 16–19 July, University of Melbourne, Melbourne.

Walker, R. (2004). *Ka Whawhai Tonu Matou. Struggle without end* (Rev. ed.). Auckland: Penguin.

Jenny Ritchie
Department of Education
Unitec Institute of Technology

COMMUNITY

DIANA MUXWORTHY FEIGE

CONFESSIONS OF A RELUCTANT PROFESSOR

In Gratitude to Service Learning

> Endangered mermaids
> Soft and sweetly gliding
> Through the concave of waves
> Calm the angry ocean.
> The manatee brings forth a peaceful end
> Surviving life,
> Enduring death.
> Perception sees a mermaid.
> Reality sees a light.

(A poem written collectively by students in response to a free-writing exercise that launches each service learning class.)

INITIAL MUSINGS

Contradictions ripple my waters. I am a loner who cherishes people's life stories; a writer frightened to expose her inner landscape; a Puerto Rican shivering in Northeastern winters; a university professor trembling in her pedagogical boots.

Halloween night a few years back a colleague asked, "What will be your costume tonight?" I paused. "I will go as myself – the Trembling, Existentially Angst-Ridden Professor." No need at all for a costume, plastic, polyester or hemp. I am the Mask. Grab my leather briefcase, hold dense, heavy labyrinths of typed, double-spaced student essays in one hand, perch the worn red pen behind one ear and I am ready to go door to door. Begging for clemency. Searching for mercy. Longing for authenticity.

A chorus of verses, laments and pleas race past my beating heart. I hear Polonius' plea, "This above all: To thine own self be true" and too easily understand Alfred J. Prufrock's laconic lament, "prepare a face to meet the faces that you meet." I quickly see Emerson's portrait of the strong, self-reliant, rugged individual and, of course, feel my mother's tender nudge, "*Mi hijita*, just be yourself." Each voice rushes past my beating heart, a cold wind stabbing a bitter October night and a brittle middle-aged heart. The costume and its sleek facade holds the weight of history. My mask is engraved with the markings of the medieval scholar, the Oxford wizard, distant, intimidating, isolated behind libraries of ancient texts, delivering expertise from behind the lectern, estranged from the glazed, glaring eyes of his awed students. It is a costume that has become a heavy cold armor. Each exhausted night I arrive home and take it off with gargantuan relief. *"Mi hijita"* now at last can come out and play.

This image of the impenetrable, impersonal authority figure is an exaggeration. But such is the power of unexamined stereotypes. And at the risk of being pitifully trite, such is the tragedy of the unexamined life. What follows is my attempt to remember my unfolding since that October night. To capture in words the slippery roads I have been traveling to unmask the mask so that I may emerge with some degree of authenticity. What follows is an inquiry into my own professional narrative. It is unabashedly reflective and personal, written in the conviction that I am not alone in the shedding of weighted stereotypes and finding validity in the resonance of stories told and patterns revealed. It is written in the belief that narrative is a critical mode of inquiry, a Moebius Loop of subjectivity and objectivity intertwined, elegant in its seamless, honest complexity. And finally, what follows is the story of liberation, a university professor out of shameful desperation, attempting to come to work each day less exhausted, more exhilarated, more a teacher.

UNFOLDING

Expertise makes me nervous. To be considered an expert in any one thing, be it how I make a decadent paella or how to nurture the knowledge, skills, and dispositions of a secondary school teacher (my assigned university task) freezes me in my tracks. The question that haunts me is: "What do I do with my expertise?" Or rather, more aptly: "What does my expertise do to me, as a teacher, scholar and learner?" The question itself reveals a covey of nagging assumptions: expertise is not innocent, expertise feeds images and defines professional roles we play whether it be in the local university community or the larger social community. Our paradigm of who the expert is impacts how the expert maneuvers his/her actions; paradigms impact praxis.

And as private as these paradigms may be, their power is no less diminished. The paradigm-fed image I carry about of the expert is my albatross. Whether it is true or false, a concoction of my own perception or a trusted, communally agreed upon verity, this image shapes my professional demeanor. In memory of Coleridge's *Ancient Mariner*, release this burden and I am free to re-imagine the teacher in the professor.

My image is that expertise assumes a certain distance between the one who knows and the one who does not know. To be a scholar immersed in the thinking, questioning and researching of a particular discipline (clearly, a necessary qualification for the professor) is concomitant to being above, beyond, out of reach with the s/he that is not sailing in that same sea of knowing. Boundaries are rigid, preferred and expected.

Yet the philosophical paradigm that sustains me contradicts this image. Other voices feed this underpinning. They are the voices of my intellectual mentors: Gregory Bateson and Mary Catherine Bateson, Maxine Greene and Deborah Meier,

Louis Schmier and Parker Palmer, Rachel Naomi Remen, and Ken Macrorie, Nel Noddings and Martin Buber, William Wordsworth and Rabindranath Tagore, Maya Angelou, Annie Dillard and Isabel Allende. On and on. Each with his/her own perspective (anthropological, epistemological, ontological, pedagogical, theological, medical, botanical, poetic). As one voice, though, sealing a resounding plea, beckoning me to emphasize the *humanity of teaching.*

The implications of this plea are enormous. They challenge the very Ground of Being. Gregory Bateson reminds me that there is no such thing as a thing, only an endless sea of interconnected relationships, a pattern that connects; his daughter Mary Catherine Bateson reminds me that lives are composed rather than planned, circular rather than linear, communal and interdependent by necessity rather than by luxury; Maxine Greene reminds me that the imagination is an integral extension of the too-often-dismissed existential dimension of learning; Deborah Meier reminds me that trust between human beings is essential to creating meaningful learning environments; Louis Schmier and Parker Palmer remind me that the inner life of the teacher is to be explored, acknowledged and validated for its power, beauty and courageous unfolding; Martin Buber and Nel Noddings remind me to care in systems/ institutions where caring is not necessarily the norm and compassion is an act of courage; Wordsworth and Tagore remind me to persist with my (hopeless) romantic idealism; Annie Dillard reminds me to see and to listen beyond the surface, each sacred acts in a sacred world; Remen and Macrorie remind me to treasure all life stories; Angelou and Allende remind me to question boundaries and keep them as permeable as possible. On and on.

Their legacy runs deeply within and perhaps I ask the impossible. Yet I am exhausted, ashamed of my own dishonesty, desperate to find peace between who I am and what I do.

SWEET RECONCILIATION

At a recent roundtable discussion with colleagues at a neighboring university, I surprised myself by candidly admitting that the primary reason I had become a service learning practitioner was utterly selfish. Survival as a professional was my motivation. Eager to find a pedagogical vehicle to re-define myself as a university professor, I turned to service learning. Perhaps here, in a pedagogy that demands curriculum and community connections, invites academic content to become alive in advocacy and action, I would be able to rip off the mask. Perhaps here I would find my-Self in the teacher and the scholar.

Dare I define service learning in one quick brushstroke (beyond saying that it is a pedagogical option that integrates curriculum and community, academics and action, service and standards)? I prefer, instead, to offer images of professor, students and community members engaged in service learning and allow the reader to emerge with his/her own impression:

Picture a cohort of university students addressing the question, "What kind of world do I want to help create?" through visual images drawn on a community mural. Imagine those same students keeping a dialectic notebook on the reading of

Elie Wiesel's *Night,* exchanged each first fifteen minutes of class. Allow days of discussion to pass grounded in free writing exercises and complementary readings (Anna Quindlen's *Homeless*, Maxine Greene's *Wide-Awakeness and the Moral Life*, Theodore and Nancy Sizer's *The Students are Watching: Schools and the Moral Contract*). A week later, those same students and their professor nail the roof of a local Habitat for Humanity home, laughing with the new homeowners, sharing lunch with all twenty volunteers. They return to class exhilarated, creating a collective montage, responding once again to the guiding, focal question. Hear the voice of one student (partial quote):

> The Students are Watching
> So I must push (my students) a lot
> Morals and learning in a classic knot
> As teacher I must realize what is possible
> Make what is demanded achievable
> I must teach my students a worthy way to live
> That to be awake is to be alive

Picture two university students with great ease facilitating a discussion in a local human rights class of eleventh and twelfth graders. They probe, "What kind of world do you want to create?" They share personal stories of how music has helped them become advocates for change. Maria takes out her guitar from behind the teacher's desk. Students are stunned. They smile. Maria sings Phil Ochs' *System of a Down*. Maria and her *compadre* Joyce hand out the lyrics of Medgar Evers' *Too Many Martyrs*. Students exchange lyrics of songs that inspire them to imagine better worlds. Together, they compose collective Found Poems from lyrics of their self-selected songs. These poems become the class anthem, collected on the Human Right's Banner that now welcomes them as they enter their classroom. Listen please to Maria's final reflections on herself as a future service learning practitioner:

> *Buddha and Me*
>
> My teacher blew in on a written forsythia, remembering April
> The cruelest month
> And I would come to rest thinking him the turtle shell below
> I thought the spring rose in his eyes
> He carried inspiration from the wreck and fed grapes of hope in poet chalk
>
> Yet humorously leans in his chair, haughtily, like the lord of certainty, dressed in red, the prince of concern, the absolute determination of significance
>
> And floats up like a broken image of hunger
> That was a teacher to me
> And now that he should be me and he my abstract notion of what teaching should be

Yet he, the symbol of my awakening I'm learning to see
His words are all around me and part of me

Because he was barely human to me

Yet my center is green and education all around for he was a vessel as I am a vessel
He floats up to me in things I can be

Tomorrow isn't such a long time and it's too quick I'll decide who I will be
And he's not the center, it's now just Buddha and me

Picture Mario, an Ecuadorian English Language Learner in a local high school, pants barely hanging on his hips, meandering into a large, cold square room. "Pappo made me come here" (the assistant principal), he says to the two university students. Mario whispers to Carlos, sitting next to him, "I am only being honest." Carlos quips, "Maybe being polite is more important than being honest." The afternoon co-curricular Empowering Book Club has begun. The high school students, guided by the two service learning students, are creating a children's book for the Mungai Foundation Children's Home in the outskirts of Nairobi, Kenya. The book is an anthology of *I Am* poems and collected childhood memories. They have titled the anthology *Soul Pieces for Kenya*. Weeks pass and Dona, one of the undaunted service learning students, helps Mario roll up his sleeves as together they dig into slippery paints and wet watercolor paper. Mario's friend runs into the room, coaxing Mario to join him. "*Vente amigo. Vamonos. Vamonos.*" (Come friend. Let's go.) Mario turns, barely looks up. "No. I want to finish." Head down and the final strokes of his *I Am* poem are completed:

   I am outgoing. I am intelligent.
   I understand that life is hard.
   I say that everyone could get out of school.
   I dream to be somebody when I'm out of high school.
   I try to play better soccer
   I hope to get a good paying job.
   I am outgoing, intelligent.

Dona writes in her final reflections, "This was a humbling moment for me.... Magic. We had won them over....We had learned to break the silence."

And I, in the midst of all this, am a provocateur. A choreographer. Nothing more, nothing less. Service learning in its demand for reciprocal learning, student voice and choice, integrated learning, collaborative efforts and civic responsibility (Berger Kaye, 2004, pp. 12-13, 37) becomes my emancipation from the lectern. I move in front of the lectern and find myself moving about, in and out of a circle of learners, in and out of the classroom's concrete walls. Roles are re-defined, expectations re-visited, pedagogical practices amended. The soul of the immigrant, the hammer and hand the new homeowner, the dreams of the destitute are the core of our inquiry. Service learning becomes more than another pedagogical option, an entrée into experiential learning; it becomes an invitation to challenge to the status quo of what teaching and learning so often are perceived to be; it becomes a call to work through the difficult re-assessment of thick, deeply engrained intellectual and professional boundaries.

RE-ENVISIONING PEDAGOGICAL POSSIBILITIES

Immediately certain words come to mind that capture the essence of these vignettes: relationships, reciprocity, community, collaboration, reflection, action, risk-taking, perseverance, courage, meaning, intimacy, trust, honesty, authenticity, exploration, awareness, wholeness...humanity. Maxine Greene (1973) writes simply and powerfully, "To teach is to engage in a profoundly human and professional responsibility" (p. 13). Teaching is ultimately a human endeavor, involving human beings in the act of becoming. To be a teacher is to act as witness to this human becoming, my own and that of my students. Being is the business of teachers; becoming is our mission, the focus of our craftsmanship. This acknowledgement of the profound humanity of teaching is what I have been so sadly, desperately missing. This acknowledgement is what service learning as a pedagogical option has given me.

The vignettes are witness to a vision of teaching and learning as being ultimately relational, more about patterns and symmetries, connections and wholes than disparate, isolated entities. And in this relational web, the expectations, roles and practices of the stereotypical classroom are re-envisioned.

EXPECTATIONS

The expectation in our service learning classroom is that we *care* for one another's learning. The "one another" is extended to the community members with whom we interact. Collaboration is the modus operandi. Partnerships are created; comfort zones are stretched so that the voice of the "other" (whomever that may be perceived to be) is heard, included, validated. The interests and skills of the participants are identified and utilized; the needs of the participants are identified and deliberate effort is made to meet those needs.

The expectation is to nurture *curiosity*. Nurture a genuine appreciation (if not hunger) for diverse perspectives. Engagement is the benchmark; questions more useful than answers. If anything, answers make us nervous. Thoughtful responses to multiple questions are far more intriguing. The earnest pursuit of doubts and queries are the risks we take. Exploration is the medium for making meaning of our learning; ambiguity is acceptable; patient and persevering flexibility of mind a prerequisite.

The expectation is to nurture *mindfulness*. The Buddhists speak of creating *sanghas*, communities of mindful practitioners, earnest seekers practicing mindfulness together. Mitchell Thomashow (2000), professor of environmental studies, muses that he thinks of his classes as *sanghas*, "temporary communities in which people can learn together by looking deeply into their lives" (pp. 12-13). To be mindful in our *sanghas*, our expectation is that we practice actively listening to one another, attending to the whispers that live silently within each other. Listening is a skill and an attitude, a responsiveness to one another. Being present is a complementary skill and disposition. Presence is perhaps the most courageous of acts, taking the risk to be attuned completely while in the process of composing one's own distinct Self.

The expectation is to nurture *transformation*. With transformation as an intent, it becomes obvious that learning involves struggle, change comes with persistence, willingness and initiative. The students repeatedly state that they want to create classrooms where "learning is fun." Within this service learning culture it is expected that this assumption will be amended: identifying and challenging one's assumptions of what is true and good is the diligent work of courageous, reflective thinkers. A caring, collaborative community develops the muscle and grace needed to embrace this remarkable, unpredictable often painful transformative process.

ROLES

If caring, curiosity, mindfulness and transformation are the expectation, then the dynamics between teacher and students, students and students in the service learning classroom must follow suit. Roles need to exemplify expectations. Paradigms defining our interactions change and how we function as a collective changes.

Teacher: It is Tuesday afternoon. Our class is preparing to go to a local soup kitchen to serve lunch to a cadre of primarily Latino immigrants. Carol asks, "Why do we have to go? Why don't those people find work and feed themselves?" A deadening silence drowns the room. We have spent hours in energetic discussions of *Night* as one document of the human struggle. We have met with a Holocaust survivor at the local Holocaust Resource Center. We have responded using a variety of modalities to the focal question "What kind of world do I want to help create?" The exclamation I hear inside me instantly is "How dare she? Idiota! De donde vino eso, mujer?!" Silence continues to breathe in the room. I tell myself to remain still. Wait. Nancy across the room responds in a sour, sarcastic tone. Carol quietly responds (and I quote recalling as nearly as possible the exact words): "I don't want to judge. I know I shouldn't, but I don't understand. I will go to the soup kitchen because I need to understand." I breathe. "That," I say to Carol and her fellow students, "is what our work together is all about." Smiles brew across the room. We wholeheartedly engage in a discussion of what it is to be open-minded (a word used so freely and unexamined) and how difficult it is to be honest with our assumptions and genuinely seek each other's perspectives.

My responsibility to the students is to be present. Tough work. Does not come instinctively. By that I mean that I am slowly learning to develop what may be considered a meditative or contemplative quality in my work – be still, beforeI jump to judgment, or even as I find myself ripping with anger and frustration, breathe. Pay attention to who is in front of me. Behold. Allow her or him to be, in their naked (figuratively of course!) Selves. Louis Schmier (1995) muses that "I truly cannot teach those whom I do not know" (p. 84). Getting to know the students is my first responsibility, designing and implementing practices and traditions that embody a culture of humanity.

Mark Engel (1972) rewards his teacher Gregory Bateson with the deeply appreciative comment, "To learn to think, you must have a teacher who can think" (p. vii). Willynilly, my responsibility as a teacher is to model dispositions of a thoughtful learner. Muddle through messy, dense, complicated, uncomfortable processes. That is my role – a fellow learner whose authority rests in the fact that I am willing to struggle through these messy processes and have some years under my belt of taking enormous leaps of faith enduring these messy processes. My authority, grounded certainly also in the expertise of a body of knowledge, lies in my willingness (and in the best of times, eagerness) to live with questions, penetrate past the easy quick answers, the superficial judgements and thrive in the quest. As Chrissy, the lost health club devotee quips, "You can't expect insights, even the big ones, to suddenly make you understand everything. But I figure: Hey, it's a step if they leave you confused in a deeper way" (Wagner, 1986, p. 39).

As teacher, my responsibility is to mentor the *sangha*. That is my role, or, more aptly, these are my multiple, intertwined roles: provocateur, mentor, observer, listener, seeker, choreographer. Hopefully more Martha Graham than Three Stooges, more Balanchine than Bergerac. Tediously, often intuitively and hopefully reflectively, I design the practices that build trust, balance freedom and structure, rigor and imagination, inviting us to interact together as a community of learners. I make effort to do this primarily in response to what I see and hear (Behold) in the students so that their voice and choice is included in the design. Trust is the heart of the *sangha*. Without trust, little movement, minimal transformation happens and genuine, thriving learning communities are non-existent.

I decided I wanted to create a learning community that would afford the students the opportunity to engage in a robust and supportive relationship with me and each other, that would allow them to cope with the challenge to grow and learn, that would emphasize self-awareness, self-development and self-expression and that would allow me to be truly *a part of the class rather than apart from it"* (Schmier, 1995, p. 27, emphasis added).

Student: Part of rather than *apart from*. The boundaries between the teacher and the student become flexible. The role of the student changes as dramatically as that of the teacher. We are co-learners, learning from each other and with each other. Another Moebius Loop of seamless interconnections is woven. In its most complete design, the boundaries of the Moebius Loop are invisible, moving rhythmically like waves in the Atlantic Ocean. "The discipline of real learning," Ken Macrorie (1988) writes, "consists of the Self and the Others flowing into each other." He adds,

> The principal reason education doesn't take better than it does is that it is a closed loop, with the knowledge and experience of the experts on one side
>
> and no way for it to flow into or over to the other side, where in darkness –

unarticulated, unreflected upon, unused – lie the knowledge and experience of students (p. 13).

The student and the teacher enter the Moebius Loop and move through it organically; the student is as much a part of his/her learning as s/he is a part of the teacher's and that of his/her fellow classmates. Macrorie admonishes, quoting Percy Shelley:

> A man to be intensely good must imagine intensely and comprehensively; he must put himself in the place of another, and of many others; the pains and pleasures of his species must become his own (p. 20).

Perhaps choreography, after all, is the most fitting metaphor. Dance is the enterprise, at its best the dancers in complete unison with one another, responding seamlessly to each other's Self.

PRACTICES

That degree of intimacy, though, takes time to nurture. I by no means claim to live in that realm of bonded unison cooperation, absolute reciprocal learning. Moments yes, here and there, but the general modus operandi is that of a fragile cooperation, on the road towards becoming this Moebius Loop. Standing together on a scaffold of a Habitat for Humanity home, the students and I build trust; engaged in peer review critiques of each other's writing, we build trust; co-teaching high school book clubs, we build trust; sharing reading response journals of *Night*, we build trust; facing the hungry Latino immigrant over a dish of *arroz con pollo*, we build trust. Caring, curiosity, mindfulness, transformation are as much expectations as they are deeds, habits of mind made visible in our habits of practice. The secret to a more humane teaching, I am slowly learning, is to muster the courage to "teach who we are" (Palmer, 1998, p. 1), making our inner landscapes visible in the pedagogy we practice. Identity and practice integrated; Self and strategies made whole.

Parker Palmer (1998) argues that "good teaching cannot be reduced to technique; good teaching comes from the identity and integrity of the teacher" (p. 10). This is so true in a vision of teaching that focuses on the humanity of teaching, the "profoundly human enterprise" that teaching is with human beings always at the center; the deeply explored inner life of the teacher guiding, inviting, choreographing that shared unfolding. But my battle I reiterate has been to find the marriage between what I am and what I do. Technique is paramount, but only when at its best it is the outcome of the hard fought battle to savor the Self.

What, then, are the practices of our service learning classroom? How is caring made visible? Curiosity nurtured? Transformation encouraged? Struggle supported? The human being in all his/her sacred complexity honored? The learning process itself in all its sacred complexity honored? The specific practices vary semester to semester but the general impulse carries across each term:

Discovery/Inquiry *as compared to delivery guides the learning, designed around essential questions that are provocative and divergent in nature.*

Ongoing reflection *as the heart and soul of this personal and professional, individual and communal inquiry*

Authentic, performance-based assessments *allowing students to direct their own inquiry, find meaning in their learning.*

Kristina called our gathering each Tuesday late afternoon a Table of Nine. That particular semester we had an unusually small covey of eight service learning students. The classroom was a large, windowless lecture room, chairs nailed to the floor. Believing that interior spaces impact culture, I re-arranged the room by bringing in one large rectangular table and gathering around it, five seats nailed to the floor and another five moveable chairs brought in from neighboring classrooms. At the center of our table was a framed picture of child reading *The Diary of Anne Frank* and occasionally a bouquet of flowers. Kristina commemorated the weekly sangha in her final reflections:

Table of Nine

Nine chairs, one table
Nine women, one dream
Attention NPR[2]
"We believe in service learning."

How can we learn from each other's experiences?
By listening.
How can literature help us understand another person?
By giving a voice.
How can I bear witness?
By speaking out.

Rachelle challenged us to
Change the Habitat for Humanity
To venture through the Night
That Mr. Wiesel so strongly advised us against.

How can tragedy change us?
By raising our awareness.
How can be we create beauty out of horror?
By doing something with that awareness.

It is our job to find that light
That shines on a place where
Loesforeribari[3] means something
When Baby Sarova is loved.

Is tolerance enough?
No.
Where does prejudice come from?
The weak.
Can people be forgiven for their actions?
God, I hope so.

Table of Nine refers to several practices that are the core of our discovery and inquiry. First, ongoing reflection: The poem is in response to a final reflective prompt asking students to identify the semester's highlights. Each class session begins with a reflective exercise, be it 1) a free-writing prompt 2) a Four Square Tool (articulating, for example, expectations, feelings, questions and concerns prior to our Heiffer International Global Village work day) 3) a Community Mural and Gallery Walk (addressing in words and drawings, for example, the simple but poignant question "What is Home?" prior to reading Anna Quindlen's essay *Homeless* and going to work at a local soup kitchen 4) a dialectic notebook shared in response to our reading of *Night* or 5) a Grab Bag Metaphor exercise in which students identify an object that metaphorically captures the essence of who they wish to be as service learning practitioners. Those metaphors become our collective wish bag, refined, deepened and broadened as the semester evolves. Metaphors have included: lighthouse, highlighter, gardener, pinecone, roadmap. Carol was a flashlight, Michael a magnifying glass, Larry silly putty, Kristina a handmade quilt.

Secondly, *Table of Nine* identifies the essential questions the learners have used as the focus of inquiry in the service learning curriculum templates they design (Examples are: Is tolerance enough? Is forgiveness possible? Of what are we afraid? What is prejudice? Who is a hero?). Using the *Understanding by Design* (Wiggins & McTighe, 2005) model of curriculum design, the students compose a unit template connecting curriculum and instruction with community-based service. Instruction is designed around a compelling, open-ended question, interdisciplinary and inquiry-based in nature. All curricular roads lead to varied responses from varied perspectives to that question. The essential questions guiding our course are twofold: "Who am I, as learner and practitioner?" and "What kind of world do I want to help create?" (borrowed from the Adelphi University/United Nations 2006 Peace Education Conference held both in Garden City, New York and the United Nations, New York City). Learners return to these questions throughout our readings, service experiences, assessments and reflective prompts.

Table of Nine also identifies the community-based experiences that are integral to the learner's transformative moments. Without them, even with its inquiry thrust, reflective emphasis and authentic performance-based assessments, the course would lack the depth of meaning it potentially holds for each student. The service, preceded and followed by research and reflection, is the venue for examining preconceived notions and stereotypes, for example, of the person without a home, the undocumented immigrant, the working poor. It is these experiences (building a home with and for a neighboring African American/Latino couple and their children or participating in a Simon Wiesenthal /New York Tolerance Center conference with New York City teachers and students) that stretch comfort zones, provoke assumptions, allow the crossing of boundaries the students don't even necessarily know they hold dear. As Maria wrote,

> Mr.(—) was the first Holocaust survivor I have met. I must admit that I was still in denial that he actually experienced the Holocaust, but then seeing the markings on his arm provided shocking proof...I did not know how to react...

> My experience in this class was nothing I expected. I didn't expect to grow and learn so much as a school practitioner and as a person. It is an experience I will never forget.

Or as Alice wrote,

> One experience that opened my mind was the Suffolk County Farm visit. The program (hunger simulation and work in the cornfields) introduced me to new ways of thinking about geography and the environment as well as the work of an agrarian lifestyle. I realized how different my lifestyle is from that, but also how similar I am to all people in terms of having physical and emotional needs and finding joy in interacting with people and animals.

Or, as Carol wrote (a poignant follow-up to the previously told story of Carol questioning why she should help "these people" at the soup kitchen),

> ... I always pictured the people being dirty, smelly, and sometimes even rude. ...when I walked in everything was organized buffet style....I quickly got into the hang of things...To my surprise, the people were nothing like I imagined. I served children workers and people who could be anyone's grandparents....I became eager to do more. I spent time with a man who was regular at the kitchen and helped him pack the things he needed before he left. I'll never forget how they all said thank you.... [I grew] as a learner because this encouraged me to stretch my boundaries and introduce myself to new opportunities.

The image of Carol, in her immaculate outfit and manicured nails, bending over to help Bill (the Inn's guest) with his crutches and heavy packages, is engrained in my heart. It is one of those moments when I as a teacher stand still in absolute delight. My ship has come in, full throttle, sails gallant to the wild winds.

Throughout this inquiry, reflection and service experiences, the students become a collective. Assessments build on that shared learning. Peer review is key to this collective process. Learners form writing circles as they revise and edit their I-Search papers, narratives that reveal the intellectual and emotional, professional and personal roads they have traveled in search of responses to purposeful, self-selected questions. Learners become writing partners as they revise and edit their articles for the university student paper or mini-grant proposals submitted to regional service learning funding networks. Checklists and rubrics are offered or created together to guide these revisions. Students conference privately with me to receive feedback prior to submitting assessments; students are encouraged to revise their assessments once a grade with further detailed feedback is given.

Other assessments include the *Inside the Service Learning Classroom* interviews (modeled after *Inside the Actor's Studio* television format) we hold with a panel of service learning practitioners in order to unpack the craft of service learning. Students also work in pairs as service learning practitioners in local schools and non-profit organizations. They facilitate Memoir Circles with high school students, helping these adolescents transform treasured moments in their life-stories into vibrant, artistic children's books for orphans in Kenya (described previously). They tutor immigrant children in the local Hispanic Counseling Center, lead Homework Helpers' programs in several local middle schools, participate in New York City high school programs mentoring terminally ill children and dancing with deaf children. Together they design activities for their respective students; assess their students' growth and accordingly revise the planned instruction. Together they laugh and cry, amazed at how scared they are the first few times they lead these children in the planned activities. "I never imagined I could have worked with someone like Larry. We are SO different. But we had so much fun together, playing off each other differences," Nancy laughed as she, Larry and I walked away down the hall after the last celebratory class session. Together they find the courage to face the unknown, within themselves and outside of themselves. It may be an act that for one person seems a small feat, but for another is huge, transformative:

> ... this class (provided me) with the encouragement as well as comfort and support that made me feel ready to take risks and try new things.... I took the risk of socializing. I'm a very socially anxious person and I usually take the easy comfortable route of avoiding interaction with my classmates. I always want to interact more, but it scares me. The atmosphere in this class allowed me to take that risk and I feel very proud and happy about the results....I am proud of myself and thankful to (my classmates) for giving me the courage to do that.

Or it may be a less tangible act, yet equally huge, transformative:

> My experience at (—) High School taught me that who I am is not hidden behind the nice clothes, heels and a portfolio. Who I am is present from the first moment I walk into the classroom...I have to know who I am and what I represent while facing my fears in becoming a teacher....

FINAL MUSINGS

Challenges persist. The pesty, itchy romantic idealism that does not leave me alone is both friend and foe. But I keep scratching away at that pesty itch, searching for ways to build that Lake Isle of Innisfree in my heart and in our classroom. Grading, for instance, in the context of desperately wishing to nurture trusting, genuinely collaborative, transformative learning environments is one persistent challenge. It is one of those so deeply engrained schooling habits that it is difficult for any of us in the United States to imagine a classroom setting without it. Goes along with overstuffed backpacks, bells ringing every 42 minutes, Friday spelling quizzes, proms and noisy cafeterias. The challenge in the context of emphasizing the humanity of teaching is to find ways to make grading a part of the humane learning experience for both teacher and learner.

Meier (2006) writes, "You cannot use the coach or expert well if he or she is also judge and high executioner" and continues, "getting a good grade, after all is getting the teacher to think you know more than you do" (p. 506). Getting good grades is a part of the game that keeps the teacher and student *apart* rather than mutually *a part* of the learning process. The numerical grade is that carrot held before the student; I want the satisfaction of growth and transformation to be that (intrinsic) carrot. Detailed feedback, copious critique and evaluation, high expectations, demanding assessments, the pain of stretching one's intellectual muscles – all of these are part of the compassionate classroom. The challenge is to find ways to attach a meaningful numerical grade to that qualitatively organic and demanding process.

Criteria checklists and rubrics have been helpful, especially when they have been designed with the students. Revision of submitted assessments once detailed feedback has been offered has helped as well. One-on-one writing conferences between myself and the students have been invaluable. The trust we build nailing roofs together, the discomfort we face meeting the Holocaust survivor, the laughter we share drawing community murals, the writing muscles we patiently carve composing *Soul Pieces for Kenya* ... each of these enliven the context in which the numerical grades are earned. Yes, with trial and error, venues are emerging that allow me to believe that a redemption of grading may be possible. Like a pesty itch in the corners of my back, I will keep scratching.

In the meantime, like Maria, I search for the Buddha in me. Like Dona, I treasure those awesome moments when together the students and I break our silence. I bow in gratitude to the muses of service learning who allow me to hope at long last that "Mi hijita" may come out and play in the classroom. The mask is off. I am forever grateful.

NOTES

[1] *Service Learning and Composition* is a required course for Grades 7-12 English Language Arts future teachers in the Adelphi University Ruth S. Ammon School of Education teacher preparation program. Students also may register from other teacher certification areas such as social studies, mathematics, languages and the varied sciences. To date, the students in this course have been primarily Caucasian women, with a growing number of Latino and African American men and women. It is this course specifically that is the heart and soul of this confessional chapter.

[2] *NPR* stands for *National Public Radio*. The student poet is referring to a class assignment in which the students compose *This I Believe* statements submitted to NPR. These statements are brief essays identifying their core values through narrative and exposition. Each week, NPR selects one *This I Believe* statement to broadcast as read by the *This I Believe* author. The students and I remain hopeful that someday soon one of the student's statements will be the one selected.

[3] In "Table of Nine, "Loesforeribari" refers to a poem shared in class written by a New York City teacher to her second grade student for whom "Loesforeribari" was the child's (phonetic) way of communicating that "Love is for everybody." We begin our service learning classes with free writing exercises; often poems written by local poets serve as exemplars of what is possible when the muse inspires and the pen is readily at hand.

REFERENCES

Berger Kaye, C. (2004). *The complete guide to service learning*. Minneapolis, MN: Free Spirit Publishing, Inc.

Engel, M. (1972). In Bateson, Gregory (Ed.), *Steps to an ecology of mind*. New York: Ballantine Books.

Greene, M. ((1973).Wide-awakeness and the moral life. In *The teacher as stranger: Educational philosophy in the modern age*. Belmont, CA: Wadsworth Publishing.

Macrorie, K. (1988). *The I-search paper*. Portsmouth, New Hampshire: Boyton/Cook Publishers.

Meier, D. (2006). Reinventing teaching. In A. Sadovnik, P. Cookson, Jr., & S. Semel (Eds.), *Exploring education: An introduction to the foundations of education* (3rd ed.). New York: Pearson Education, Inc.

Palmer, P. (1998). *The courage to teach*. San Francisco: Jossey-Bass.

Quindlen, A. (2001). *Homeless*. Re-printed (2008). Miami, FL: Dade-Monroe Teacher Education Center/Middle School Lesson Plans, Homeless Resources.

Schmier, L. (1995). *Random thoughts: The humanity of teaching*. Madison, WI: Magna Publications, Inc.

Sizer, T., & Sizer, N. (1999). *The students are watching: Schools and the moral contract*. Boston: Houghton Mifflin Company.

Thomashow, M. (2000). The sacred learner. *Antioch New England Graduate School Bulletin*. Keene, New Hampshire: Antioch New England Publications.

Wagner, J. (1986). *Signs of intelligent life in the universe*. New York: Harper and Row, Publishers.

Wiesel, E. (1986). *Night*. New York: Bantam Books.

Wiggins, G., & McTighe, J. (2005). *Understanding by design* (2nd ed). Alexandria, VA: Association for Supervision and Curriculum Development.

Diana Margaret Muxworthy Feige
Ruth S. Ammon School of Education
Adelphi University

DONNA GRACE AND RHONDA NOWAK

PLACE-CONSCIOUS LEARNING

Bringing Local Culture and Community into the Curriculum

On a recent sunny, breezy morning in Hawai'i, I entered a second grade classroom to visit one of my student teachers. She was concerned about the scripted reading program the school was using and asked me to observe a lesson. As I sat down in the back of the room, the lesson began with a group recitation of the "rules" for the 'oi/oy' sound. The children were then asked to define the 'oi/oy' words from their spelling list, on which they would be tested at the end of the week. Following this, the students opened their language arts text books to a story about squirrels. They were instructed to take turns, each orally reading a paragraph of the story, going child by child, row by row around the room. The children had already read this story with the teacher the day before, and would read it again a third time the following day.

As the reading commenced, some children stumbled and struggled through their designated paragraph. Others spoke so quietly, it was almost impossible to hear. Another lost her place and had to be reminded to follow along in the text with her finger. Apart from the reader, the majority of the children looked bored, distracted, and disengaged. The story about squirrels had little meaning for the children, since these animals do not live in Hawai'i. The quality of writing was dry, factual, and uninspiring. Following a question and answer period about squirrels, the children moved on to silently complete the accompanying workbook pages. I wondered what the children were learning during this time, other than to dislike reading.

As language arts faculty members, in the College of Education, at the University of Hawai'i, Manoa (UHM), Rhonda and I (Donna) shared mutual concerns about the impact of the No Child Left Behind Legislation, implemented in the U.S.A in 2002, on the literacy curricula in Hawai'i's elementary school classrooms. We became increasingly disturbed by the simplistic, pre-packaged, scripted curricula we saw being implemented in many public schools. With ever-increasing time and attention being paid to testing, accountability and a narrowing of the curriculum, literacy instruction was being reduced to drill and practice, low level thinking skills, and the robotic repetition of teachers' pre-scripted instruction. In the process, many important areas of students' lives and learning were being ignored, including children's abilities to question texts, consider multiple perspectives, make connections between their in and out-of-school interests and experiences, engage in inquiry, explore and debate ideas, and to think critically about the world in which they live.

During this time, Rhonda and I were also participants in a faculty reading group where we read and discussed books on varying topics about which we wanted to learn more. Critical place-based pedagogy was one of these topics. As we read, we resonated with the view of critical place-based educators who argued for curricula that supported students in developing and practicing skills, strategies, and habits of mind/action that enable them to actively participate in a democratic society and to become more thoughtful stewards of the Earth's resources; to become aware of and appreciate the physical, cultural, historical, and spiritual characteristics of the community that surrounds them. What makes it unique? What makes it special? What problems can be identified, and how can we work together to solve them? Such critical and creative engagement with one's local place is typically lacking in the current view of education that seeks to prepare students to work and function in a consumer-oriented society where they "learn to earn."

In contrast, we learned that the aim and intent of critical place-based education is to prepare children and youth not only to sustain the cultural and ecological integrity of the places they inhabit, but also to critique relations of power within these spaces. As we read and discussed the literature on this topic, it was clear that critical place-based pedagogy offered a much-needed move away from a standardized, generic curriculum, toward teaching and learning practices that value diversity, community, and the uniqueness of particular geographical places and the people who inhabit them. Differing from traditional place-based inquiries that typically focus on the environmental and native aspects of place, critical place-based pedagogy considers the importance of immigrant as well as native perspectives, and emphasizes the interrelationships among environmental, socio-cultural, economic, and political aspects of place. We appreciated the promotion of holistic and systemic thinking, problem posing, and problem solving, and began thinking about how we could incorporate this approach into our teaching.

Despite the potential benefits of critical place-based pedagogy, it was clear from our review of the literature that specific classroom practices that actualize this approach remain in a fledgling state (Brooke, 2003; Gruenwald, 2003; Gruenwald & Smith, 2008; Haymes, 1995). Thus, inspired by our readings and discussion on this topic, Rhonda and I joined together in an inquiry project with the intent of exploring the value and challenges of integrating critical place-based theory and practice into the graduate courses that we teach. For Rhonda, this took place in a week-long course in a summer 2007 Inquiry Institute co-sponsored by the Hawai'i Writing Project (an affiliate of the National Writing Project, U.S.A.) and the College of Education at UHM. I incorporated critical place-based pedagogy in a 2007 Media Literacy course in the graduate department of Curriculum and Instruction. In both our projects, we implemented the instructional model for place-based critical inquiry (PBCI) developed by Rhonda. Figure 1 depicts the model's five recursive teaching and learning phases: Connect, Wonder, Construct, Act, and Reflect. Collaboration is an essential component of the PBCI process. In the following we share the insights, "ah ha's," and enigmas that we experienced as we embarked upon this journey.

RHONDA'S STORY

Kapi'olani Park is nestled at the base of Diamond Head crater in Waikiki, on the island of Oahu, in the state of Hawai'i. Perhaps one of the most photographed landmarks in Honolulu, the extinct volcano towers over the park like a sentinel. In contrast, it's the local residents who primarily make use of the 100-acre park named after Kapi'olani, consort of King David Kalakaua (1874-1891). Residents spend relaxing weekends picnicking under the park's plentiful shower and banyan trees, attending a concert at the Waikiki Band Shell, or watching their children play soccer in one of the playing fields. Few residents, however, spend much time thinking about the park as another kind of playing field – one that has hosted a succession of social and environmental controversies since the park was dedicated "to the people" by the "Merrie Monarch" in 1877 (Weyeneth, 2002). Such controversies include recreational versus passive use of parkland, commercialism on park grounds, and preservation of historical sites.

It was at Kapi'olani Park on a warm, windless morning in summer 2007 that I first met with a dozen kindergarten through high school teachers to explore inquiry-based teaching and learning. The teachers represented some of the racial diversity of Hawai'i, including Asian, Pacific Islander, Caucasian, and mixed-race ancestry. Half were locals, born and raised in Hawai'i, while the other half were from various states on the mainland who had lived in the islands for varying lengths of time. They ranged in classroom experience from two to twenty-five years and worked with children and adolescents in a range of school settings. Two teachers worked in private Christian schools, one worked in a privately endowed school for Hawai'ian and part-Hawai'ian children, and the rest worked in public schools in rural, suburban, and urban communities throughout O'ahu and the Big Island.

The inquiry institute is an advanced program offered jointly by the Hawai'i Writing Project and College of Education at UHM. It is intended to support teachers in practicing and then fostering students' critical thinking through place-based inquiry, while also meeting state literacy standards. Based on their program applications, teachers were interested in the inquiry institute because they were looking for ways to move writing in their classrooms toward more authentic and meaningful purposes. As one high school teacher wrote:

> I am interested in inquiry for teaching and learning because with my kids, I need to start with what they know and what they may be interested in finding out. It's important for them to feel some ownership and take the lead and responsibility for what they learn, with guidance from me. It seems that asking questions is how we make sense of the world we live in, and could be a more interesting way to go about learning for my students.

My intention was to spend the week examining ways to practice purposeful reading and writing in the context of inquiry; however, I also wanted to introduce the teachers to a conceptual basis and instructional model for integrating inquiry into a larger context of critical place-based pedagogy (Gruenewald, 2003). I wanted the teachers to become familiar with an alternative direction for teaching and learning that questions the traditional isolation of schooling from community life

(Gruenewald & Smith, 2008). Figure 1 depicts the instructional model for place-based critical inquiry that I used for the summer institute.

There were sure to be challenges within the constraints of a weeklong institute. However, the teachers and I were going to continue our collaborations through distance education the following fall as they designed and implemented action research projects. Hopefully, they would incorporate elements of place-based critical inquiry with students in their classrooms and then study how students responded to such a curricular approach. First, though, it was important for teachers to learn about place-based critical inquiry themselves.

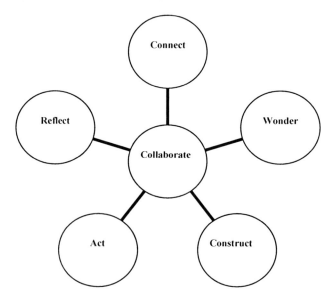

Figure 1. Place-based critical inquiry process

Kapi'olani Park turned out to be an excellent choice for introducing teachers to the concept of "making the familiar strange" through place-based critical inquiry. All of the teachers had visited the park before, some of them on several occasions. During the Connect phase when teachers considered and discussed their background experiences and knowledge of the park, one teacher wrote:

> I have had many experiences at Kapi'olani Park, especially because I used to work at Waikiki Elementary, which is right nearby. Last year, I walked my students through the park on our way to and from the Aquarium. I have also enjoyed walking and biking around the park for exercise.

Yet, teachers were less knowledgeable about the potential for using the park as a point of entry into an inquiry project that could evolve into an examination of geographical, environmental, historical, sociocultural, political, and/or economical issues. I wanted the teachers to use a critical lens to think about the forces that have combined to shape the physical landscape of the park as well as its social and environmental policies. In essence, I hoped they would "celebrate and critique local place" (Brooke, 2003, p. 63).

One purpose for the Connect phase is to build initial background knowledge about these various possibility spaces for studying the park, so I created and played a slideshow that depicted a mosaic-like perspective: the Victorian bandstand, trash overflowing from bins, an art show, tourists with cameras, flowering trees, homeless people, man-made ponds, lacrosse games, and traffic. I intentionally designed the slideshow without printed text to allow the teachers to formulate their own interpretations of the park through the visual images. The slideshow supported the teachers in thinking about the park as something more than a place for recreation or peaceful interaction with nature. These connections led to richer explanations on their inquiry think sheets about why the park is important to them and to others in the community. After viewing the slideshow, Jeannine added:

> The park is also important for many homeless people, as it is their home. Rhonda shared a picture of a man who cares for one section of the park. So, maybe some people feel some kind of love or emotional connection to the park.

We then moved on to the Wonder phase of the place-based critical inquiry. The overarching purpose for this phase is to use background knowledge to generate initial wonderings about the park, which are subsequently shaped into the selection of an inquiry topic and inquiry questions. The teachers embarked on a "wonder walk" through the park, prior to which we discussed the importance of noticing details and jotting down observations in their field journals using multiple senses. When the teachers returned from their wonder walk through the park, several of them expressed surprise about all they had never noticed before. In some cases, these surprises led to their inquiry topic. Later that day, we used our multisensory observations and notes to create Five Senses poems. Debbie became intrigued with the old-fashioned lampposts in the park. Here is her poem and accompanying visual image:

Figure 2. Lamppost in Kapiolani Park

Lamppost in the Ironwoods
Dark green, straight and elegant,
Ornate and proud,
Strong and silent,
It stands
Trying to blend in, but failing,
Delicate, yet substantial,
Exquisite, yet straightforward,
Side by side with ironwoods
Swaying gently in the breeze.
It stands
As man's attempt
To illuminate a dark world.

One challenge several teachers encountered during the Wonder phase was developing critical inquiry questions about the park. After the teachers noted their questions on the inquiry think sheets, we analyzed the kinds of questions they raised. Almost all of the questions were what Barell (2003) calls "gathering" questions for which teachers expected to observe, describe, and accumulate information about their inquiry topics. I wanted the teachers to move beyond gathering questions to include "processing" questions that would lead them to make their own interpretations. Even further, I wanted teachers to pose "applying" questions, which would help them to shift their thinking toward more critical analysis and to use what they learned to take action.

I felt it was important for the teachers to understand that the questions they posed at the outset of their inquiries would have a great impact on the direction in which their projects would go. Their inquiries could end up being just another fact-gathering exercise. Hopefully, their revised questions would lead to deeper more critical inquiries about Kapi'olani Park and the people, places, and politics connected to it. Tammy, for example, had initially noted her curiosity about the history of the parkland. After we discussed the different levels of questioning, she also wondered,

> What are some of the political issues and controversies associated with the park? The walk got me thinking a lot about assumptions with the word "park" (usually positive) in comparison to some of the issues (i.e. recreational open space vs. preservation of urban open space, or burial grounds).

Next, we explored the idea of texts as artifacts (Pahl & Rowsell, 2005) that could include print, digital, image, sound, and motion based modalities. I asked the teachers to locate and use at least three different types of informational resources for their inquiries about the park. The last activity within the Wonder phase involved teachers in making predictions about possible challenges they would encounter during their inquiries. I was surprised to learn that some teachers felt intimidated by using people in the community as informational resources. Some of this was due to time constraints; however, teachers also felt reluctant to tap into community knowledge because they were uncomfortable with approaching officials. As one teacher wrote,

> I think there is one member of the Kapi'olani Park Preservation Society whose job is to manage/care for the trees. I would like to call him and ask him some questions but I am going to be reluctant to do it because I am shy to talk to him.

The Construct phase of the inquiry process began the following day. The purpose of this phase is to construct personal meaning about selected inquiry topics through critical analysis of informational resources. We discussed the exploratory nature of inquiry – how arriving at answers to their questions was not as important as using their questions as a starting point, and then staying open to new directions that might present themselves along the way. I reminded them of Parker's (2007) advice:

> Often, you may not find an answer to your initial question, the one that started the inquiry; but that question can lead you to a world of new questions, and that is its primary importance...As Judith Lindfors says of inquiry, "Exploring, not answering, is central." (p. 3)

In the current educational climate where knowing the right answers is so highly regarded, it is easy to understand why some teachers were uneasy with the ambiguity of the inquiry process. However, the most important community problems are messy ones, with ill-defined origins and even murkier solutions that require a collaborative and process-oriented approach.

Within place-based critical inquiry, analysis of text shifts from merely summarizing information to critically evaluating it in terms of usefulness, credibility, and underlying agendas explicitly or implicitly set forth by the authors. I hoped through their experiences with place-based critical inquiry, the teachers would come to challenge the notion that informational resources provide unbiased facts and would recognize, instead, that all authors write subjectively from their own worldviews. Thus, it is important for readers to question what other worldviews are not represented in the text.

Most of the teachers were unfamiliar with practicing this type of critical reading, an approach Freire and Macedo (1987) call reading the word and the world. To support them in this process, teachers analyzed and critiqued their informational resources by responding to questions such as the following: What were the social, economic, and political events happening at the time this text was written that shaped the information in it? Who is providing this information? What are their values and perspectives? What do they have to gain from providing the information this way? Who are others who might have different perspectives? How are they positioned in this text? Where might information from other perspectives be found?

Teachers found the process of critical analysis time-intensive, yet thought provoking. Takyin said she spent hours at the library and on the Internet searching for information about the Waikiki Shell from differing perspectives. She critiqued one of her resources, a letter to the editor in the Honolulu Advertiser:

> [This is] probably someone from the community who does not want the taxpayers' money to go to waste since the [Band] Shell needs to be maintained even though it's not providing revenue for the city. It could also be one of the vendors taking part in the show. This person would want to encourage others to come to the show to gain profit for his/her business.

Takyin also considered opposing perspectives:

> People who are not in favor of the commercialism of Kapi'olani Park would not agree with this article.

Some teachers, like Takyin, used their critical evaluations of the informational resources to develop a richer, more complex, synthesis of key ideas across texts. We used a synthesis sheet to organize recurring concepts, conflicting information, surprises, and new questions. This last writing activity within this phase led naturally to considerations about how to articulate our meaning making to others during the next part of the inquiry process.

During the Act phase, my intention was to support teachers in recognizing writing as a form of action within place-based critical inquiry. Even further, I wanted teachers to position their inquiry texts within a framework of place-conscious praxis – using reflection and action to transform the world around them (Freire, 1970). This proved to be a difficult task within the time constraints of the summer institute, yet it was valuable to discuss how the teachers' writing could serve the larger community by building citizens' understandings about the issues surrounding Kapi'olani Park.

Some teachers interpreted this charge more literally and produced, for example, an informational slideshow for children featuring animals at the park's zoo, and a brochure about trees in the park that could be used by community residents as a walking guide. Other teachers took a more critical stance. For example, Debbie created a slideshow in which she challenged the city's actions of erecting a new bandstand and installing man-made ponds in the park without first conducting an environmental study or soliciting input from community residents. On one slide she wrote:

> The city's attorneys claimed that the pond built in 2000 was considered landscaping under the 1983 Master Plan. Is the city going to continue not to solicit public opinion or environmental assessments in the planning process for future projects?

Kim wrote a poem in which she critiqued placement in the park of a burial mound for Hawai'ian ancestral remains uncovered during the development of Waikiki:

Kähi Häli`a Aloha
The place of loving remembrance
Nestled in the heart of Waikiki

Forgotten in plain sight
Trapped in a prison – surrounded by commercialization
Signs of disrespect:
"DO NOT LEAVE TRASH ON WALLS"

"DO NOT CLIMB ON ANY PART OF BURIAL MOUND"
Byproduct of ongoing excavation and construction
Meant to dignify and honor
Smell and taste the salty spray of the sea and tears
Kähi Häli`a Aloha
The place of loving remembrance

Jocelyn combined images and a poem for two voices with which she criticized long-standing neglect of the Natatorium (a memorial built in 1927 in honor of servicemen from Hawai'i who were killed in WWI). Part of the poem reads:

I am the Natatorium
War Memorial   corroding
Olympic   crumbling
Ocean-fed saltwater
                                cracking
Swimming pool
- 2400
- witnessed Duke, Buster, Johnny Wesmueller
      Remember me
      Fix me

Christine created a mini-documentary in which she examined the history and economical feasibility of the Dillingham fountain located at one end of the park. She noted:

> In 1967, the fountain cost $55,000 and took three months to build. In 1997, it cost $400,000 to restore and six months to finish. Currently, the fountain costs about $6,000 a year to upkeep. Would Louise Dillingham approve of the money being spent on the fountain? Do you?

After the teachers shared their inquiry texts during the last day of the summer institute, we engaged in reflective dialogue about Kapi'olani Park and the place-based critical inquiry process. During the Reflect phase, teachers identified overarching issues related to various aspects of the park and brainstormed how these issues are connected to more global concerns. One teacher wrote,

> The theme of historical significance/preservation comes up whenever anyone proposes changes and/or development in an area. This theme connects to the global issue of preserving historically significant sites. Controversy also surrounds all of the decisions that are made about historical sites. There are always people with differing views that are passionate about their beliefs.

Not surprisingly, a recurring theme among the issues that were raised involved power relationships among various stakeholders associated with the park. Teachers now asked questions such as the following: What other social-environmental controversies are occurring at the park? How have these controversies come to be?

Who is allowed to make decisions about the park, and who is not invited to the table? Whose interests are best served by this arrangement? What other, more equitable, arrangements might be forged by an informed citizenry? I hoped these kinds of questions would become a habit of mind for the teachers as they continued to explore local places, people, and politics through critical inquiry with their students.

We had come full circle in our place-based critical inquiry process. Now, and rightfully so, we left the summer institute with more questions about our inquiry topics and place-based education than what we had started with. But these wonderings were different. They reflected a deeper understanding about the possibilities a place-based critical pedagogy holds for supporting students in connecting their literacies to the world around them. Rather than seeing Kapi'olani Park, or any park, as merely a place to spend time on the weekends, the teachers recognized the potential of using familiar community settings as a way to engage their students in meaningful cross-curricular inquiry. They were excited about the deeper levels of learning they could foster if they and their students became more knowledgeable about their own communities, and then used these funds of knowledge to reflect on the ways in which local issues represent microcosms of universal concerns. Susan wrote,

> As the park reflects Hawai'i's own problems, it also mirrors global issues: pollution, homelessness, tourism, commercialism, and racism. For example, we saw lots of litter in the park, which brings up issues of people feeling connected to their communities so they will take care of the land. It also brings up the whole issue of global warming and how the greenhouse effect is increasing because people continue to allow waste to affect our atmosphere.

Importantly, the teachers' reflections showed they also recognized that place-based critical inquiry provides a much-needed space in the school curriculum to develop students' voices as informed community members and the leaders of tomorrow. After the teachers shared their inquiry presentations and we discussed common themes among their inquiry topics, Jennine noted,

> There is always tension between the 'old days' and the present. How can that tension be alleviated or lessened? From the presentations, I would argue that the greater voice that diverse community members have in the process of change, the happier the community will be in the end because more of the stakeholders will have contributed input.

As I think back on the challenges encountered and the insights that were formed during the inquiry institute, the importance of collaboration stands out. Many of the teachers commented on how much they benefited from the opportunity to build their understandings with others, even during the short time we spent together in the institute. In fact, some of the teachers decided to focus on increasing student collaboration as their action research project in order to lay the foundation for inquiry in their classrooms. At first, I was a little disappointed that they did not feel ready to implement more of what they had learned in the inquiry institute.

However, I realized that collaboration is at the heart of inquiry, just as it is at the heart of community involvement and active participation in a democratic society. I am encouraged by the teachers' willingness to step outside of their scripted school literacy programs and engage students in authentic conversations about local people, places, and politics. I believe these conversations inspire the kind of critical thinking in the service of community *kuleana* – responsibility - that our state standards, standardized curriculum, and standardized tests cannot adequately achieve.

DONNA'S STORY

> February 19, 2007, Honolulu – A violent road-rage altercation between Native Hawai'ians and a white couple near Pearl Harbor…is provoking questions about whether Hawai'i's harmonious "aloha" spirit is real or just a greeting for tourists. (*USA Today*)

According to the 2005 Census Bureau report, Hawai'i is the most ethnically diverse state in the nation, with no ethnic majority. The population consists of a unique mix of Hawai'ians, part-Hawai'ians, Filipinos, Koreans, Micronesians, Japanese, Chinese, Okinawans, Caucasians, African-Americans, Hispanics, and others. We have the highest percentage of residents listing themselves as being of more than one race, and approximately one in two marriages are inter-racial. Considering this, Hawai'i, in many ways, is a model of racial tolerance and acceptance. Rates of murder and other violent crimes are low, and incidents such as the one described at the beginning of this story are not common. Although road rage incidents occasionally occur, visitors are always surprised at the courtesy shown by most Hawai'i drivers to one another. For the most part, people of different ethnic backgrounds exist side by side, treating one another with respect and aloha. However, racial tensions exist, and Hawai'i is not necessarily the happy "rainbow society" that it is perceived to be. Race and ethnicity are important components of identity and social relations in Hawai'i and often trigger preconceptions and stereotypes.

Distinctions are often drawn between locals - primarily non-whites who have been born and raised in the islands, and non-locals - particularly military personnel and other whites or African-Americans from the mainland. Anti-western sentiments have a lengthy history in Hawai'i, due to the involuntary nature of Hawai'i's incorporation into the United States, the deleterious impact of western contact on Hawai'ians, and the subordination and discriminatory treatment of the early immigrant plantation workers. Moreover, there are clear links between ethnicity and social, political and economic status in Hawai'i. Caucasians and Japanese Americans are two of the most affluent ethnic groups living in Hawai'i, and Native Hawai'ians continue to rank lowest in the state in terms of health, education, and economic well-being, and highest in infant deaths, incarceration, and suicide rates.

Caucasians, commonly referred to as haoles,[1] are sometimes perceived negatively, not because of who they are as individuals, but because of white economic privilege and the history of American domination in Hawai'i. The small number of African-

Americans in the state are often military personnel, and sometimes disdained because of the association with American imperialism, the illegal overthrow of the Hawai'ian monarchy, and the temporary nature of their residence in Hawai'i. Although these racial tensions usually subside below the surface, occasionally they erupt in violence such as that described in the newspaper quote.

Although incidents involving this degree of violence are not the norm, Hawai'i did record six "hate crimes" in 2006, up from one or two incidents in previous years. Thus, there is cause for concern. However, in a tourist-driven state, incidents such as this don't generate much public discussion. As quoted further on in the above-mentioned newspaper article, racial tensions are like "news about shark attacks…people are afraid they might lose customers."

More commonly, negative racial attitudes are conveyed in non-violent form, such as being shunned socially, or being the butt of racial slurs. Such incidents are not confined only to whites or African-Americans. In another study I conducted (Grace, 2006), six and seven year old children in Hawai'i schools reported being teased and called names based on their ethnicity:

> I don't like it when kids be mean to me because I'm Japanese.
> They call me Filipino.
> They call me my ethnicity.
> Sometimes people make fun of me.
> I heard the word "nigger" in hip hop music.
> Kids sometimes make "Japanese eyes" (stretching eyelids to look slanted).

As these comments demonstrate, although race relations are better here than in many places, there is still work to be done. Notions of ethnicities as already-read texts need to be disrupted, and long standing silences about racism need to be broken. If we are to improve social relations and cultural understandings, it is important to provide time and space to think and talk about such issues in the classroom and elsewhere. This belief led to the development of an assignment I implemented in the graduate course in Media studies that I taught in fall, 2007. Informed by the literature on critical place-based pedagogy, I constructed a mid-term project in which the students would articulate and examine their thoughts and perceptions about the notion of Hawai'i as a melting pot. My intent was to provide a way for them to decode the images and ideologies of "their own concrete, situated experiences with the world" (Gruenewald, 2003, p. 5), and probe into issues regarding racial tensions and relations in the state.

The assignment incorporated the five phases discussed by Rhonda for place-based critical inquiry: connect, wonder, construct, act, and reflect. In the Connect phase, the students wrote a personal narrative about an incident, situation, or event in their life that depicted their perspective on the topic of Hawai'i as a melting pot, thereby connecting place with self and community (Woodhouse & Knapp, 2000). Second, in the Wonder phase, they were asked to consider alternative perspectives on the topic, and reasons that might underlie differing views. Third, in the Construct phase, the students engaged in further inquiry and research and constructed meaning about the topic. Next, either individually or with others, the students developed their explorations into a creative, multi-modal project utilizing sound, images, and text (Act phase). Finally, they wrote a final reflection on the project, including their thoughts about the project overall, their own presentation, and the presentations of others (Reflect phase). These reflections were assessed on a credit/no credit basis, because I did not want earning a grade to influence what they had to say.

In order to safely and openly examine and discuss controversial issues such as this, the classroom community needs to be one in which an ethic of caring, respect and affirmation is fostered. I try hard to establish this type of climate in all of the courses that I teach. In the media course, we began each session with activities that helped us get to know one another better on a personal level. Each class also included small group discussions of the readings, with members rotating through different groups each week, and food was often brought to share as we talked, worked, and learned together. The students and I were on a first-name basis, and the atmosphere was informal and relaxed. Because the course was student-centered and project-based, more time was spent in student, rather than teacher talk.

The twelve students in the course were of diverse racial and ethnic backgrounds. Eight were "local" or born and raised in the islands, and four were non-local, having lived in Hawai'i from three to ten or more years. Of the locals, three were Japanese-American, one was Chinese-American, one was Okinawan, another was Vietnamese, and two were of mixed Hawai'ian and Asian ancestry. The non-local group was comprised of an Australian, a Filipino from Manila, a Mexican from California who had married a "local" Hawai'ian, and a Caucasian from the mainland. They were all current or former elementary or secondary teachers. This particular mix of students and their personal histories and individual experiences surely shaped the data gathered from this project in certain ways. Thus no claims for generalization of the results are implied.

I, myself, am a white, middle-class female who moved to Hawai' in 1990. At that time, one of our daughters was three years old and the other was five. Both daughters were educated in the Hawai'i public schools, and grew up with friends from a mix of ethnic backgrounds. My husband and I have also been fortunate to have many friends, neighbors and colleagues representing a variety of ethnicities, and have felt accepted in both our personal and professional lives. However, being a haole, and being fairly well read in post-colonial literature, I am conscious (and understanding) of the negativity often associated with Caucasians from the mainland. Therefore, this awareness may have influenced my perceptions and interpretations of this project. In fact, my own positionality as a white, non-local, probably explains the surprise I felt when I read the students' initial narratives.

I had anticipated a range of responses to the assignment, and expected some of the students to critique the discourse of Hawai'i as a melting pot as a myth. That did not happen. Of the twelve students, nine of them adamantly agreed with the metaphor. Of the three who somewhat differed, Elston, a local, male, described the state's ethnic mix as a 'salad' rather than a melting pot, where different cultures got along but maintained their own customs. After moving to Hawai'i and taking her first job here, Colleen, the woman from Australia, wrote:

> I had the feeling that I was not welcome in the clicky conversations that went on in the office. The local staff did not appear friendly and would often respond to my questions with monosyllabic grunts.

However, she eventually gained acceptance and concluded that Hawai'i was indeed a grand melting pot. A third student, of part-Hawai'ian ancestry, was the only one who took exception to this descriptor. She wrote:

> Call it lingering xenophobia if you must, but it is clear to me that there is no effort put into being tolerant of others that are unlike ourselves, nor is there an effort to mingle and enjoy the viewpoints of others. We merely coexist in a semblance of harmony.

The majority of the students, however, firmly viewed Hawai'i as a melting pot, as seen in the sample of comments below.

> Hawai'i truly is a melting pot of cultures, languages, people and lifestyles. These things make up our local culture, which is unique and unlike any other place in the world.

> Our multiculturalism is evident in every aspect of life. At weddings, it's common to see the bride and groom do the money dance which is a Filipino custom. The lion dance is from the Chinese culture, and giving a banzai toast comes from Japan. At most celebrations, leis are given, which were originally made by the Hawai'ians.

> The plate lunch [a popular menu special] speaks for itself. Where else could you get a combination of Kalbi Korean short ribs and teriyaki chicken served with rice and macaroni salad?! Only in Hawai'i will you find Korean, Japanese and American all on one plate!

These comments certainly characterize much of what is so special about living in Hawai'i. Without a doubt, we have a rich and wonderful multicultural mix of people, food, customs and celebrations. However, that doesn't mean that we don't have problems. In the celebration of diversity that characterized most of the students' narratives, many silences were also evident. Only one of the students alluded to issues related to racial tensions or relations, despite awareness of situations like the beating described previously that had occurred only a few months before.

In thinking about this, I realized that the students, most of whom were locally born and raised, viewed the topic of Hawai'i as a melting pot through their own personal experiences. This was validated in a few of the students' comments. According to one student, "My personal life defined my ideas of Hawai'i as a melting pot." Another observed that, "It seemed that everyone's work came from who they are and how they felt about living in Hawai'i." And as cultural insiders in Hawai'i, locals tend not to experience prejudice or racism to the extent experienced by other groups. At this point, a critical lens was largely lacking.

In the next part of the project, the intent, as mentioned by Rhonda, was to "make the familiar strange," and engage in some "critical wonderings." Thus, the students were asked to entertain the notion of alternate perceptions on the topic of Hawai'i as a melting pot that might differ from their own. They were encouraged to conduct further investigation; to step out of their own personal space and read, think, and talk with others about the topic. Following this, the students moved on to construct meaning from their investigations, before proceeding to develop their inquiries into culminating multimodal class presentations to be shared with the class. Although some students maintained their initial views on the topic, for others, shifts had clearly taken place in their thinking. Only four of the twelve students still claimed that Hawai'i is a melting pot, citing similar reasons as were shared in their first narratives – the blending of cultures, harmony in diversity, and the aloha spirit. Another four students shifted just a bit, and developed the related theme of a mosaic of cultures living side by side, respecting each others' traditions. As Astrid wrote:

> Hawai'i is a mosaic; a picture made of many bits of different-colored stone or glass. Just as each bit of stone or glass shines with its own color, each ethnic group retains its unique qualities. Together, they form something new: a multicultural mosaic.

An additional four students changed from their initial stance on the topic. Nikki and Dawn, two local females, created a Power Point presentation with the text written in the local dialect of Pidgin-English. One of their slides had the caption, "*We stay almos' dea, but not everybody get Aloha*," (We're almost there, but not everyone has the Aloha spirit). On this slide were the five following links to newspaper reports: (1) Kill a Haole Day (2) Hate Crimes (3) Rise in Shelter Utililization by Micronesians in Hawai'i (4) When Homeless is Better than Home, and (5) Hawai'i's Micronesians Assail Housing Report. These students concluded that "*We need to instill the values of Aloha in our youth to become the true 'melting pot' of tomorrow.*" Joe, a Caucasian from the mainland, uncritically supported the notion of Hawai'i as a melting pot in his first narrative. For his final project, however, he created a video in which he interviewed several of his high school students on the topic. A few of these students expressed negative views about mainlanders and tourists, and both the African-American and the Hispanic males interviewed stated that they felt racial prejudice and discrimination definitely have a presence in Hawai'i. In his conclusion, he stated that Hawai'i may not be a melting pot for everyone. Gregoria, the Latina female from California, also videotaped interviews with friends and acquaintances who shared differing views on the topic. Some of her interviewees felt that Hawai'i was a melting pot, and some strongly felt otherwise. She said that conducting these interviews opened her eyes to new interpretations of the topic.

The projects were all well done, and the multiple perspectives presented had an impact not only on those who viewed the presentations, but also on those who produced them. The interviews were particularly powerful. In their final, written reflections, every student in the class indicated that their thinking had changed in some way throughout the process of completing and seeing the different presentations:

> I realized that my experiences as an immigrant to Hawai'i were very different from others. I know now that my dark hair and yellow-tinged complexion made assimilating less troublesome. Mine was a face similar to those they had seen before.
>
> Growing up, I often heard statements by teachers, students, and friends that Hawai'i is a melting pot and accepted it as truth. Exploration of this notion went unchallenged. However, after completing this project, my views have changed. I realized the importance of questioning concepts before accepting them as truth.
>
> After the presentations, I thought a lot more about the topic. I am beginning to suspect that the melting pot concept may be the result of a good public relations campaign on the part of the Hawai'i Visitors Bureau. It is a nice package: sandy pristine beaches, Hawai'ian music, and friendly people of mixed ethnicity, all getting along with each other. But we have our troubles like everywhere else. The difference is that because so much of our state's livelihood depends on the tourism industry, we have to work harder at keeping our dirty laundry hidden away.
>
> This project really made me think twice! It's hard to overcome many stereotypes because we have grown up hearing them from our peers, parents, and the media. If we can teach our children to respect each other and not judge others by the color of their skin or the shape of their eyes, maybe then we can begin to accept each other for who we are, and really become a melting pot.

In reflecting upon this project myself, I appreciated the opportunity to learn from and with my students. Listening to the students' voices broadened my level of awareness and understanding of relationships and experiences in Hawai'i, just as I hope and think occurred for most of the students as well. By hearing each others' stories, we became closer to one another, and strengthened bonding in the classroom. As one student wrote:

> This project really illustrated the concept of building a classroom community. Whether we worked in pairs or individually, viewing the final product really helped me learn more about my classmates – where they are from, what they feel, what they are going through and their own perspectives.

I also realized the importance of beginning critical inquiry and engagement in social issues much earlier, and not waiting until students reach university to critically question taken-for-granted assumptions about those we share space and place with on this earth. Unfortunately, in Hawai'i, as elsewhere, what often takes place in the name of multicultural education is a superficial focus on food, festivals, holidays and heroes that essentialize or trivialize difference and may actually reinforce ethnic stereotypes rather than diminish them. Within the school discourse of "same but different," dominant structures of power and privilege remain unchanged and unchallenged. Perhaps we need to move beyond a "celebration of differences" in schools, to address the ways in which racism, inequalities, and relations of power impact the lives of children and those around them. If, as educators, we seek to promote ways of living together better in the world, we might consider breaking some of the silences in school lessons and discussions of diversity, and promoting an ethic of social justice in which issues of race, class, gender, language, politics, and economics are salient.

FINAL REFLECTIONS

With the national trend of standardized, pre-packaged, and generic curriculum, education is rapidly becoming "place-less" (Brooke, 2003). By bringing place-consciousness into the teaching and learning process, Rhonda and I saw first-hand that learning can be more meaningful, relevant and engaging when it moves beyond the four walls of the classroom. Through experiencing and reflecting on these projects and our students' responses, we were offered a brief glimpse of what might be possible. We plan to continue revising and reworking our teaching in ways that affirm our students' abilities to identify and solve social and environmental problems, contribute to the welfare of others, and positively impact our local communities. We hope that our university students will, in turn, incorporate place-based critical inquiry in their work with K-12 students, and, in the words of Gruenwald (2008, p.viii), find ways "to more deeply connect children and young people to the places where they live," so that the "caring, knowledge, responsibility, and skill required to make those places healthy and humane" can emerge.

As language arts teacher educators, we look forward to the day when we can walk into more elementary school classrooms where we see children reading and writing about things that matter to them, discussing and debating ideas, inquiring into issues they are concerned about, and believing that they can make a difference in their communities and in the lives of others. Perhaps place-based critical inquiry can help make that dream a reality.

NOTES

[1] Haole (how-lee) is a Hawai'ian term that originally meant foreigner. Today, it typically refers to Caucasians, and sometimes is used in a derogatory manner.

REFERENCES

Barell, J. (2003). *Developing more curious minds*. Alexandria, VA: Association for Supervision and Curriculum Development.
Brooke, R. (Ed.). (2003). *Rural voices: Place-conscious education and the teaching of writing*. New York: Teachers College Press.
Freire, P., & Macedo, D. (1987). *Literacy: Reading the word and the world*. Westport, CT: Bergin & Garvey.
Freire, P. (1970). *Pedagogy of the oppressed*. New York: Continuum International Publishing Group, Inc.
Grace, D. (2006). *Video pen pals: Interpreting children's constructions of their ethnicities*. Paper presented at the American Educational Research Association, San Francisco.

Gruenewald, D. A. (2003). The best of both worlds: A critical pedagogy of place. *Educational Researcher, 32*(4), 3–12.

Gruenewald, D. A., & Smith, G. A. (Eds.). (2008). *Place-based education in the global age.* New York: Lawrence Erlbaum Associates.

Haymes, S. N. (1995). *Race, culture, and the city: A pedagogy for black urban struggle.* New York: State University of New York Press.

Pahl, K., & Rowsell, J. (2005). *Literacy and education: Understanding the new literacy studies in the classroom.* London: Paul Chapman Publishing.

Parker, D. (2007). *Planning for inquiry: It's not an oxymoron!* Newark, DE: National Council of Teachers of English.

USA today racial tensions are simmering in Hawaii's melting pot. Retrieved January 13, 2007, from http://www.usatoday.com/printedition/news/20070307/1a_cover07.art.htm

Weyeneth, R. R. (2002). *Kapi'olani park: A history.* Honolulu, HI: Kapi'olani Park Preservation Society.

Donna Grace
Institute for Teacher Education
University of Hawai'i at Manoa

Rhonda Nowak
Institute for Teacher Education
University of Hawai'i at Manoa

ELITE BEN-YOSEF

TODAY I AM PROUD OF MYSELF

Telling Stories and Revaluing Lives

BEGINNINGS

I was an elementary school special education teacher who studied literacy and became a college professor. In this learning process I became aware of both the power of language and the power of literacy to give voice to marginalized groups in society. One day I discovered Hope House, which is a home for recovering women established to help those in need of a place to live while recovering from mental illness, drug and alcohol abuse, incarceration and other traumas. I approached the home's director and suggested volunteering to teach a weekly literacy class for the residents. I had never worked with adults before, let alone women recovering from trauma, but when I brought up the idea, the light in the director's eyes and the strong hug she enveloped me in, just threw me right into the water, where I learned to swim.

At the time I began the class there were about twenty women in residence, but only two showed up, actually – down – as we congregated in the basement which serves as the living room for the house: Sula,[1] was in her mid 20s and could not read or write at all. Originally from Honduras, she had recently given birth to a boy who she was not allowed to keep, but whom she would be able to visit at the office of social services during Christmas. Isaiah was what Sula talked about all the time and it was for his sake that she desperately wanted to learn to read and write.

Maru came too. Her father had sent her to the U.S. from Africa to study, but she got involved in drugs and prostitution and is now, in her late 40s, getting her life back on track. Maru read and wrote some English with great difficulty (the difficulty stemming in part from her need for prescription glasses, which she never had). She had no knowledge of reading and writing in her native language, but a desire for knowledge was burning inside her and since the day we started, she never missed a class. Other women in the house said that they knew how to read and didn't need to participate. I believe they also wanted to check out the situation before committing, so in the weeks that followed, new residents would join us, then leave. One woman, in particular, would come down quietly and sit on the side, listening but refusing to join our circle or to participate in our discussions. After some time she would go upstairs, just as quietly as she came.

I needed to get more participants in order to begin a constructive dialogue. So I sent a message to all the women that for our next meeting I would bring a video and popcorn. Ten women showed up and we watched *Vera Drake*.[2] Since this is not an easy film to watch (the pace is slow, dialogue in British English is limited and includes many silences, the topic is back-street abortions and the protagonist is an anti-heroine), and since I believe in critically reading films as texts which are sources of information and knowledge, I didn't let the women watch quietly. During the whole film I modelled critical reading by making comments, pointing things out and posing questions, encouraging the women to do the same. (Some cooperated but others were annoyed and complained about not being able to just watch the movie in peace.) At our next meeting, six women arrived, creating the continuing core of our group, and a very strong discussion developed, originating in the film and moving out into the world.

CHALLENGES

What are the challenges a teacher faces in a situation focused on nurturing voice? First, creating relationships of trust with the students by establishing the classroom as a safe space for everybody to feel free to open up, think and say what is on their minds and in their hearts. The process involves "…honouring learners' silences as well as their words, bearing witness by being a caring listener, balancing expressions of pain with those of joy and humour, and offering content and activities that allow learners to share as much or as little information about themselves as they choose" (Kerka, 2002, p. 3). It also involves being sensitive to the students' physical, emotional and material needs, helping them become "available for learning" (Horseman, 2000; Ben-Yosef, 2002). One woman would agree to sit only on the softest chair, so we made it into a joke and accommodated her wish; another kept falling asleep as a side effect of her medication; our youngest and most troubled student had a very short attention span, so she would get up and leave suddenly, and after a while one of the other students would bring her back down until she left again. Two of the women didn't have winter coats, so I brought coats from home. When I travelled or entertained I always brought cakes or chocolates to share with the students, and sometimes I "snuck" coffee in, since I knew they all craved coffee but were allowed to drink house coffee only in the mornings. We were creating a community of learners that was framed by the space and activities we shared, but was also growing from the inside in the form of a web of strengthening personal relationships (myself included) originating in sharing of stories, experiences and secrets, learning from each other and caring for one another.

The second, yet concurrent, challenge relates to the use of texts appropriate in this specific situation, texts that can help shatter the silence and transform the learner from object of oppression to agent of one's own life (Freire, 1997). Maxine Green (1988) writes that mutuality, concern and the affirmation of other are not in themselves enough to bring about such transformation. What is needed is to challenge the language of texts that are couched in dominant male discourse, a language that denies body and feeling, and silences women's ways of knowing. We must use texts to unconceal, to create clearings and spaces where decisions can be made, where questions can be raised.

Between Sula, who was learning her ABCs, and Jill (the quiet one) who was an avid reader of historical fiction, there were diverse levels of literacy, interest and need. My aim was to include everyone in the critical discourse and for them to, ultimately, be empowered to produce, transform and reproduce meaning (Freire & Macedo, 1987). To this end I looked for materials that would be relevant to the students' lives, provide incentives for reading, critical thinking and a free exchange of ideas while, hopefully, motivating writing. I was hoping the women would be able to find voice and tell their stories as part of a process of self-exploration to promote identity construction, visibility and shattering the silence pervading the experiences of women who have been marginalized (Baird, 2001; Ben-Yosef, 2008).

And the long term goals? Bringing the learners to a place from which they could produce their own knowledge constructed upon their own reality (Quigley, 1999); teaching them to use literacy for the purpose of "acquiring a sense of self worth and self preservation, a sense of being part of society" (Baird, 2001, p. 177). And most of all, I wished to encourage them to recover their voices that had been silenced. As Barbara wrote:

My voice was silenced from the time I was a little girl
I am now a voice trying on truth for a change,
looking to drop the lies, to become more honest,
lighter to carry myself from place to place.
I am now 50 plus and have chosen to stop running and hiding.
because I can't hide me from me.
There is much work to be done,
to live my life free from self doubt and embarrassment.
It's time to shake the past off my shoulders,
to get busy living in the here and now, right now!

READING THE WORLD AND THE WORD

Texts that would relate to the students' own experiences would enable them to access the larger concept of critical reading. Helen Frost's book *Keesha's House* (2003) fit our need. It tells the story (in verse) of a teen who established a safe-house for herself and other runaways. All the women could relate to the stories in the book (many of them, including myself, had teenaged children or had gone through experiences similar to those described in the book), and Frost's writing is discrete while the events described are far enough removed from the students' actual experiences so as not to intimidate the reader. After reading the first chapter I modelled responding to the language and structure of the text (repeated words, broken sentences, metaphors), as well as to the plot as a mirror of my life and as window into issues in our society. When the students took up responding, lively and insightful discussions took place, largely about experiences that the women had (either similar or different from those that we read about) but also moving into larger social issues such as abortion, discrimination and bias, power and powerlessness, coming of age, lives in prison, etc.

When we read about a teenage girl who had to leave home because she was pregnant and her parents couldn't handle it, Sula told how she had twins at age 11 after being raped by her brother. Her mother proceeded to throw her out of the house, beginning many years of living on the streets. When we read about a boy whose parents couldn't accept the fact that he was gay, Lily told about the support she had received from her mother for her own lifestyle: "As long as you're happy," she would always tell her daughter. When we read about one of the girls implying that she had already been in jail once before, Davina told how other inmates would taunt her because she liked to read when she was in prison. After watching the movie *Vera Drake* (Leigh, 2004), Jill talked about the other side of the issue, having been an OBGYN nurse and encountering women in the hospital who had back-room abortions that went bad, and the how staff were desperately trying to save their lives. The story about a girl who didn't feel safe in the house because her mother's new husband would come into her room at night without permission, led Lidia to tell about being abused for years by her grandfather when her mother was hospitalized for long periods of time. She had never talked about this before, she told us, because she felt ashamed, embarrassed, not good enough. Bobbie described severe abuse beginning at age eight which led her to run away from home and begin a life of drugs and addiction. She wrote:

> *My life and mind have always been in a spin, like a tornado.*
> *Don't know where I'm going, but I know where I've been –*
> *I've been through a lot in life that shouldn't have been.*
> *I search for a magic carpet to carry me through to the clouds,*
> *Trying to find my rainbow of happiness on the other side...*

Our reading and discussions were very productive in terms of critical reading and in terms of opening up and telling stories: talking about lives and naming issues and experiences. After watching *Five People You Meet in Heaven* (a film based on Mitch Albom's book) and discussing friendship, which was one of the issues we found in the text, Polly said that she had just realized the strong bonds of friendship she had forged with two of the other residents, friendships the likes of which she had never formerly had with other women. Due to a traumatic event in her past, she never wanted to befriend other women, yet now, under the new circumstances of her life, living at Hope House with women in circumstances similar to her own, she has opened up and is thriving in these relationships which are helping her cope and deal with her life.

On another occasion, Ivy was responding to the writing prompt, "A typical day for me is…", and after describing a typical day she put down her paper and said:

> I went to visit my mother today. She lives in an abandoned house and abuses drugs and I've been going to visit her since I came out of prison…but sometimes she really embarrasses me! She wants to walk down the street with me and then she goes around telling everyone, "This is my daughter;

this is my daughter." She's a bag lady and she's telling everyone that I'm her daughter! I want to run away but people keep telling me she's my mother and I have to put up with her!

Dorie was sitting next to Ivy and couldn't take her eyes off her. When Ivy stopped her story, Dorie said quietly, "That's what happened to me with my mother. I never told anyone about this before, but my mom is mentally ill and all the years when I was growing up she would tell people at the store, 'This is my daughter,' and I thought, 'Where can I hide?'" As our meeting came to an end, Dorie and Ivy, who had been living in the house together for five months and had never exchanged more than a greeting, stayed seated, talking, sharing stories. As I turned to say goodbye, I saw them hugging and crying on each other's shoulders.

We also made strides towards becoming more sensitive to "the art of words": learning about the power of language as we learned about the power a reader has over texts and their interpretation (Rosenblatt, 1995). Davina described how reading has changed for her as a result of our classes:

I never used to read but I started reading in prison because I needed something to do. Now I read because I like to. I read and I understand what the writer is doing. I understand why he is writing something or describing something in a certain way. In the past I hated these descriptions, but today I just can't get enough.

Polly mentioned something similar when talking about reading films. She complained jokingly that after learning to "read" the videos in our classes, she can't view movies anymore without questioning and responding to the story in real time, a habit that annoys her fellow viewers.

STALLED WRITING

Writing in our context was more difficult. Whereas the students had much they wanted to talk about and felt comfortable enough doing so, the effort involved in writing about their lives was too great for some of them, as was the intimidation of "formal" writing: fear of making spelling or grammar mistakes, not knowing "how" or what to write, and maybe even fear of the teacher's critique, as they were used to in school experiences in the past. The only exception at this time was Lily, whose elder son was in prison, and although he had been there for several years, she had never visited him because she had been in prison herself. She had never written to him, either, because, she said, all she had to tell was bad news and she was afraid of making spelling mistakes. Now that she was out of prison and getting her life back in order, she decided to write her son a letter that she would have me correct before sending. Together we went over the letter (which needed minimal correction) in which she apologized for not writing before. She told her son that she was in recovery and doing well. Two weeks later Lily received a reply from her son asking that she come visit him.

From my own studies and work with undergraduate struggling readers, I learned about the connection between writing personal histories and developing a sense of self, of agency. I believed that writing their stories in their own voices would help the women make deeper meaning of their lives, getting away from the negative categories they were condescendingly placed in by society and social institutions with which they came into contact (Ben-Yosef, 2008, 2009). I wanted them to use their developing critical reading skills to reread into their lives and find the positive, the strengths, the significant moments; to revalue their lives, which society refuses to value, and to have the students recognize "...that they can legitimately hold on to parts of the past even as they move into the future" (Silin, 2006, p. 3).

Michael Morpurgo writes about his experience of writing while travelling with his parents on a sailboat (*Peggy Sue*) when he was 12 years old (Morpurgo, 2002, p. 23):

> At school I had never been much good at writing. I could never think of what to write or how to begin. But on the *Peggy Sue* I found I could open up my log and just write. There was always so much I wanted to say. And that's the thing. I found I didn't write it down at all. Rather, I said it. I spoke it from my head, down my arm, through my fingers and my pencil, and onto the page. And that's how it reads to me all these years later, like me talking.

Maybe if my students could speak their lives onto the page, as young Michael did, writing would be easier for them, a more natural process?

At about the same time I saw Briski and Kaufman's (2004) documentary *Born into Brothels* where they shows Briski's work with children of prostitutes in Calcutta's red light district. A photographer herself, she gave the children disposable cameras to document their lives, and the results in terms of both photography and literacy, were significant and illuminating.

Maybe the use of disposable cameras to document their lives would jump-start writing for my students?

WRITING FROM THE INSIDE

I sent word that I would be coming with cameras so that anyone wishing to get one should make sure to be in the house that afternoon. I gave each student (and any of the other residents that wanted one) a disposable camera that they were to use by taking pictures of anything they decided was significant in their lives. When the pictures were developed and returned to the photographers, I asked them each to pick a picture and tell us why she chose to take it. At first I wrote down their stories and later, I recorded them on video.[3] After telling their stories, the students wrote them down. Lucy took several photos of the flowers in the back yard and told us:

> First I took pictures of the flowers when they were very small and about two weeks later, when they had grown. I did that because they remind me of myself. When I got clean this time I was very immature, but now I feel that I'm growing each day, like the flowers.

TODAY I AM PROUD OF MYSELF

Ann took a picture of an abandoned house and wrote:

> I chose to take a picture of an abandoned house because two years ago when I was drinking, I lived in an abandoned house. I had abandoned myself and my life. I didn't care where I lived. All I needed was to drink.

While talking about her writing, Davina said that she is beginning to think that she is actually happy she went to prison. It was a slap in the face, so hard that it centred her life. It had taught her a lesson that no amount of preaching or threatening had been able to do in the past: she now knows that she does not want to go to prison ever again, so she will keep away from the things that got her into trouble. Her older brother, on the other hand, is now facing a second, very long prison term. For him, she says, the first time around was not hard enough. Davina felt empowered by the changes she has made to her life, and she was now in charge of the upkeep of Hope House and its yard:

> *Before Hope, I was a prisoner in my own mind,*
> *an inmate locked up like a caged animal.*
> *Today I am that no longer.*
> *Today I feel empowered by giving back to the house*
> *that showed me love and has given me strength.*
> *Hope House has given me back my life and respect from my family.*
> *Hope House has given my parents a daughter,*
> *who has grown into a respectable citizen.*
> *Who would have thought that I would hear from my mom,*
> *the words I always needed to hear:*
> *"YOU SOUND REAL GOOD, I LOVE YOU."*

She also took a picture of a dog she befriended down the street, and wrote:

> *I've always loved dogs.*
> *It's almost like they understand me,*
> *and I can understand their need and desire to be loved.*
> *This is Chew, my best friend. I tell him everything, although not in words.*
> *When I feel happy, upset or just plain down, I go and sit with Chew.*
> *I don't have to talk,*
> *I can sit still and let my higher power speak to me in the stillness.*
> *When I was young I was told that I was adopted from Canada,*
> *that I'm Mohawk Indian and French Canadian.*
> *Indians believe in spirit guides and so do I.*
> *I feel that certain dogs trust me because they know*
> *I have the Wolf spirit by my side.*
> *The wolf is the teacher, the pathfinder and moon dog of my soul.*

Ann took a picture of homeless men sleeping in the park.

> *I took a picture of 2 guys sleeping in the park because*
> *I remember when I used to sleep in the park.*

*I would get a blanket from Free Lunch and
lie down on the blanket,
under a tree,
on the grass,
because I was drunk.
I can laugh at it now, but then it wasn't funny.
I was sad and alone,
with no one to talk to,
no one to listen to me.
I would pray to God, ask why I was living like that,
and I stopped believing in God.
Now I do believe, again,
but I have to remember those days to stay sober.*

Nadine talked about a photo of the tattoo she had on her right shoulder:

*This is a picture of my newly acquired tattoo,
a cross with a butterfly in the middle,
and in the 4 corners it says:
Only By God's Grace.
I remember lying in a foetal position on the cold concrete of a gas station,
excruciating pain.
I remember wanting so much to be out of pain,
wanting someone to make it go away,
wanting to die.
I remember waiting,
waiting for an ambulance
yelling at the sky: GOD, PLEASE MAKE IT STOP!
In the emergency room they decided to discharge me,
again, as they had done a week before.
The drug levels in my blood were so high,
they thought I was expendable.
"There's nothing more we can do for her," they said.
"She's bleeding on your floor," my boyfriend said.
"You're very lucky he came with you," they told me after the surgery:
entopic pregnancy, internal bleeding, severe blood loss.
The butterfly in the middle symbolizes
a new beginning.
It is an excruciating process to become a butterfly,
an exhausting process.
It isn't easy and it takes a lot of work,
but to become that butterfly
I must work on getting out of the cocoon.*

TODAY I AM PROUD OF MYSELF

Maru had a friend take a picture of her in her African dress. She wrote:

That's the way I used to be when I wasn't using.
I used to be a beautiful mother.
But when I was using I was nobody.
Today I am doing the right thing.
Getting a new foundation for life.
Finding myself by myself has given me power.
Today, when I look at myself in the mirror, I laugh.
I am somebody:
Jesus loves me and I love myself.
Today I am proud of myself.
I am a powerful woman.
I hold my head high.

IN CLOSING THIS CHAPTER

Erin had joined us only sporadically. She was always off to her favourite meeting just as we were coming into the house. One day, as we crossed paths by the door she handed me the following piece:

I come from my grandmother's dreams

A girl. Finally. The pink and white blanket envisioned a generation ago can be knit. Only the best yarn will do.

Dreams can come true

Erin, you still do? Ha! Yes, every day I put cream on my elbows too. Feel how smooth. Let me see yours. Oh, yes. You are a lady too. You are smart. You will graduate, get a good job. Now why don't you marry this one? He will have you, support you, be good to you. Oh, I am talking, talking – the flowers! Why do you do this, baby? So much money! Oh, Erin, I love you. I love your brother too, but you – ah, you know it.

I became my grandmother's nightmare

Kicked out of college. For drugs! What is this? Marijuana now. Then it will be heroin. Is she addicted? The soap opera showed it – the girl addicted to drugs, meeting the dealer in a dark alley, selling her body. Not Erin. Why won't her mother, her father save her, make her be good?

There is no cure for nightmares

You must do as I say Erin. Go back to school. Be a mentch. Leave this – this place. Who is this man? You MUST LISTEN to me. You're lucky. You have parents that love you, that want you home. My parents died in the war when I was 14. I was alone. Fourteen. Go, go home. Erin, please. What is wrong with you? What are you doing in this place? You are too bony. Eat. You need to eat, eat. I will cook for you.

I am waking up

I give her eulogy, high. Everyone says how beautiful it was. Reminds me how grandma stitched her every stitch with love. Back at his studio I rip the sweater off to look for a fresh vein. The needle rocks me to sleep. I dream that I'm clean, back in school, happy, bringing my grandma flowers, making her proud.

Dreams can come true

Happy Mother's Day grandma. I love you. I miss you so much! I'm 9 months clean. I wish you were here to see me like this. I'm trying so hard to be a mentch. I'm gonna go back to school, be an art teacher or an art therapist. I guess you know what I am doing now (not like you didn't have ideas when you were here. I know you knew it all). I'm sorry I hurt you so bad. I know you forgive me. I just wish I'd been good enough that you could've visited me, told me stories before bed.

And the flowers weren't much.

I wanted to.

I love you.

Our project is ongoing. New women join and veterans leave. Some go back to their old lives; some succeed in opening a new page and forging a new space for themselves. We celebrate anniversaries of "being clean," of being out of prison. Coffee has become a standard feature as have outings to plays and museums. Some of our students are open and expressive, like Bonnie, who at the slightest prompt would carry all of us into her last prison stay where she went through a harsh and humiliating boot camp experience, while others are reticent, like Ivy, who keeps saying she can't talk yet because it still hurts too much.

Writing has become easier, a more natural process of telling lives. Stories have become fuller, including dreams of future possibilities. In an effort to communicate with others we have posted the writings on the web at www.LiteracyAndLife.blogspot.com where there is also a short video showing our writing and learning process. You are invited to visit the site and listen to the stories, all of which were used, published and posted with the participants' full consent.

NOTES

[1] All names are pseudonyms
[2] The movie tells the story of Vera Drake, a cleaning woman who gave abortions free of charge to "girls who needed help" in 1950's England.
[3] I created a short video documenting the photography project. It can be found on the web at www.LiteracyAndLife.blogspot.com.

REFERENCES

Baird, I. C. (2001). Education, incarceration and the marginalization of women. In V. Sheared & P. A. Sissel (Eds.), *Making space: Merging theory and practice in adult education*. Bergin & Garvey.

Ben-Yosef, E. (2009). Portraits and possibilities: Empowerment through literacy. In M. Miller & R.P. King (Eds.) *Empowering women in literacy: Voices from experience*. Charlotte, NC: Information Age Publishing.

Ben-Yosef, E. (2008). Raising voices through the arts: Creating spaces for writing for marginalized groups of women. *Perspectives: The New York Journal of Adult Learning*.

Briski, Z., & Kaufman, R. (Directors and Producers). (2004). *Born into brothels: Calcutta's red light kids* (motion picture). USA: THINKFilm.

Freire, P. (1997). *Pedagogy of the oppressed*. New York: Continuum.

Freire, P., & Macedo, D. (1987). *Literacy: Reading the word and the world*. CT: Bergin & Garvey.

Frost, H. (2003). *Keesha's house*. New York: Farrar, Straus & Giroux.

Green, M. (1998). *The dialectic of freedom*. New York: Teachers' College Press.

Horsman, J. (2000). *Moving forward: Approaches and activities to support women's learning*. Toronto, ON: Parkdale Project Read. Retrieved from http://www.jennyhorsman.com/Movingforward.pdf

Kerka, S. (2002). Trauma and adult learning. *Eric Digest*, no. 239. Retrieved from http://www.ericdigests.org/2003-4/trauma.html

Leigh, M. (Director) & Simon Channing-Wilson (Producer). (2004). *Vera Drake* (motion picture). United Kingdom: New Line Cinema.

Morpurgo, M. (2002). *Kensuke's kingdom*. New York: Scholastic Press.

Quigley, A. B. (1999, Fall). Naming our world, claiming our knowledge: Research-in- practice in adult literacy programs. *The Alberta Journal of Educational Research, XLV* (3), 253–262.

Rosenblatt, L. M. (1995). *Literature as exploration*. New York: Modern Language Association of America.

Silin, J. G. (Ed.). (2006). Introduction. In *Welcoming the stranger: Essays on teaching and learning in a diverse society*. Occasional Papers #17. Bank Street College of Education.

Elite Ben-Yosef
Ruth S. Ammon School of Education
Adelphi University

ABOUT THE AUTHORS

Elite Ben-Yosef taught special education prior to earning a Ph.D in Literacy Studies with a focus on marginalized groups of learners. She believes that every child wants to learn and can do it well if teachers only take the time to find the right approach. Her goal in teaching preservice teachers is to open minds to possibilities of providing equal learning opportunities to all students by focusing on the individual learner's strengths and literacies. On a voluntary basis, Elite teaches literacy to adult women and to youth at a juvenile detention facility. Her latest publication is "Portraits and Possibilities: Empowerment through Literacy," in M. Miller & K.P. King (Eds.) *Empowering Women in Literacy: Views from Experience*, 2009, Information Age Publishing.

Diane Caracciolo earned an Ed. D. in Art Education from Teachers College, Columbia. She is an Assistant Professor of Curriculum and Instruction at Adelphi University, where she teaches and coordinates a series of *Exploring the Arts* courses for prospective educators. She has published in the areas of Indigenous educational studies and arts education. She is interested in exploring ways to support the imagination through arts-based learning. She is a former Waldorf high school English and theatre teacher.

Diana M. Feige, Ph.D. is a sojourner, an unsettled idealist more comfortable with questions than with answers. Born of Puerto Rican and English parents, she spent her youth in Puerto Rico in a bicultural fest, weaving varied languages, dispositions and traditions. New England became her home in her college years, graduating first from the University of New Hampshire and years later from Harvard Divinity School/Harvard University and Teachers College/Columbia University. Her first professional venture was as a high school teacher; for the last fourteen years she has been teaching and mentoring Adelphi University (Garden City, New York) students as they navigate their academic and professional roads towards becoming school practitioners.

Donna J. Grace is a Professor and member of the language arts faculty at the University of Hawaii at Manoa. She is also Co-director of the Institute for Teacher Education in the College of Education. Donna received her Ed.D. in Curriculum and Instruction from the University of Hawaii, and holds a Masters Degree in Early Childhood Education from the Ontario Institute for Studies in Education. She was also an elementary school teacher for ten years. Donna's teaching and research interests center around cultural studies, media studies, critical literacy, and early childhood education.

Rob Linné earned a Ph.D. in Language and Literacy Studies at the University of Texas at Austin and now teaches in the Adolescence Education program at Adelphi University in New York. Courses he has developed at Adelphi include Youth

Literacies: Literature, Culture, and the Arts; Teaching Writing in the Secondary School; and Immigrant Experience in Fiction and Film. His research interests focus on media culture and youth while his most recent work examines how class is portrayed in film and literature, especially in relation to labor issues. Rob has co-edited, with Leigh Benin and Adrienne Sosin, *Organizing the Curriculum: Perspectives on Teaching the US Labor Movement,* published by Sense in 2009.

Anne M. Mungai, Ph. D. is an Associate Professor, Chair of the Department of Curriculum and Instruction and director of Special Education programs at Adelphi University. She has served as a consultant to several schools that have started inclusion and has provided service to schools as a professional developer and field researcher in the areas of cognition, and classroom instruction with racially, ethnically, and linguistically diverse populations. Her research agenda over the last several years has revolved around the concept of multicultural issues, inclusion issues, staff development, gender issues and learning. She is the co-editor of *Pathway to Inclusion: Voices from the Field* published by University Press of America. She is also interested in comparative education and is the author of the book *Growing up in Kenya: Rural Schooling and Girls* published by Peter Lang.

Rhonda Nowak, Ph.D. is Assistant Professor of Literacy Teacher Education at the University of Hawaii at Manoa. She teaches undergraduate and graduate courses in literacy, language arts, and assessment. She is also Director of the Hawaii Writing Project, state affiliate of the National Writing Project. She has worked with teachers in several K-12 schools in the areas of her research interests, which include literacy and inquiry across the curriculum, authentic literacy assessment, and teacher collaboration. She has published in the areas of literacy curriculum, instruction, assessment and teacher education.

Michael O'Loughlin, Ph.D. is a Professor at Adelphi University where he is on the faculty of the Ruth S. Ammon School of Education. He is also a faculty member and supervisor at the Derner Institute of Advanced Psychological Studies, and in the Postgraduate Programs in Psychoanalysis and Psychotherapy at Adelphi. He has a clinical practice in New Hyde Park, New York. His most recent work includes a book. co-edited with Richard Johnson, *Rethinking Childhood Subjectivity,* to be published by SUNY Press in 2009, and a book, *The Subject of Childhood,* published by Peter Lang Publishing in 2009.

Frances V. Rains, Ph.D. (Choctaw/Cherokee & Japanese) is an Associate Professor in the Native American and World Indigenous Peoples Studies at Evergreen State College. Her research interests include critical race theory, Indigenous Knowledge, white privilege/racism, American Indian history & social justice issues. Her in-press chapter, with Melody Bidtah [Port Gamble S'Klallam Nation], Lovera Black Crow [Elwha Klallam Nation], Kara Horton [Port Gamble S'Klallam] and Toni Jones [Nooksack Nation], entitled, "American Indian Mothers Speaking from the Heart: Public Schools and their Children" will be published by Teacher College Press in the edited book, *Teaching Bilingual/Bicultural Children: Teachers Talk about Language and Learning*. The editors are Lourdes Diaz Soto and Haroon Kharem. Another chapter, "The Color of Social Studies: A Post-Social Studies Reality Check" was published in 2006, in *The Social Studies Curriculum: Purposes, Problems and Possibilities, 3rd Edition,* by SUNY Press, with E. Wayne Ross as editor.

Jenny Ritchie, Ph.D. is an Associate Professor in Early Childhood Teacher Education at Te Whare Wānanga o Wairaka, Unitec Institute of Technology in Auckland, New Zealand. She came to her academic career in early childhood education from a background of a wide range of teaching experience in the field, and as a parent of six children. Her doctoral research focused on the implications of honouring the indigenous culture and language within early childhood education and teacher education in Aotearoa. Recently she completed, with Cheryl Rau and other co-researchers, two studies funded by the Teacher Learner Research Initiative (TLRI), Whakawhanaungatanga: partnerships in bicultural development in early childhood care and education; and Te Puawaitanga – partnerships with tamariki and whānau in bicultural early childhood care and education. In both her teaching and research she focuses on supporting early childhood educators to enhance their practice in terms of applying an awareness of cultural and social justice issues.

Steve Sharra is currently a Visiting Assistant Professor of peace and justice studies in the Department of Philosophy at Michigan State University (MSU). He has a Ph.D. in Teacher Education from MSU, and an MA in English Education from the University of Iowa. Steve's research interests are in peace education, teachers' autobiographical writings, African perspectives on peace and social justice, and Pan Africanism. Steve taught in Malawian primary schools, and was an educational editor at the Malawi Institute of Education. He attended the University of Iowa as an Honorary Fellow in Writing and a writer-in-residence, in 1997 and 1998. Steve has published a children's novel, *Fleeing the War*, which won first prize in Malawi in 1995. He served as president of the Malawi Writers Union, 1996-98. In addition to being a blogger, he is also a Global Voices Online country author for Malawi.

Kryssi Staikidis is an Assistant Professor in Art Education at Northern Illinois University. She holds an Ed.D. in Art and Art Education from Teachers College Columbia University, a Master of Fine Arts in Painting from Hunter College, and a Bachelor of Science degree in Anthropology and Art History from Columbia University. Her research interests are in the areas of indigenous pedagogy, art studio practice as a site for research, and visual culture/critical pedagogy in the classroom.

Dalene M. Swanson is an Adjunct Professor, University of British Columbia, and a SSHRC Postdoctoral Scholar, University of Alberta. She is a Faculty Associate of the Centre of Culture, Identity and Education, UBC. Her interests span curriculum studies, mathematics education; teacher education; narrative methodologies; critical theory/pedagogy; indigeneity; socio-cultural and political perspectives in education; and issues of social, ecological and global justice. Dalene was born and educated in South Africa, and holds degrees in mathematics and education from the Universities of Cape Town and British Columbia. She researches from poststructural and postcolonial perspectives. Dalene's doctoral research was in South African schools with socio-economic, cultural and historical differences. Her narrative-based dissertation at UBC, which draws on the concept of Ubuntu, addresses critical issues in mathematics education and curriculum studies, and contests hegemonic practices in schools and society. Dalene received four prominent international awards in Qualitative Research and Curriculum Studies for this research. Website: www.ualberta.ca/~dalene/index.html

AUTHOR OF FOREWORD:

Ngũgĩ wa Thiong'o was born in Kenya in 1938 into a large peasant family. He is currently Distinguished Professor of English and Comparative Literature and Director of the International Center for Writing and Translation at the University of California, Irvine. He is a novelist, essayist, playwright, journalist, editor, academic and social activist and a recipient of eight Honorary Doctorates. His works include: *Weep not Child; The River Between; A Grain of Wheat; Secret Lives; Petals of Blood; Caitaani Mũtharabainĩ* (English trans: *Devil on the Cross); Detained: A Writers Prison Diary; Matigari Ma Njirũũngi* (English trans: *Matigari); Homecoming; Decolonising the Mind; Moving the Centre; Struggle for Cultural Freedoms; Writers in Politics; Penpoints, Gunpoints and Dreams; The Black Hermit; This Time Tomorrow; The Trial of Dedan Kimathi* (with Micere Mugo); *Ngaahika Ndeenda,* (with Ngũgĩ wa Mĩriĩ, English trans: *I Will Marry When I Want); Murogi wa Kagogo* (English trans: *Wizard of the Crow);* and *Something Torn and New.* Ngũgĩ has also written the *Njamba Nene* series for children, and he now edits the Gĩkũyũ language journal, *Mũtiiri.*

INDEX

A

Africa, 24, 25, 27, 33–37, 42, 47, 54, 56,
Afrikaans, 5, 16, 19n6, 20nn.7–10, 12–13
AIDS, 35, 42, 90–91, 93, 97
Airline Ambassadors International (AAI), 46
allotment system, 78n8, 79
Aloha, 172, 173, 175, 179
Aotearoa, xiv, 135–144, 197
art education, xiv, 105, 113, 117–123, 195, 197
Auckland, 197
Austin, 93–95, 195
autobiographical narratives, xi, 27, 29–32, 35–37, 64

B

Bannock Nation, 75, 76
Battiste, M., 113, 114
bicultural development, 144n4, 197
boarding schools, military-style, 74, 78, 79
Brooklyn, 94–96, 103, 125
Bureau of Indian Affairs, 78, 79, 81, 82, 115n5

C

Carlisle, 78, 79
Caroline Wambui Mungai Foundation, *see* CWMF
Chipembere, H.M., 25, 26, 36
Chiume, K., 23, 25, 26, 36
collaboration, 104, 121, 130, 154, 166, 174, 175, 196
colonialism, ix, xii, 19n3, 24–25, 32–33, 55–56, 114, 140
colonizers, xiii, 71–75, 80–84, 85n4
community, ix, xi–xv, 3–11, 13, 15, 17, 18, 20n15, 26, 28, 31–36, 40–42, 45–47, 62, 93, 103, 104, 108–110, 112–114, 115n11, 118, 119, 121, 129, 130, 131nn.1, 4, 135–137, 147–192
curriculum, xiv, 19n3, 24, 26–29, 32, 35–37, 47, 110–111, 113–114, 115n10, 135, 137, 142, 151, 159, 165, 174–175, 181, 195–198
CWMF (Caroline Wambui Mungai Foundation), xii, 41–42, 45

D

Derrida, J., 19nn.2, 4, 5, 57
dictatorship, 25, 27, 30–31, 33, 34

drug dealers, 6, 8, 9
Dublin, 60

E

education
   early childhood education, xiv, 41, 135–142, 144n1, 195, 197
   peace education, 26, 27, 29, 32, 35, 159, 197
   public education, 65n8, 103, 105, 110–113, 165, 167, 177
educational research, xii, xiv, 13, 141, 144n4
educators, non-indigenous, 104, 107, 110–114, 137
ethnicities, 19n3, 175–177, 180
ethnography, collaborative, 115n3, 131n2

F

Freire, P., 26, 97, 137, 171, 172, 184, 185
Freud, S., 64, 65n12

G

gay, xiii, 89–99, 186
genocide, cultural, xiii, 54, 55, 69, 70, 80, 84
government, federal, 75, 80, 82, 83
Greene, M., 150–152, 154, 184

H

Hawai'i, xiv, 165–167, 173–180, 181n1
HIV, 35, 43, 45
Homelands
   Osage, 79, 80
Hope House, 183, 186, 189
human rights, 12, 80, 98, 152

I

Ignatiev, N., 58
Indigenous
   communities, 9, 11, 104, 119, 135, 138
   peoples, xi, xiii, 10, 13, 33, 39, 54, 72, 78–80, 83, 84n1, 103–107, 110–112, 114, 115n2, 115n8, 115n10, 135, 137, 141, 196,
injustice, xiii, 12, 27–30, 35, 70, 74, 77, 79–80, 83–84, 96–97, 99, 111, 135
inquiry, xii, xiv, 27, 34–35, 37, 105–106, 110, 114, 131n3, 150, 154, 157–160, 165–176, 180–181, 196

INDEX

interviews, 19n3, 31, 115n8, 127, 138, 160, 179
Ireland, xii, 53–60, 65n5

K

Kapi'olani Park, 167, 168, 170–174
Kaqchikel cultures, 124

kaupapa, 140, 141
Kenya, xii, 26, 34, 36, 40–47, 153, 160, 162, 196, 198
Kristeva, J., 53, 60

L

Lacanian Psychoanalysis, 65n10
Lassiter, L.E., 115n3, 131n2
literacy, xv, 28, 56, 165–167, 175, 183, 185, 188, 192, 192n3, 195, 196
lived experiences, xi, xiv, 4, 9, 64, 119–121, 123, 129
London, 53
Long Island, xiii, 94, 98, 103–105, 107–113, 114n1, 115nn.2, 4, 6, 8

M

Malawi, 23–37, 37nn.2, 4, 197
manaakitanga, 139, 140, 142
Māori
  families, 135, 136, 139, 142
  language, 135–138, 143
  legends, 138
  values, 138–139, 141–142
Maya cultures, 124, 125, 130
McCloud, J., 81, 83
Meier, D., 150, 151, 161
melting pot, 176–180
mentors, 119–125, 127, 129, 130, 142, 150
Meriam Report, 79
Musopole, A., 27, 33, 34

N

Narratives
  autobiographical, xi, 27, 30–32, 35–37
Native
  Americans, 111, 113, 175
  communities, 73, 79, 104
  Hawai'i, 175
  Nations, 69–72
  Native women, xiii, 69–74, 76–77, 79–81, 83–84, 85n4
  peoples, 69–71, 73, 77–80, 82–84, 84n1, 85n8, 103–107, 110–112, 114, 115nn.2, 8, 10
Nduluzi, 27–29

New York City, 94, 99, 126, 159, 161, 162n3
New Zealand Council for Educational Research, 114n4
non-Indians, 75, 77, 81, 85n8
Northern Cheyenne, 82
Northern Paiutes, 75, 76
Norton, C.v., 82

O

orphaned children, xii, 42
Osage, 79, 80

P

paintings, 31, 95, 117–130, 131n4, 132n5, 197
Paiutes, 75–76
Palmer, P., 151, 157
partnering, xiii, 103–116, 114n1, 115n8
PBCI, *see* place-based critical inquiry
peace education (*see* education, peace)
pedagogy, xii, 17, 24, 26, 27, 32, 35–37, 61, 64, 65nn.11, 14, 107, 120, 137, 139, 151, 157, 166, 167, 174, 176, 197–198
Pinde, 27n3, 28, 29
place-based critical inquiry (PBCI), 166, 168, 169, 171, 172, 174, 181
place-based pedagogy, critical, 166, 167, 174, 176
Place-Conscious Learning, xiv, 165–181
powwow, 108–109, 115n7
psychoanalysis, 57, 65nn.9, 10, 196
public schooling (*see* education, public)

Q

qualitative research, 18, 198
queer, 90

R

race, xiii, 3, 19n3, 20n6, 25, 40, 53, 56, 75, 91, 93, 149, 175, 176, 196
racial formation, 56, 57
Rafael, P., 119–123, 125–131, 131n4
Rappaport, D., 77–80
Rau, C., 141, 144n4, 197
reservation, 74–76, 79, 81–82, 85n8, 104, 107–110, 112, 115n7
rights, 11–12, 71, 79–82, 84, 85n4, 97–98, 108, 112, 115n11, 116n12, 152

S

sanghas, 154–155, 158
scholarship, xi–xiii, 26, 28, 32–35, 59, 62, 63
schooling communities, 13, 19n3

schools
　elementary, 14, 110, 111, 165, 181, 183, 195
　mission, 14, 33, 53, 54, 74, 107, 113, 154
　public, 3, 65n9, 103, 105, 110–113, 165, 167, 177, 196
service learning, xiv, 149–162, 162n1, 162n3
Shinnecock
　Shinnecock Hills, 107–108
　Shinnecock Museum, 105, 107, 108, 110, 112, 113
Sindima, H., 27, 28, 32–34
skollies, 6n12, 7
Smith, L.T., 131n2, 137, 140, 143
Sonneborn, L., 72, 74–81
South Africa, xii, 3–5, 9–15, 17, 19n3, 20nn.6, 9, 10, 14, 25–27, 34, 36, 136, 198
stereotypes, 62, 70, 71, 74, 77, 84, 96, 111, 112, 150, 159, 175, 180
structural violence, 24, 27, 28, 35, 36
subjectivity, 19n2, 54, 60–64, 65n9, 150, 196
subjugation, 9, 11, 54
Sula, 183n1, 185–186
Sullivan, G., 61, 65n5, 123n5, 132nn.5, 6

T

Takyin, 171–172
Te Tiriti, 137–138, 143
Te Whāriki, 137, 139, 142
teacher autobiography, xii, 23–37

tribes, 65n4, 77, 79, 81, 112, 135, 137, 143
Tutu, D., 10–12, 26, 41

U

ubuntu (includes Ubuntu, uBuntu), xi–xiii, xv, xvn1, 3–20, 19n2, 24, 26–27, 33, 37, 39–49, 198
uMunthu, xii, 23–37, 37n4

W

wairua, 139, 143
Waitangi, 137, 138, 143
Waldman, C., 75–77, 81, 85n8
Wangige, 41, 45–46
Wembayi, 30, 31
whakapapa, 139, 143
whanaungatanga, 139–143, 144n4, 197
whanaungatanga approach, 139, 140, 142
whiteness, 58, 59
Winnemucca Hopkins, S., 74–76, 80
women, elder, 69, 70, 83, 195
women's councils, 72
workshops
　professional development, 113, 138
　writing, 24, 27
worldviews, xiv, 63–64, 171

Z

Zimbabwe, 26, 34, 36, 37
Zitkala-Sa, 78–80